WHAT'S IN
A BRAND NAME?

Now you can find out exactly how many calories are in all your favorite brand-name foods! Now you can plan your diet with the help of the complete slimming guide to supermarket shopping!

"PERENNIAL DIETERS! COMPULSIVE CALORIE COUNTERS! WEIGHT WATCHER DROPOUTS! YOU ARE *MY* KIND OF PEOPLE AND THIS IS *OUR* LITERARY EVENT OF THE DECADE. . . . WITH THE DEDICATION OF A SCIENTIST, CORINNE NETZER HAS PENETRATED THE CALORIC MYSTERY OF THE SUPERMARKET."
—Gael Greene, *Life* magazine

"HELP HAS APPEARED IN A PAPERBACK BOOK THAT TAKES NOTE OF SUPERMARKET REALITIES. . . . NOW THOSE WHO ARE OVERWEIGHT CAN COUNT CALORIES IN ALMOST ALL PREPARED OR CONVENIENCE FOODS AND COMPARE VARIOUS BRANDS AS WELL."
—Morris Fishbein, M.D., *Medical World News*

THE BRAND-NAME CALORIE COUNTER

CORINNE T. NETZER

A DELL BOOK

Published by
Dell Publishing Co., Inc.
1 Dag Hammarskjold Plaza
New York, New York 10017

Dell ® TM 681510, Dell Publishing Co., Inc.

ISBN: 0-440-10676-1

Printed in the United States of America

First printing—May 1981

ACKNOWLEDGMENTS

The Brand-Name Calorie Counter would have been impossible to compile without the assistance and good will of the American food industry and I would like to express my wholehearted thanks to the many companies and the dozens of people who had to answer my apparently unending requests for more and more information; without them this book could never have been written.

In addition I would like to thank my editor, Elaine Chaback, for her infinite patience.

C.T.N.

INTRODUCTION

I love food and I've honestly never been able to decide which I really prefer more—eating or cooking. They both give me an enormous amount of pleasure, and frankly, I'm considered a good cook and a terrific hostess. All this would lead you to believe I must be a perennial fatty. Not so—but you *can* believe that I truly am a perennial dieter, *always* fighting The Battle of the Bulge. More often than not I'm on a diet during the year (let's forget Thanksgiving and Christmas holidays . . . after all, a person has to live!).

The initial *Brand-Name Calorie Counter* came out because I was again on one of my diets, again trying to "hold that line" and again faced with a regimen of four ounces of lean beef or breast of chicken or fillet of sole. I knew there was another world out there in the supermarket, something that would satisfy my need, my craving for variety. And so I began to compile the first of these books.

This is the third edition of *The Brand-Name Calorie Counter* and it has been necessary to make changes, revisions, and additions simply because the food industry is constantly changing and adding products, and because the American way of food and life is changing.

You can find almost anything your heart (or your palate) desires in your local supermarket—either canned, boxed, glassed, or frozen. And it will be as good as, if not better than, anything you can whip up at home. In these days, when more and more women are working outside the home, it is a blessing to know that you don't have to slave for hours over a hot stove to come up with a satisfying dinner after a hard day at work—which leads me back to dieting.

You may want to substitute a slice of *La Pizzeria* pepperoni pizza (164 calories) for that aforementioned lean beef, or you may want to reward yourself at dessert time with a piece of *Sara Lee* strawberry cream cheese cake (214 calories). The point is to take the boredom and the misery out of dieting while still "toeing the line." You need variety; otherwise, if you're like me, you'll get tired of the drudgery and the routine, and just plain give up.

More and more people are "eating out" these days, and so I've added a super-bonus section of Fast Food and Chain Restaurants. It seems to me just because you're dieting doesn't mean you have to suffer and be denied a *McDonald's* cheeseburger (306 calories), or an *Arby's* roast beef sandwich (350 calories); you can take your diet right to the restaurant.

I've tried to represent all the largest chains in the country, but you might find that the one you like best is not included. This may be because the information is not available (nutritional analyses are really quite expensive), or because the product (i.e., burger, taco, pizza) may vary greatly from one restaurant location to another. In future editions, as more data becomes available, I'll be adding more listings to this section, and to all the others.

You will find that there are many ways to use this book. For instance, you might decide to make substitutions in whatever diet you are on; or you might decide to take a stab at a food new to you; or try a totally new brand. You might also decide not to vary your diet by as much as a crispy green bean. The choice is really *yours*. But whatever you may decide, you will be armed with all the facts, because this book contains the specific caloric information you need to start your diet, to stay on it, to maintain your plan, and to just plain eat well.

C.T.N.

CONTENTS

WHAT YOU SHOULD KNOW
ABOUT USING THIS BOOK

WHERE TO FIND WHAT

Most calorie counters list foods alphabetically. This counter does not. It lists foods categorically. This means that all cereals are grouped together; so are all frozen dinners, all pizzas, all fruits, all wines, and so on. For example—and more important, for convenience—if you want to find the caloric content of various soups, you don't have to hop-scotch from A (asparagus) through V (vichyssoise); you simply turn to the chapter titled "Soups, Broths and Chowders," and there you will find all soup listings.

Occasionally, you may have trouble deciding what category a food belongs in; occasionally, too, the same food, in different forms, appears in more than one category. To locate hard-to-categorize and multiple-listed foods quickly, just flip to the index.

BE CAREFUL ABOUT MAKING COMPARISONS

It is only natural that you will want to use this counter to compare the caloric content of different foods and different brands. In many instances, you can make comparisons accurately by merely glancing at the listings. For example, all soft drinks are listed in the same measure (eight fluid ounces); therefore, you can easily compare the caloric content of *Coca-Cola* with that of *Dr Pepper*, or *Schweppes Bitter Lemon*, or whatever.

To facilitate easy comparison, categories have been listed in a uniform measure whenever it was possible or feasible to do so. However, it was neither feasible nor sensible to list certain foods in a uniform measure. For example, all data on crackers could have been presented in a measure of one ounce, but that would have meant you would have to weigh a *Triscuit* to learn its caloric content. For practicality's sake, crackers, cookies, bread, rolls, and various other foods are listed by the piece—in the size packaged by the manufacturer. This means you can easily determine the calories in a single cracker, but you cannot compare different brands and varieties of crackers accurately. Why? Because, unless you weigh every cracker, you have no way of knowing if they are the same size.

To get the most from this book—and your diet—you must recognize that similar foods aren't necessarily packaged in the same or even similar sizes. For example, consider two brands of chocolate-covered marshmallow cookies, *Mallomars* and *Pinwheels*, both manufactured by *Nabisco*. I've listed all cookies by the piece (one cookie, as packaged), and if you check, you'll find that a *Mallomar* has 55 calories, while a *Pinwheel* has 140 calories. However, while it is true that one *Pinwheel* has more than twice as many calories as one *Mallomar*, it is also true that by the pound or by the ounce the caloric content of the two is almost identical. The answer to this seeming mystery is simple: The size of one *Pinwheel* is more than double the size of one *Mallomar*.

The point here is simple but important. If you're not certain that products are the same size, *don't make comparisons; they may not be accurate*.

You can, of course, compare any foods that are listed in the same standard measure. You can compare the calories in a half cup of apricots with the calories in a half cup of prunes; or the calories in one ounce of Muenster cheese with the calories in one ounce of Swiss cheese. However, what you cannot do (and it took me forever to understand this) is compare foods that are listed in dissimilar units of measure. Because even doctors and home economists sometimes confuse measures by capacity with measures by weight, it should be noted also that you can't, for example, accurately compare four ounces of custard with a half cup of ice cream. Four ounces is a measure of how much something weighs. Half a cup is a measure of how much space something occupies. The units of measure are dissimilar and, therefore, not comparable. Think of it this way: Eight ounces of puffed rice cereal contains approximately 880 calories and fills the capacity of about 16 eight-ounce measuring cups; an eight-ounce cup of puffed rice contains about 55 calories and weighs half an ounce. Clearly, eight ounces of puffed rice and an eight-ounce cupful of puffed rice are not the same!

Sometimes, exactly eight ounces of a food exactly fills the capacity of an eight-ounce cup, but more often it does not—which is why you shouldn't try to compare foods listed by weight with foods listed by volume. Just remember: The capacity of a standard eight-ounce measuring cup is eight *fluid* ounces, not eight *weight* ounces.

As noted before, you can compare foods listed in a similar measure—and you can, of course, convert a unit of measure to a smaller or larger amount. You may find the charts below helpful in making conversions.

EQUIVALENTS BY CAPACITY
(all measures level)
1 quart = 4 cups
1 cup = 8 fluid ounces
= ½ pint
= 16 tablespoons
2 tablespoons = 1 fluid ounce
1 tablespoon = 3 teaspoons

EQUIVALENTS BY WEIGHT
1 pound = 16 ounces
3.57 ounces = 100 grams
1 ounce = 28.35 grams

You don't have to know that there are 28.35 grams in an ounce to use this book, but you may find the information handy when shopping or comparing package sizes. By federal law, the net weight (or volume) of a packaged food must be printed on the food's can, box, wrapping, etc. Most containers list a food's net weight in ounces or pounds; however, labels now include the weight in metric measure, as well, and a few labels will only give the metric weight. A label might read, for example, "Net weight 222 grams." The only way you can determine that the net weight of that food is somewhat less than eight ounces is by knowing how many grams equal one ounce.

PAY ATTENTION TO PACKAGE SIZES

To get full value from *The Brand-Name Calorie Counter*, it's important that you pay attention to package sizes. Specifically, whenever the caloric content of a food is listed by one ounce, you must check the food's label to learn how much the product weighs—and then multiply its weight in ounces by the number of calories per ounce. Cheeses, for example, are listed in a one-ounce measure. To determine the caloric content of an eight-ounce package of *Dorman's* American cheese, simply multiply eight by 106 and you will see that the entire package contains 848 calories.

Pay attention to weights, too, whenever a product is listed by the whole package. For example, as this book goes to press, the weight of *Green Giant's* beef stew entree is nine ounces, and the data herein pertains to the full nine ounces. Should *Green Giant* increase or decrease the amount of stew in their frozen entree, the data should be adjusted accordingly.

PAY ATTENTION TO PACKAGE DIRECTIONS

You will find many products listed in *The Brand-Name Calorie Counter* that require some home preparation: condensed soups, salad dressing mixes, sauce mixes, potato mixes, and many more. For convenience, the data on the majority of these products is given for the "finished" food when it is *prepared according to the package directions.* Should you make a change in a package recipe, bear in mind that you may also change the caloric content of the finished food. If, for example, a package recipe calls for a cup of whole milk and you substitute a cup of skim milk, the prepared food will have a lower caloric content than is listed here. There is no reason why you shouldn't vary package directions; the point is, if you do so, be sure to determine how the change will affect the caloric content of the prepared food.

SOURCES AND ACCURACY OF DATA

The caloric values in this book are based on data obtained from producers and processors of all brand-name foods, as well as from label information. Every care has been exercised to evaluate the data as accurately and fully as possible; every effort has been made to present the material clearly and usefully.

Consumers should be aware, however, that a variety of factors can, to some extent, affect the accuracy of any and all analyses of food. For example, apples grown in different regions of the country may differ slightly in composition; therefore, the calories shown for any product that contains apples must be considered average or typical. Seasonal changes can also affect the composition of an apple; so, too, can the maturity of the crop when picked. For these and similar reasons, and because there is no practical way to analyze every sample of a processed food, it is an accepted practice within the food industry—and within the United States Department of Agriculture—to present nutritive data that is typical or "proximate."

As this revised, unabridged edition of *The Brand-Name Calorie Counter* goes to press, the data has been checked to see that it is as up-to-date as possible. However, just as you strive to vary or improve your recipes, so do home economists in the food industry; in addition, economic factors sometimes cause a difference in how a food is packaged (for example, the size of a cookie may decrease or increase) and, therefore, the caloric content may change. Because of these reasons, it is impossible to guarantee that some of the data won't change in time. As needed, corrections will be made in later editions of the book. Until then, you must be on the lookout for changes yourself. In particular, if you find that a favorite food is suddenly labeled "New" or "Improved," you may want to write the producer directly to ask if the food's caloric content has changed.

ABBREVIATIONS IN THIS BOOK

cond. ....condensed
fl. ....fluid
" ....inch
lb. ....pound
oz. ....ounce
pkg. ....package
semicond. ....semicondensed
tbsp. ....tablespoon
tsp. ....teaspoon

CHAPTER 1

EGGS, PANCAKES, CEREALS AND OTHER BREAKFAST FOODS

EGGS
See also "Frozen Breakfasts"

	CALORIES
imitation, fat-free (*Egg Beaters*), ¼ cup	40
omelets:	
cheese, freeze-dried** (*Mountain House*), 1.2 oz. dry	180
cheese, mix*	
(*McCormick/Schilling* Seasoning Mix), 1 serving	168
w/bacon, mix (*Durkee*), 1 pkg. dry	128
w/bacon, mix* (*Durkee*), yield from ½ pkg.	310
Mexican, freeze-dried**	
(*Mountain House*), 1.45 oz. dry	220
puffy, mix (*Durkee*), 1 pkg. dry	112
puffy, mix* (*Durkee*), yield from ½ pkg.	302
western, mix** (*Durkee*), 1 pkg.	170
western, mix*	
(*McCormick/Schilling* Seasoning Mix), 1 serving	164
scrambled:	
precooked, freeze-dried**	
(*Mountain House*), 1 oz. dry	180
mix** (*Durkee*), 1 pkg.	124
w/bacon, precooked, freeze-dried**	
(*Mountain House*), 1.05 oz. dry	180
w/bacon bits, freeze-dried**	
(*Mountain House*), 1.1 oz. dry	170

Eggs, scrambled, continued

    w/bacon bits, mix** *(Durkee)*, 1 pkg. 181
    w/butter, freeze-dried**
       (Mountain House), 1.1 oz. dry 160

  * *Prepared according to package directions*
** *Prepared according to package directions, with water*

FROZEN BREAKFASTS, one whole package
See also "Eggs," "French Toast" and "Pancakes & Waffles"

                                   CALORIES
French toast, w/sausages *(Swanson)*, 4½-oz. pkg. 300
pancakes and sausages *(Swanson)*, 6-oz. pkg. 500
scrambled eggs and sausages, w/coffee cake
  (Swanson), 6¼-oz. pkg. 460

FRENCH TOAST, one slice*,
except as noted
See also "Frozen Breakfasts"

                                     CALORIES
frozen:
    (Aunt Jemima) 85
    (Downyflake) 135
    cinnamon swirl *(Aunt Jemima)* 97
freeze-dried *(Mountain House)*, ⅓-oz. serving 50
mix** *(McCormick/Schilling Batter Mix)* 119

  * *As packaged or prepared*
** *Prepared according to package directions*

PANCAKES & WAFFLES
See also "Frozen Breakfasts"

                                     CALORIES
pancake batter, frozen:
    plain *(Aunt Jemima)*, 4" pancake* 70
    blueberry *(Aunt Jemima)*, 4" pancake* 68
    buttermilk *(Aunt Jemima)*, 4" pancake* 71
pancake, frozen *(Downyflake)*, 1 pancake** 80

Pancakes & Waffles, continued

pancake and waffle mix:

plain (*Aunt Jemima* Complete), ⅓ cup 198
plain (*Aunt Jemima* Complete), 4″ pancake* 67
plain (*Aunt Jemima* Original), ¼ cup 108
plain (*Aunt Jemima* Original), 4″ pancake* 73
plain (*Hungry Jack* Complete), 4″ pancake* ...:......60
plain (*Hungry Jack* Extra Lights), 4″ pancake* 67
plain (*Hungry Jack* Panshakes), 4″ pancake* 83
plain (*Log Cabin*), 4″ pancake* 60
plain (*Log Cabin* Complete), 4″ pancake* 60
blueberry (*Hungry Jack*), 4″ pancake* 110
buckwheat (*A & P*), ¼ cup 110
buckwheat (*A & P*), 4″ pancake* 63
buckwheat (*Aunt Jemima*), ¼ cup 107
buckwheat (*Aunt Jemima*), 4″ pancake* 67
buttermilk (*Aunt Jemima*), ⅓ cup 175
buttermilk (*Aunt Jemima*), 4″ pancake* 100
buttermilk (*Aunt Jemima* Complete), ⅓ cup 236
buttermilk (*Aunt Jemima* Complete), 4″ pancake* 80
buttermilk (*Betty Crocker*), ⅓ cup 170
buttermilk (*Betty Crocker*), 4″ pancake* 93
buttermilk (*Betty Crocker* Complete), ½ cup 210
buttermilk (*Betty Crocker* Complete), 4″ pancake* 70
buttermilk (*Hungry Jack*), 4″ pancake* 80
buttermilk (*Hungry Jack* Complete), 4″ pancake* 60
buttermilk (*Log Cabin*), 4″ pancake 77
sweet grain (*Hungry Jack*), 4″ pancake* 67
whole wheat (*Aunt Jemima*), ⅓ cup 142
whole wheat (*Aunt Jemima*), 4″ pancake* 83

waffles, frozen:

plain (*Aunt Jemima* Original Jumbo), 1 waffle** 86
plain (*Downyflake*), 1 waffle** 60
plain (*Downyflake* Hot 'N Buttery), 1 waffle** 65
plain (*Downyflake* Jumbo Homemade Size), 1 waffle** ..85
plain (*Eggo*), 1 waffle** 120
blueberry (*Aunt Jemima* Jumbo), 1 waffle** 86

waffles, frozen, continued

blueberry (*Downyflake*), 1 waffle** 90
blueberry (*Eggo*), 1 waffle** 130
bran (*Eggo*), 1 waffle** 170
buttermilk (*Aunt Jemima* Jumbo), 1 waffle** 86
buttermilk (*Downyflake*), 1 waffle** 85
buttermilk, round (*Downyflake*), 1 waffle** 100
strawberry (*Eggo*), 1 waffle** 120

* *Prepared and/or cooked according to package directions*
** *As packaged*

CEREALS & CORN PRODUCTS, DRY (UNCOOKED)
See also "Cereals, Cooked," "Cereals, Ready-to-Eat"
and "Flour"

CALORIES

barley, pearled, regular or quick
(*Quaker Scotch Brand*), ¼ cup 172
corn grits or hominy:
(*Quaker* Instant), 1 packet 79
white, regular or quick (*Aunt Jemima*), 3 tbsp. 101
white, regular or quick (*Quaker*), 3 tbsp. 101
white, quick (*3-Minute Brand*), ½ oz. 100
artificial cheese flavor (*Quaker* Instant), 1 packet 104
imitation bacon bits (*Quaker* Instant), 1 packet 101
imitation ham bits (*Quaker* Instant), 1 packet 99
corn meal:
white (*Aunt Jemima*), 3 tbsp. 102
white (*Quaker*), 3 tbsp. 102
white, bolted, mix (*Aunt Jemima*), ⅙ cup 99
white, self-rising (*Aunt Jemima*), ⅙ cup 98
white, self-rising, bolted (*Aunt Jemima*), ⅙ cup 99
yellow (*Aunt Jemima*), 3 tbsp. 102
yellow (*Elam's* Stone Ground), 1 oz. 105
yellow (*Quaker*), 3 tbsp. 102
cracked wheat (*Elam's*), 1 oz. 102

Cereals & Corn Products, Dry (Uncooked), continued

farina:

(*Cream of Wheat*), 1 oz. 100
(*Cream of Wheat* Instant), 1 oz. 100
(*Cream of Wheat* Mix 'n Eat), 1-oz. packet 100
(*Cream of Wheat Quick*), 1 oz. 100
(*H-O*), ⅙ cup 108
(*Malt-O-Meal*), 1 oz. or 3 tbsp. 100
(*Quaker* Hot 'n Creamy), ⅙ cup 101
w/baked apple and cinnamon
   (*Cream of Wheat* Mix 'n Eat), 1¼-oz. packet 130
w/banana flavor and spice
   (*Cream of Wheat* Mix 'n Eat), 1¼-oz. packet 130
w/cocoa and toasted malt
   (*Malt-O-Meal*), 1 oz. or 3 tbsp. 100
w/maple flavor and brown sugar
   (*Cream of Wheat* Mix 'n Eat), 1¼-oz. packet 130
w/toasted malt (*Malt-O-Meal*), 1 oz. or 3 tbsp. 100

oatmeal or oats:

(*Elam's* Scotch Style), 1 oz. 108
(*Elam's* Steel Cut), 1 oz. 109
instant (*H-O*—box), ⅓ cup 85
instant (*H-O*—packet), 1 packet 105
instant (*H-O* Sweet & Mellow), 1 packet 150
instant (*Quaker*), 1 packet 105
instant (*3-Minute Brand*), 1 packet 110
old fashioned (*H-O*), ⅓ cup 92
quick (*H-O*), ⅓ cup 89
quick or old fashioned (*Harvest Brand*), ⅓ cup 110
quick or old fashioned (*Quaker*), ⅓ cup 109
quick or old fashioned (*Ralston*), ⅓ cup 110
quick or old fashioned (*3-Minute Brand*), ⅓ cup 110
w/apple and brown sugar (*H-O* Instant), 1 packet 120
w/apple and brown sugar
   (*3-Minute Brand* Instant), 1 packet 120
w/apple and cinnamon (*Quaker* Instant), 1 packet 134
w/bran and raisins (*Quaker* Instant), 1 packet 153

oatmeal or oats, continued

w/bran and spice (*H-O* Instant), 1 packet 145
w/cinnamon and spice (*H-O* Instant), 1 packet 170
w/cinnamon and spice (*Quaker* Instant), 1 packet 176
w/maple and brown sugar (*H-O* Instant), 1 packet 165
w/maple and brown sugar (*Quaker* Instant), 1 packet ...134
w/raisins and spice (*Quaker* Instant), 1 packet 159
masa harina (*Quaker*), ⅓ cup 137
masa trigo (*Quaker*), ⅓ cup 149
tortilla flour, *see "Flour," page 44*
wheat, toasted (*Wheatena*), ¼ cup 120
whole wheat (*Quaker Pettijohns*), ⅓ cup 100
whole wheat (*Ralston* Instant and Regular), ¼ cup 110

CEREALS, COOKED*, about ¾ cup,
except as noted
See also "Cereals & Corn Products, Dry (Uncooked)"
and "Cereals, Ready-to-Eat"

CALORIES

barley, pearled, quick (*Quaker Scotch Brand*) 172
barley, pearled, regular (*Quaker Scotch Brand*) 129
farina:
   (*Cream of Wheat*) 100
   (*Cream of Wheat* Instant or Quick) 100
   (*Cream of Wheat* Mix 'n Eat)** 140
   (*Quaker* Hot 'n Creamy), 1 cup 101
   prepared w/milk (*Pillsbury*) 225
   prepared w/water (*Pillsbury*) 90
   w/baked apple flavor and cinnamon
     (*Cream of Wheat* Mix 'n Eat)** 170
   w/banana flavor and spice
     (*Cream of Wheat* Mix 'n Eat)** 170
   w/maple flavor and brown sugar
     (*Cream of Wheat* Mix 'n Eat)** 170

Cereals, Cooked, continued

oatmeal and oats:

instant (*H-O*—box) 130

instant (*H-O*—packet) 110

instant (*H-O* Sweet & Mellow) 150

instant (*Quaker*) 105

old fashioned (*H-O*) 140

quick (*H-O*) 130

quick or old fashioned (*Quaker*), ⅔ cup 109

w/apple and brown sugar (*H-O* Instant) 120

w/apple and cinnamon (*Quaker* Instant) 134

w/bran and raisins (*Quaker* Instant) 153

w/bran and spice (*H-O* Instant) 150

w/cinnamon and spice (*H-O* Instant) 170

w/cinnamon and spice (*Quaker* Instant) 176

w/maple and brown sugar (*H-O* Instant) 160

w/maple and brown sugar (*Quaker* Instant) 163

w/raisins and spice (*Quaker* Instant) 159

whole wheat (*Quaker Pettijohns*), ⅔ cup 100

* *Prepared according to package directions*
** *Prepared according to package directions, with 2 oz. whole milk*

CEREALS, READY-TO-EAT, one ounce
and approximate cup measure*, except as noted
See also "Cereals & Corn Products, Dry (Uncooked)"
and "Cereals, Cooked"

CALORIES

bran and high-fiber:

(*All-Bran*), 1 oz. = ⅓ cup 70

(*Bran Buds*), 1 oz. = ⅓ cup 70

(*Bran Chex*), 1 oz. = ⅔ cup 110

(*Corn Bran*), 1 oz. = ⅔ cup 109

(*Cracklin' Bran*), 1 oz. = ⅓ cup 120

(*Elam's* Miller's Bran), 1 oz. 87

bran and high-fiber, continued

(*Kellogg's* 40% Bran Flakes), 1 oz. = ⅔ cup 90

(*Most*), 1 oz. = ¾ cup 110

(*Nabisco* 100% Bran), 1 oz. = ½ cup 70

(*Post* 40% Bran Flakes), 1 oz. = ⅔ cup 90

(*Van Brode* 40% Bran), 1 oz. = ⅝ cup 100

w/raisins (*Kellogg's* Raisin Bran), 1.3 oz. = ¾ cup 120

w/raisins (*Post* Raisin Bran), 1 oz. = ½ cup 90

w/raisins (*Ralston* Raisin Bran), 1 oz. = ½ cup 100

w/raisins (*Van Brode* Raisin Bran), 1 oz. = ¾ cup 120

corn:

(*Cocoa Puffs*), 1 oz. = 1 cup 110

(*Corn Chex*), 1 oz. = 1 cup 110

(*Corn Total*), 1 oz. = 1 cup 110

(*Country Corn Flakes*), 1 oz. = 1 cup 110

(*Featherweight* Corn Flakes), 1 oz. = 1 cup 110

(*Kellogg's Corn Flakes*), 1 oz. = 1 cup 110

(*Kellogg's* Sugar Frosted Flakes), 1 oz. = ⅔ cup 110

(*Kix*), 1 oz. = 1½ cups 110

(*Pops*), 1 oz. = 1 cup 110

(*Post* Honeycomb), 1 oz. = 1⅓ cups 110

(*Post Toasties* Corn Flakes), 1 oz. = 1¼ cups 110

(*Ralston* Corn Flakes), 1 oz. = 1 cup 110

(*Ralston* Sugar Frosted Flakes), 1 oz. = ¾ cup 110

(*Sugar Corn Pops*), 1 oz. = 1 cup 110

(*Trix*), 1 oz. = 1 cup 110

(*Van Brode* Corn Flakes), 1 oz. = 1¼ cups 110

(*Van Brode* Corn Flakes low sodium),
    1 oz. = 1¼ cups 110

(*Van Brode* Sugar Toasted Corn Flakes),
    1 oz. = ⅝ cup 110

brown sugar and honey flavor
    (*Body Buddies*), 1 oz. = 1 cup 110

chocolate flavor (*Crazy Cow*), 1 oz. = 1 cup 110

chocolate chip flavor (*Cookie Crisp*), 1 oz. = 1 cup 110

corn, continued

fruit flavor, natural

(*Body Buddies*), 1 oz. = ¾ cup 110

oatmeal flavor (*Cookie Crisp*), 1 oz. = 1 cup 120

strawberry flavor (*Crazy Cow*), 1 oz. = 1 cup 110

vanilla wafer flavor (*Cookie Crisp*), 1 oz. = 1 cup 110

corn bran, *see "bran and high-fiber," above*

granola and "natural" cereals:

(*C. W. Post* Family Style Cereal), 1 oz. = ¼ cup 130

(*Country Morning*), 1 oz. = ⅓ cup 130

(*Heartland*), 1 oz. = ¼ cup 120

(*Quaker* 100% Natural), 1 oz. = ¼ cup 139

w/almonds (*Sun Country*), 1 oz. = ¼ cup 125

w/apple and cinnamon

(*Quaker* 100% Natural), 1 oz. = ¼ cup 135

w/cinnamon and raisins

(*Nature Valley*), 1 oz. = ⅓ cup 130

w/coconut (*Heartland*), 1 oz. = ¼ cup 130

w/coconut and honey

(*Nature Valley*), 1 oz. = ⅓ cup 150

w/fruit and nuts (*Nature Valley*), 1 oz. = ⅓ cup 130

w/raisins (*C. W. Post* Family Style), 1 oz. = ¼ cup ...130

w/raisins (*Heartland*), 1 oz. = ¼ cup 120

w/raisins (*Sun Country*), 1 oz. = ¼ cup 125

w/raisins and dates

(*Country Morning*), 1 oz. = ⅓ cup 120

w/raisins and dates

(*Quaker* 100% Natural), 1 oz. = ¼ cup 134

toasted oat mixture (*Nature Valley*), 1 oz. = ⅓ cup ...130

oats:

(*Alpha-Bits*), 1 oz. = 1 cup 110

(*Cheerios*), 1 oz. = 1¼ cups 110

(Cinnamon *Life*), 1 oz. = ⅔ cup 105

(*Froot Loops*), 1 oz. = 1 cup 110

(*Frosty O's*), 1 oz. = 1 cup 110

oats, continued

    (*Honey-Nut Cheerios*), 1 oz. = ¾ cup 110
    (*Life*), 1 oz. = ⅔ cup 105
    (*Lucky Charms*), 1 oz. = 1 cup 110
    (*Post* Fortified Oat Flakes), 1 oz. = ⅔ cup 100
    (*Toasty O's*), 1 oz. = 1¼ cups 110
rice:
    (*Cocoa Krispies*), 1 oz. = ¾ cup 110
    (*Featherweight* Crisp Rice), 1 oz. = 1 cup 110
    (*Kellogg's* Frosted Rice), 1 oz. = 1 cup 110
    (*Malt-O-Meal* Puffed Rice), 1 oz. = 2 cups 100
    (*Quaker* Puffed Rice), 1 oz. = 2 cups 110
    (*Ralston* Crispy Rice), 1 oz. = 1 cup 110
    (*Rice Chex*), 1 oz. = 1⅛ cups 110
    (*Rice Krinkles*), 1 oz. = ⅞ cup 110
    (*Rice Krispies*), 1 oz. = 1 cup 110
    (*Van Brode* Cocoa Rice), 1 oz. = ¾ cup 110
    (*Van Brode* Crisp Rice), 1 oz. = 1 cup 110
    (*Van Brode* Crisp Rice—Low Sodium), 1 oz. = 1 cup ..110
    (*Van Brode* Sugar Frosted Rice), 1 oz. = ¾ cup 110
wheat:
    (*Buc Wheats*), 1 oz. = ¾ cup 110
    (*Crispy Wheats 'N Raisins*), 1 oz. = ⅞ cup 100
    (*Frosted Mini Wheats* w/sugar), 1 oz. = 4 biscuits 110
    (*Frosted Mini Wheats* w/brown sugar and cinnamon),
      1 oz. = 4 biscuits 110
    (*Malt-O-Meal* Puffed Wheat), 1 oz. = 2 cups 100
    (*Nabisco* Shredded Wheat), ⅞-oz. biscuit 90
    (*Nabisco* Shredded Wheat—single service),
      ¾-oz. biscuit 80
    (*Nabisco Spoon Size* Shredded Wheat), 1 oz. = ⅔ cup ..110
    (*Pep*), 1 oz. = ¾ cup 110
    (*Quaker* Puffed Wheat), 1 oz. = 2 cups 108
    (*Quaker* Shredded Wheat), 1.3 oz. = 2 biscuits 104
    (*Sunshine* Shredded Wheat), 1 biscuit** 85
    (Super *Sugar Crisp* Wheat Puffs), 1 oz. = ⅞ cup 110
    (*Toasted Mini-Wheats*), 1 oz. = 5 biscuits 110

wheat, continued

(*Total*), 1 oz. = 1 cup 110
(*Van Brode* Wheat Flakes), 1 oz. = ¾ cup 110
(*Wheat Chex*), 1 oz. = ⅔ cup 110
(*Wheaties*), 1 oz. = 1 cup 110
wheat bran, *see "bran and high-fiber," above*
wheat germ (*Kretschmer*), 1 oz. = ¼ cup 110
wheat germ, w/sugar and honey
(*Kretschmer*), 1 oz. = ¼ cup 107
miscellaneous mixed grains:
(*Apple Jacks*), 1 oz. = 1 cup 110
(*Cap'n Crunch*), 1 oz. = ¼ cup 121
(*Cap'n Crunch* Crunchberries), 1 oz. = ¼ cup 120
(*Cap'n Crunch* Peanut Butter), 1 oz. = ¼ cup 127
(*Concentrate*), 1 oz. = ⅓ cup 110
(*Count Chocula*), 1 oz. = 1 cup 110
(*Franken Berry*), 1 oz. = 1 cup 110
(*Grape-Nuts*), 1 oz. = ¼ cup 100
(*Grape-Nuts* Flakes), 1 oz. = ⅞ cup 100
(*King Vitaman*), 1 oz. = ¾ cup 120
(*Product 19*), 1 oz. = ¾ cup 110
(*Quisp*), 1 oz. = 1⅙ cups 121
(*Special K*), 1 oz. = 1¼ cups 110
(*Team Flakes*), 1 oz. = 1 cup 110

* *Note the variance in cup measurements*
** *As packaged*

BREAKFAST BARS & BEVERAGES

CALORIES

bars, clusters and squares:
(*Nature Valley* Breakfast Squares), 2 bars* 380
almond (*Nature Valley* Granola Bars), 1 bar* 110
almond (*Nature Valley* Granola Cluster), 1 roll* 140
almond crunch (*Carnation* Breakfast Bar), 1.44-oz. bar ..200
caramel (*Nature Valley* Granola Cluster), 1 roll* 140

bars, clusters and squares, continued

    chocolate chip (*Carnation* Breakfast Bar), 1.49-oz. bar ..200
    chocolate crunch
      (*Carnation* Breakfast Bar), 1.49-oz. bar 200
    cinnamon (*Nature Valley* Granola Bar), 1 bar* 110
    coconut (*Nature Valley* Granola Bar), 1 bar* 120
    oats and honey (*Nature Valley* Granola Bar), 1 bar* ..110
    peanut (*Nature Valley* Granola Bar), 1 bar* 120
    peanut butter crunch
      (*Carnation* Breakfast Bar), 1.51-oz. bar 210
peanut butter and chocolate chips (*Crunchola*), 1 bar* 160
    raisin (*Nature Valley* Granola Cluster), 1 roll* 140
    yogurt and granola, orange (*Crunchola*), 1 bar* 140
    yogurt and granola, strawberry (*Crunchola*), 1 bar* 140
cereal beverage (Instant *Postum*), 6-fl.-oz. glass 10
drinks, breakfast, *see "Flavored Milk Beverages," page 53*

* *As packaged*

CHAPTER 2

BREADSTUFFS, CRACKERS AND FLOUR PRODUCTS

BREADS, one slice, as packaged*, except as noted
*See also "Sweet Breads, Mixes," "Rolls, Biscuits & Muffins"
and "Breadsticks"*

	CALORIES
barbecue, w/sesame seeds (*Jane Parker*)	45
bran and high-fiber:	
(*Arnold Bran'nola*)	90
(*Brownberry* Whole Bran)	75
(*Monk's* Hi-Fibre)	50
(*Oroweat Bran'nola*)	93
(*Pepperidge Farm* Honey Bran)	58
brown, canned (*B & M*) ½" slice	78
brown, w/raisins, canned (*B & M*) ½" slice	78
buttermilk (*Jane Parker*)	75
corn and molasses (*Pepperidge Farm*)	70
cracked wheat:	
(*Northridge*)	70
(*Pepperidge Farm*)	70
(*Taystee*)	80
(*Wonder*)	75
date-nut (*Thomas'*)	90
flatbread, *see "Crackers," page 46*	
French:	
(*Jane Parker*)	70
(*Francisco*—long, sliced)	60

French, continued

   (*Francisco*—mini loaves), ⅓ of loaf 200
   (*Francisco*—round, sliced) 85
   (*Francisco*—square, sliced) 110
   (*Pepperidge Farm* Brown & Serve), 1-oz. slice 75
   (*Wonder*) 75
gluten (*Oroweat*) 70
gluten (*Thomas' Glutogen*) 30
(*Hillbilly*) 70
(*Hollywood*—dark) 70
(*Hollywood*—light) 70
Italian (*Pepperidge Farm* Brown & Serve), 1-oz. slice 75
Italian, w/sesame seeds (*Jane Parker*), 1-oz. slice 75
oatmeal:
   (*Brownberry*) 80
   (*Northridge*) 70
   (*Pepperidge Farm*) 65
pumpernickel:
   (*Arnold*) 75
   (*Brownberry* Sandwich Dark Bread) 75
   (*Oroweat* Bavarian Pumpernickel) 69
   (*Oroweat* Bohemian Pumpernickel) 100
   (*Pepperidge Farm* Family) 75
   (*Pepperidge Farm* Party Pumpernickel), 2 small slices ...45
(*Profile*—dark) 75
(*Profile*—light) 75
protein (*Thomas' Protogen*—fresh) 45
protein (*Thomas' Protogen*—frozen) 55
raisin:
   (*Arnold* Raisin Tea Loaf) 70
   (*Brownberry* Raisin Cinnamon) 85
   (*Brownberry* Raisin Nut) 95
   (*Jane Parker*) 80
   (*Monk's*) 90
   (*Northridge* Royal Raisin Nut) 85
   (*Oroweat* Raisin Nugget) 85

raisin, continued

(*Pepperidge Farm*) .... .75

(*Thomas'* Cinnamon Raisin Loaf) .... .60

(*Roman Meal*) .... .70

rye:

(*Arnold*) .... .75

(*Arnold* Diet Rye) .... .50

(*Arnold* Seeded Rye) .... .75

(*Arnold* Soft Rye) .... .75

(*Brownberry* Extra Thin) .... .65

(*Grossinger's*) .... .70

(*Oroweat* Buffet Rye), 2 small slices .... .50

(*Oroweat* Dark Rye) .... .65

(*Oroweat* Dill Rye) .... .70

(*Oroweat* Hearth Rye) .... .61

(*Oroweat* Russian Rye) .... .70

(*Oroweat* Swedish Rye) .... .51

(*Pepperidge Farm* Family Rye) .... .80

(*Pepperidge Farm* Jewish Rye) .... .65

(*Pepperidge Farm* Party Rye), 2 small slices .... .35

(*Pepperidge Farm* Seedless Rye) .... .80

(*Wonder*) .... .75

sourdough (*Di Carlo*) .... .70

wheat:

(*Arnold* American Granary) .... .70

(*Arnold* Brick Oven Wheat—1-lb. loaf) .... .60

(*Arnold* Brick Oven Wheat—2-lb. loaf) .... .80

(*Arnold* Honey Wheat Berry) .... .90

(*Arnold* Melba Wheat) .... .40

(*Arnold* Natural Wheat) .... .65

(*Arnold* Small Family Wheat) .... .60

bran, *see "bran and high-fiber," above*

(*Brownberry* Health Nut) .... .85

(*Brownberry* Natural Wheat) .... .85

(*Brownberry* Great Grains) .... .70

cracked, *see "cracked wheat," above*

wheat, continued

(*Fresh Horizons*) 50
(*Fresh & Natural*) 70
(*Home Pride* Butter Top) 75
(*Home Pride* Wheatberry) 70
(*Northridge*) 70
(*Northridge* Thin Sliced) 45
(*Oroweat* American Granary) 70
(*Oroweat* Honey Wheat Berry) 85
(*Oroweat* Low-Sodium) 70
(*Oroweat* Soya) 67
(*Oroweat* Sprouted Wheat) 65
(*Oroweat* Thin Sliced) 45
(*Oroweat* Wheat Nuggets) 79
(*Pepperidge Farm* Honey Wheatberry) 60
(*Pepperidge Farm* Sprouted Wheat) 65
(*Pepperidge Farm* Wheat—1½-lb. loaf) 90
(*Pepperidge Farm* Wheat Germ) 60
(*Taystee*) 80
(*Wonder*) 75

wheat, whole:

(*Arnold* Stoneground 100%) 55
(*Jane Parker* 100%) 70
(*Monk's* Stone Ground) 80
(*Oroweat* 100%) 94
(*Northridge* 100%) 70
(*Pepperidge Farm*) 70
(*Pepperidge Farm* Very Thin) 40
(*Thomas'*) 50
(*Wonder* 100%) 70

white:

(*Arnold* Brick Oven White—1-lb. loaf) 65
(*Arnold* Brick Oven White—2-lb. loaf) 85
(*Arnold* Country White) 95
(*Arnold* Hearthstone White—2-lb. loaf) 85

white, continued

(*Arnold* Hearthstone Country White—1-lb. loaf) 70
(*Arnold* Melba White) 40
(*Arnold* Small Family White) 65
(*Brownberry* Extra Thin) 70
(*Brownberry* Sandwich) 75
(*D'Agostino*) 75
(*Fresh Horizons*) 50
(*Home Pride* Butter Top) 75
(*Jane Parker* Low-Sodium) 75
(*Jane Parker* Thin Sliced) 70
(*Monk's*) 70
(*Northridge*) 70
(*Northridge* Honey Egg) 70
(*Northridge* Low Sodium) 70
(*Northridge* Soya Nut) 67
(*Northridge* Thin) 45
(*Oroweat* Old Style) 75
(*Pepperidge Farm* Family White) 75
(*Pepperidge Farm* Thin Sliced) 75
(*Pepperidge Farm* Toasting) 85
(*Pepperidge Farm* Unsliced), 1-oz. slice 85
(*Pepperidge Farm* Very Thin) 40
(*Pepperidge Farm* Sandwich) 65
(*Taystee*) 75
(*Taystee* Low-Sodium) 75
(*Wonder*) 75
(*Wonder* Low-Sodium) 70
w/buttermilk (*Wonder*) 75
Vienna bread (*Francisco*—long, sliced) 34
Vienna bread (*Jane Parker* Dutchtop) 75

* *Be careful about comparing the calories in brands of presliced bread. Bread is packaged in different size slices and, to be accurate, you must be sure you're comparing slices of the same size. (See "What You Should Know About Using This Book," pages 11–16)*

SWEET BREADS, MIXES*
See also "Breads" and "Rolls, Biscuits & Muffins"

	CALORIES
applesauce spice (*Pillsbury*), 1/16 of loaf	120
apricot nut (*Pillsbury*), 1/16 of loaf	110
banana (*Pillsbury*), 1/16 of loaf	120
blueberry nut (*Pillsbury*), 1/16 of loaf	110
cherry nut (*Pillsbury*), 1/16 of loaf	120
cornbread:	
(*Aunt Jemima* Easy Mix), ⅙ of cornbread	220
(*Ballard*), ⅛ of cornbread	160
(*Dromedary*), 2″ × 2″ square piece	130
cranberry (*Pillsbury*), 1/16 of loaf	120
date (*Pillsbury*), 1/16 of loaf	130
nut (*Pillsbury*), 1/16 of loaf	120
oatmeal raisin (*Pillsbury*), 1/16 of loaf	120

* Prepared according to package directions

ROLLS, BISCUITS & MUFFINS,
one piece*, except as noted
See also "Breads" and "Cakes, Cookies, Pies & Pastries"

	CALORIES
bagels, frozen:	
plain (*Lender's*)	150
plain, small (*Lender's Bagelette*)	70
egg (*Lender's*)	150
garlic (*Lender's*)	160
onion (*Lender's*)	160
onion, small (*Lender's Bagelette*)	70
pizza, see "Pizza, Frozen," page 169	
poppy seed (*Lender's*)	150
pumpernickel (*Lender's*)	160
raisin (*Lender's* Raisin 'n Honey)	200

agels, frozen, continued

rye (*Lender's*) 150
sesame seed (*Lender's*) 160
iscuits (*Wonder*) 105
iscuits, mix** (*Bisquick*), 2 oz. or ½ cup 240
iscuits, refrigerated:
(*Ballard Oven Ready*) 50
(*1869 Brand* Baking Powder) 100
(*1869 Brand* Baking Powder—prebaked) 100
(*1869 Brand* Butter Tastin') 100
(*Hungry Jack* Butter Tastin') 95
(*Hungry Jack* Flaky) 90
(*Pillsbury* Country Style) 50
(*Pillsbury* Prize) 65
(*Tenderflake* Baking Powder Dinner Biscuits) 55
buttermilk (*Ballard Oven Ready*) 50
buttermilk (*1869 Brand*) 100
buttermilk (*1869 Brand*—prebaked) 100
buttermilk (*Hungry Jack* Extra Rich) 65
buttermilk (*Hungry Jack* Flaky) 80
buttermilk (*Hungry Jack* Fluffy) 100
buttermilk (*Pillsbury*) 50
buttermilk (*Pillsbury* Big Country) 90
buttermilk (*Pillsbury Extra Lights*) 60
buttermilk (*Tenderflake* Dinner Biscuits) 55
uns, *see "rolls" below*
heese, bake and serve
(*Jane Parker* Hot Slices), 1 section 85
innamon (*Jane Parker* Hot Slices), 1 section 85
Jane Parker Hot Slices—white), 1 section 80
Jane Parker Hot Slices—half and half), 1 section 80
uffins:
blueberry (*Howard Johnson's Toastee*) 121
blueberry (*Thomas' Toast-r-Cakes*) 110
bran (*Arnold Bran'nola*) 160
bran (*Thomas' Toast-r-Cakes*) 120
corn (*Howard Johnson's Toastee*) 112

rolls, continued

cloverleaf (*Jane Parker*) 85
club (*Pepperidge Farm*) 120
crescent (*Pepperidge Farm* Butter Crescent) 130
deli style (*Arnold* Deli Twist) 110
deli style (*Pepperidge Farm*) 180
dinner (*Arnold*) 60
dinner (*Arnold* Party Rolls) 55
dinner (*Home Pride*) 90
dinner (*Pepperidge Farm*) 65
dinner (*Pepperidge Farm* Golden Twist) 120
dinner (*Pepperidge Farm* Hearth) 60
dinner (*Pepperidge Farm* Old Fashioned) 37
dinner (*Pepperidge Farm* Party Rolls) 35
dinner (*Wonder*) 105
dinner, bake and serve (*Jane Parker*) 60
finger (*Pepperidge Farm*) 60
flaky, bake and serve (*Jane Parker*) 95
frankfurter or hot dog (*Arnold*) 110
frankfurter or hot dog (*Jane Parker*) 90
frankfurter or hot dog (*Pepperidge Farm*) 120
frankfurter or hot dog (*Taystee*) 120
frankfurter or hot dog (*Wonder*) 160
French (*Pepperidge Farm—4-pack*) 230
French (*Pepperidge Farm—9-pack*) 110
French, bake and serve (*Jane Parker*) 80
French, brown and serve (*Francisco*) 90
French, brown and serve
   (*Pepperidge Farm—large*), ½ roll 200
French, brown and serve
   (*Pepperidge Farm—small*), ½ roll 130
French, brown and serve (*Wonder*) 85
French, sweet, brown and serve (*Francisco*), 3″ roll 100
French, sweet, brown and serve (*Francisco*), 6″ roll 240
gem style, brown and serve (*Wonder*) 85
(*Jane Parker* Enriched) 65
(*Jane Parker* Enriched—sliced) 100

rolls, continued

hamburger (*Arnold*) 110

hamburger (*Jane Parker*) 90

hamburger (*Pepperidge Farm*) 110

hamburger (*Taystee*) 120

hamburger (*Wonder*) 160

hoagie (*Jane Parker*) 200

hoagie, Italian (*Jane Parker*) 150

kaiser (*Francisco*) 180

kaiser and hoagie (*Wonder*), ½ roll 230

pan roll (*Wonder*) 105

parkerhouse (*Pepperidge Farm*) 60

sandwich (*Arnold*) 130

sandwich (*Pepperidge Farm*) 140

sandwich, soft (*Arnold*) 110

sandwich, wheat (*Oroweat*) 200

sesame seed (*Pepperidge Farm* Buns) 120

sesame seed (*Pepperidge Farm* Sesame Crisp) 70

twin, bake and serve (*Jane Parker*) 85

variety (*Francisco*) 100

rolls, frozen:

croissant (*Sara Lee*) 109

dinner (*Sara Lee* Party Rolls) 55

parkerhouse (*Sara Lee*) 73

sesame seed (*Sara Lee*) 55

rolls, mix** (*Pillsbury* Hot Rolls) 95

rolls, refrigerator:

(*Butterflake*) 110

crescent (*Ballard*) 95

crescent (*Pillsbury*) 95

dinner, white (*Pillsbury* Bakery Style) 90

dinner, wheat (*Pillsbury* Bakery Style) 90

frankfurter wrap (*Pillsbury* Wiener Wrap) 60

frankfurter wrap, cheese (*Pillsbury* Wiener Wrap) ...60

* *As packaged*
** *Prepared according to package directions*

BREADSTICKS, one piece*, except as noted

CALORIES

lightly salted (*Pepperidge Farm* Snack Sticks), ½ oz.	60
plain (*Stella D'Oro*)	41
plain (*Stella D'Oro* Dietetic—salt free)	42
pumpernickel (*Pepperidge Farm* Snack Sticks), ½ oz.	55
onion (*Stella D'Oro*)	39

sesame:

(*Flavor Tree*), ½ oz.	79
(*Flavor Tree* Low-Sodium), ½ oz.	81
(*Pepperidge Farm* Snack Sticks), ½ oz.	60
(*Stella D'Oro*)	53
(*Stella D'Oro* Dietetic—salt-free)	57
sesame-bran (*Flavor Tree*), ½ oz.	82
whole wheat (*Pepperidge Farm* Snack Sticks), ½ oz.	55

* *As packaged*

CROUTONS, ¼ cup, except as noted
See also "Crumbs & Meal" and "Stuffing & Stuffing Mixes"

CALORIES

plain:

(*Bel-Air*)	30
(*Brownberry* "Buttery" Toasted)	45
(*Pepperidge Farm*), ⅓ oz.*	47
bacon (*Bel-Air*)	40
Caesar salad (*Brownberry*)	45

cheese:

(*Brownberry*)	45
Cheddar (*Pepperidge Farm*), ⅓ oz.*	43
Italian (*Bel-Air*)	50
cheese-garlic (*Bel-Air*)	50
cheese-garlic (*Pepperidge Farm*), ⅓ oz.*	47
garlic (*Bel-Air*)	40

Croutons, continued

herb seasoned (*Croutettes*), .7 oz.** 70
onion-garlic (*Brownberry*) 45
onion-garlic (*Pepperidge Farm*), ⅓ oz.* 47
seasoned:
  (*Bel-Air*) 45
  (*Brownberry*) 45
  (*Pepperidge Farm*), ⅓ oz.* 47

* *Approximately ¼ cup*
** *Approximately ½ cup*

CRUMBS & MEAL, one ounce, except as noted
See also "Croutons" and "Stuffing & Stuffing Mixes"

CALORIES

breadcrumbs:
  (*Colonna*), 2 tbsp. 29
  (*Jane Parker*), 2 tbsp. 28
  (*Wonder*) 108
  flavored, Italian style (*Jane Parker*), 2 tbsp. 29
  seasoned (*Contadina*), 2 tbsp. 50
corn-flake crumbs (*Kellogg's*) 110
corn meal or grits, *see "Cereals & Corn Products, Dry,"*
  page 22
cracker crumbs:
  (*Keebler*) 106
  (*Premium* Saltines) 120
  graham (*Keebler*) 122
  graham (*Nabisco*) 140
  graham (*Sunshine*) 119
matzo meal (*Manischewitz*) 110

STUFFING & STUFFING MIXES
See also "Croutons" and "Crumbs & Meal"

CALORIES

stuffing, dry:
    cornbread (*Pepperidge Farm*), 1 oz. 110
    cube (*Pepperidge Farm*), 1 oz. 110
    herb (*Pepperidge Farm*), 1 oz. 110
    chicken and herb, pan style
    (*Pepperidge Farm*), 1 oz. 110
    seasoned, pan style (*Pepperidge Farm*), 1 oz. 110
stuffing mixes*:
    (*Bell's*—6-oz. pkg.), ½ cup 220
    (*Bell's*—16-oz. pkg.), ½ cup 233
    chicken (*Stove Top*), ½ cup 170
    chicken (*Uncle Ben's*), ½ cup 177
    cornbread (*Stove Top*), ½ cup 170
    cornbread (*Uncle Ben's*), ½ cup 176
    herb seasoned (*Croutettes*), ½ cup 130
    pork (*Stove Top*), ½ cup 170
    traditional sage (*Uncle Ben's*), ½ cup 177
    with rice (*Stove Top*), ½ cup 180

* *Prepared according to package directions*

SEASONED COATING MIXES, one envelope, as packaged

CALORIES

for chicken:
    (*Shake 'n Bake*) 279
    barbecue style (*Shake 'n Bake*) 366
    crispy country mild (*Shake 'n Bake*) 318
    Italian flavor (*Shake 'n Bake*) 286
for fish (*Shake 'n Bake*) 226
for hamburger (*Shake 'n Bake*) 163
for pork (*Shake 'n Bake*) 260
for pork and ribs, barbecue style (*Shake 'n Bake*) 290

FLOUR, one cup, except as noted
See also "Cereals & Corn Products, Dry (Uncooked),"
"Yeast, Baker's" and "Baking Powder & Cornstarch"

	CALORIES
all-purpose (*Pillsbury*)	400
bread (*Pillsbury*)	410
buckwheat (*Elam's* Pure), 4 oz.*	401

cake:

(*Swans Down*)	400
self-rising (*Presto*)	400
self-rising (*Swans Down*)	360
(*King Midas*)	400
(*Occident*)	400
(*Peavey* High Altitude Hungarian)	400
plain (*Ballard*)	400

tortilla:

(*Pinata*), 4 oz.*	320

rye:

medium (*Pillsbury*)	420
wheat (*Pillsbury* Bohemian)	400
whole (*Elam's* Stone Ground 100%), 4 oz.*	405
sauce and gravy (*Pillsbury*), 2 tbsp.	50

self-rising:

(*Ballard*)	380
(*Aunt Jemima*)	400
(*Pillsbury*)	380
unbleached (*Pillsbury*)	380
unbleached (*Pillsbury*)	400
unbleached, white, w/wheat germ (*Elam's*), 4 oz.*	414

whole wheat:

(*Elam's* Stone Ground), 4 oz.*	416
(*Pillsbury*)	400

* *Approximately 1 cup*

YEAST, BAKER'S

CALORIES

active, dry (*Fleischmann's*), ¼-oz. pkg. 20
active, dry (*Fleischmann's*—in jars), ¼ oz. 20
active, fresh (*Fleischmann's*), 6-oz. pkg. 15
household (*Fleischmann's*), ½ oz. 15

BAKING POWDER & CORNSTARCH

CALORIES

baking powder (*Calumet*), 1 tsp. 2
baking powder (*Davis*), 1 tsp. 5
cornstarch (*Argo/Kingsford's/Duryea's*), 1 tbsp. 35

CRACKERS, one piece*, except as noted
See also "Chips, Puffs & Similar Snacks"

CALORIES

(*American Harvest*) 16
animal crackers, *see "Cookies," page 223*
arrowroot, *see "Cookies," page 223*
bacon flavor (*Keebler* Bacon Toast) 16
bacon flavor (*Nabisco* Bacon Thins) 11
butter flavor:
    (*Hi-Ho*) 19
    (*Keebler* Club) 16
    (*Keebler* Town House) 17
    (*Nabisco* Butter Thins) 14
    (*Ritz*) 17
    (*Tam-Tams*) 14
    (*Sunshine* Banquet Wafers) 14
butter flavor-sesame (*Nabisco* Sesame Snack) 17
cheese filled (*Frito-Lay's*), 1½-oz. pkg. 200

Crackers, continued

cheese-filled sandwich (*Cheez Waffles*), 1 oz. 140
cheese flavor:
    (*Cheese Nips*) 6
    (*Cheese Shindig*) 7
    (*Cheez-It*) 6
    Cheddar (*Pepperidge Farm* Goldfish), ¼ oz. 35
    Cheddar (*Pepperidge Farm* Goldfish Thins) 18
    Parmesan (*Nabisco* Cheese Swirls) 11
    Parmesan (*Pepperidge Farm* Goldfish), ¼ oz. 35
    Swiss (*Nabisco* Cheese Snack) 10
cheese sandwich, peanut-butter filled (*Cheda-Nut*) 38
(*Chicken In A Biskit*) 10
(*FFV* Ocean Crisp) 58
(*FFV* Snack Crackers) 17
flatbread:
    (*Ideal* Ultra-Thin) 12
    (*Ideal*) bran 19
    whole grain (*Ideal*) 19
garlic (*Manischewitz* Garlic *Tams*) 13
garlic (*Old London* Melba Rounds) 10
graham crackers, *see "Cookies," page 226*
matzo: one sheet or piece:
    (*Manischewitz* American) 115
    (*Manischewitz* Egg 'n Onion) 112
    (*Manischewitz* Matzo Cracker) 8
    (*Manischewitz* Matzo Thins) 91
    (*Manischewitz* Passover Matzo) 129
    (*Manischewitz* Passover Egg Matzo) 132
    (*Manischewitz* Passover Thin Tea Matzo) 103
    (*Manischewitz* Passover Whole Wheat Matzo) 118
    (*Manischewitz* Thin Salted) 95
    (*Manischewitz* Thin Tea Matzo) 103
    (*Manischewitz* Unsalted) 112
    (*Manischewitz* Whole Wheat with Bran) 110
melba toast (*Old London*) 17

Crackers, continued

onion flavor:
   (*Keebler* Onion Toast) 15
   (*Nabisco* French Onion) 12
   (*Manischewitz* Onion *Tams*) 13
   green (*Pepperidge Farm Goldfish*
      Mixed Suite), ¼ oz. 35

oyster:
   (*Dandy*) 3
   (*Oysterettes*) 3
   (*Sunshine*) 4
   (*Zesta*) 2

peanut butter (*Frito-Lay's*), 1½-oz. pkg. 210
pizza (*FFV*) 15
pizza (*Pepperidge Farm Goldfish*), ¼ oz. 35
potato (*Keebler* Potato Crisp) 16
potato (*Tater Puffs*) 7
pumpernickel (*Keebler* Pumpernickel Toast) 15
pumpernickel (*Old London* Melba Toast) 17

rye:
   (*Finn Crisp* Bread Wafers) 20
   (*Keebler* Rye Toast) 16
   (*Nabisco* Rye Wafers) 20
   (*Pepperidge Farm Goldfish* Thins) 17
   (*Ry-Krisp*) 25
   (*Wasa* Lite Rye Crisp Bread) 30
   (*Wasa* Golden Rye Crisp Bread) 37
   (*Wasa* Hearty Rye Crisp Bread) 54
   dark, with caraway (*Finn Crisp* Bread Wafers) 20
   seasoned (*Nabisco* Rye Wafers) 23
   seasoned (*Ry-Krisp*) 30
   seasoned (*Wasa* Rye Crisp Bread) 34

saltines:
   (*FFV*) 13
   (*Krispy*) 12
   (*Krispy* Unsalted) 13

saltines, continued

    (*Pepperidge Farm Goldfish*), ¼ oz. 35
    (*Pepperidge Farm Goldfish* Thins) 17
    (*Premium*) 12
    (*Premium* Unsalted) 12
sesame:
    (*FFV* Sesame Crisp) 14
    (*Keebler* Savory Sesame) 13
    (*Keebler* Sesame Toast) 16
    (*Old London* Melba Toast) 20
    (*Teeko* Glazed Sesame Crisp) 22
    (*Wasa* Crisp Bread) 60
sesame-cheese (*Pepperidge Farm Goldfish*
    Mixed Suite), ¼ oz. 35
sesame-garlic (*Pepperidge Farm Goldfish*), ¼ oz. 35
(*Skittle Chips*) 14
(*Sociables*) 10
soda and water biscuits:
    (*Crown Pilot*) 70
    (*Jacob's* Biscuits for Cheese) 35
    (*Jacob's* English Cream) 110
    (*Jacob's* Large Water Biscuits) 35
    (*Milk Lunch*) 28
    (*Royal Lunch*) 55
    (*Sea Toast*) 65
    (*Waldorf* Low-Sodium) 14
soup and oyster, *see "oyster," above*
sourdough (*Wasa* Toast) 45
taco (*Pepperidge Farm Goldfish*), ¼ oz. 35
toast peanut butter (*Frito-Lay's*), 1½-oz. pkg. 210
(*Uneeda*) 22
(*Wasa* Mora Crisp Bread) 333
(*Wasa* Sport Crisp Bread) 43
(*Waverly*) 18
wheat:
    (*FFV* Stoned Wheat Wafers) 15
    (*Keebler* Wheat Toast) 16

* As packaged

CHAPTER 3

CREAM, MILK AND MILK BEVERAGES

MILK, eight fluid ounces, except as noted
See also "Cream" and "Flavored Milk Beverages"

	CALORIES
buttermilk, .5% fat (*Meadow Gold*)	105
buttermilk, 1.5% fat (*Foremost*)	110
condensed, canned:	
(*Borden Dime Brand*), ½ cup	504
(*Borden Eagle Brand*), ½ cup	500
(*Borden Magnolia Brand*), ½ cup	504
dry nonfat, reconstituted*:	
(*A & P*)	80
(*Carnation*)	80
(*Foremost Milkman*)	97
(*Pet* Instant)	80
(*Sanalac*)	80
evaporated, canned:	
(*A & P*), ½ cup	170
(*Borden*), ½ cup	173
(*Carnation*), ½ cup	170
(*Pet*), ½ cup	170
(*Wilson's*), ½ cup	170
filled (*Dairymate*), ½ cup	150
lowfat (*Carnation*), ½ cup	110
skimmed (*Carnation*), ½ cup	100
skimmed (*Pet*), ½ cup	100
half and half, *see "Cream," page 51*	

Milk, continued

skim or lowfat:

(Borden Lite Line) 120
(Borden Pro-Line) 140
(Foremost Profile) 99
(Foremost Profile Nonfat) 91
(Foremost So-Lo) 133
(Hood Nuform Lowfat) 110
(Hood Silouet Skim) 110
(Light n' Lively) 110
(Meadow Gold) 87
(Viva) 137

whole:

(A & P) 150
(Dellwood) 150
(Hood) 150
3.3% fat (Foremost) 148
3.3% fat (Meadow Gold) 150
3.5% fat (Borden) 150
3.5% fat (Foremost) 153
3.7% fat (Sealtest) 157

CREAM, one tablespoon
See also "Milk" and "Creamers, Non-Dairy"

CALORIES

half and half:

10.5% fat (Foremost) 19
10.5% fat (Sealtest) 19
12% fat (Foremost) 21
12% fat (Meadow Gold) 30

heavy, whipping*:

(Foremost) 54
36% fat (Meadow Gold) 50
36% fat (Sealtest) 52

Cream, continued

light, table or coffee:

   18% fat (*Foremost*) 28

   18% fat (*Sealtest*) 28

   20% fat (*Foremost*) 31

medium, whipping* (*Sealtest*) 44

sour, *see "Sour Cream," page 52*

whipped, *see "Dessert Toppings," page 243*

* *Unwhipped (volume is approximately doubled when whipped)*

SOUR CREAM, one tablespoon
See also "Cream"

                                         CALORIES

plain or regular:

   (*Breakstone*) 29

   (*Hood*) 25

   (*Meadow Gold*) 29

   (*Sealtest*) 30

   18% fat (*Foremost*) 19

   20% fat (*Foremost*) 21

half and half:

   (*Hood Nuform*) 20

   10.5% fat (*Foremost*) 19

   12% fat (*Foremost*) 21

imitation (*Pet*) 25

CREAMERS, NON-DAIRY, one tablespoon, except as noted
See also "Cream"

                                         CALORIES

dry form:

   (*Ann Page*) 36

   (*Coffee-mate*) 30

   (*Coffee-mate*), 1 packet 16

dry form, continued

   (Cremora) 36
   (IGA) 33
   (Pet) 30
liquid form:
   *(Coffee-mate)** 13
   (Coffee Rich) 20
   (Coffee Twin) 18
   (Jerzee), 1 fl. oz. 43
   (Poly Rich), 1 fl. oz. 43
   (Sanna) 24
   half and half *(Meadow Gold)* 27
whipped, *see "Dessert Toppings," page 253*

* *Liquid reconstituted: 2 parts water and 1 part dry form*

FLAVORED MILK BEVERAGES,
eight fluid ounces, except as noted
See also "Eggnog, Nonalcoholic"
and *"Cocoa & Flavored Mixes, Dry"*

                                              CALORIES

banana, canned *(Sego)*, 10-fl.-oz. can 225
butterscotch, canned *(Slender)*, 10-fl.-oz. can 225
butterscotch, canned *(Sego)*, 10-fl.-oz. can 225
cherry-vanilla, mix* *(Foremost* Instant Breakfast) 290
chocolate:
   drink, .7% fat, dairy pack *(Foremost)* 161
   drink, 2% fat, dairy pack *(Meadow Gold)* 185
   milk, dairy pack *(Sealtest)* 200
   milk, 3.3% fat, dairy pack *(Foremost)* 218
   milk, 3.3% fat, dairy pack *(Meadow Gold)* 200
   milk, lowfat, dairy pack *(Hood)* 160
   canned *(Borden* Dutch Chocolate Drink),
      7¾-fl.-oz. can 200
   canned *(Borden* Frosted Shake), 7½-fl.-oz. can 270

chocolate, continued

    canned (*Slender*), 10-fl.-oz. can 225
    canned (*Sego*), 10-fl.-oz. can 225
    canned (*Sego* Dutch and Very Chocolate),
      10-fl.-oz. can 225
    mix* (*Carnation* Instant Breakfast) 280
    mix* (*Foremost* Instant Breakfast) 290
    mix* (*Pillsbury* Instant Breakfast) 290
    mix* (*Slender*), 6 fl. oz. 225

chocolate fudge:

    canned (*Borden Frosted Shake*), 7½-fl.-oz. can 270
    canned (*Slender*), 10-fl.-oz. can 225
    mix* (*Foremost* Instant Breakfast) 290

chocolate malt:

    canned (*Slender*), 10-fl.-oz. can 225
    canned (*Sego*), 10-fl.-oz. 225
    mix* (*Carnation* Instant Breakfast) 280
    mix* (*Pillsbury* Instant Breakfast) 290
    mix* (*Slender*), 6 fl. oz. 225

chocolate marshmallow, canned (*Slender*), 10-fl.-oz. can ..225
chocolate marshmallow, canned (*Sego*), 10-fl.-oz. can 225
cocoa, *see "Cocoa & Flavored Mixes, Dry," page 265*
coffee:

    milk, low fat, dairy pack (*Hood*) 160
    canned (*Borden Frosted Shake*), 7½-fl.-oz. can 270
    canned (*Slender*), 10-fl.-oz. can 225
    mix* (*Carnation* Instant Breakfast) 280
    mix* (*Foremost* Instant Breakfast) 290
    mix* (*Slender*), 6 fl. oz. 225

strawberry:

    canned (*Borden* Frosted Shake), 7½-fl.-oz. can 270
    canned (*Sego*), 10-fl.-oz. can 225
    mix* (*Carnation* Instant Breakfast) 280
    mix* (*Foremost* Instant Breakfast) 290
    mix* (*Pillsbury* Instant Breakfast) 290

Flavored Milk Beverages, continued

vanilla:

    canned (*Borden* Frosted Shake), 7½-fl.-oz. can 270

    canned (*Slender*), 10-fl.-oz. can 225

    canned (*Sego*), 10-fl.-oz. can 225

    canned (*Sego* Very Vanilla), 10-fl.-oz. can 225

    mix* (*Carnation* Instant Breakfast) 280

    mix* (*Foremost* Instant Breakfast) 290

    mix* (*Pillsbury* Instant Breakfast) 290

    mix* (*Slender*), 6 fl. oz. 225

* *Prepared according to package directions, with whole milk*

EGGNOG, NONALCOHOLIC, four fluid ounces

CALORIES

canned:

    4.7% fat (*Borden*) 132

    6% fat (*Borden*) 154

    8% fat (*Borden*) 171

dairy pack:

    6% fat (*Foremost*) 206

    6% fat (*Meadow Gold*) 164

    6% fat (*Sealtest*) 174

CHAPTER 4

YOGURT

YOGURT & YOGURT DRINKS, one serving*
See also "Frozen Yogurt"

CALORIES

plain:
    (*Breyer's*), 8 fl. oz. 160
    (*Colombo*), 8 oz. 150
    (*Dannon*), 8 fl. oz. 150
    (*Foremost*), 8 fl. oz. 150
    (*Friendship*), 8 oz. 150
    (*Hood Nuform*), 8 oz. 150
    (*Yoplait*), 6 oz. 130
apple:
    (*Colombo* Shake), 6 oz. 150
    (*Yoplait*), 6 oz. 190
    crisp (*New Country*), 8 oz. 240
    Dutch (*Dannon*), 8 fl. oz. 260
    spiced (*Colombo*), 8 oz. 240
    spiced (*Hood* Swiss Style), 8 oz. 240
apricot (*Dannon*), 8 fl. oz. 260
apricot (*Foremost*), 8 fl. oz. 250
banana:
    (*Colombo* Sundae Style), 5 oz. 140
    (*Dannon*), 8 fl. oz. 260
    split (*Hood* Firm 'N Fruity), 5 oz. 140
banana-strawberry (*Colombo*), 8 oz. 235

Yogurt & Yogurt Drinks, continued

banana strawberry (*Colombo* Lite Lowfat), 8 oz. 190
blackberry (*Foremost*), 8 fl. oz. 250
blueberry:
    (*Breyer's*), 8 fl. oz. 270
    (*Colombo*), 8 oz. 250
    (*Colombo* Lite Lowfat), 8 oz. 190
    (*Colombo* Sundae Style), 5 oz. 140
    (*Dannon*), 8 fl. oz. 260
    (*Foremost*), 8 fl. oz. 250
    (*Friendship*), 8 oz. 225
    (*Hood* Firm 'N Fruity), 5 oz. 150
    (*Hood* Swiss Style), 8 oz. 230
    (*Meadow Gold* Swiss Style), 8 oz. 245
    (*Meadow Gold* Western Style), 8 oz. 249
    (*Sweet 'N Low*), 8 oz. 150
    (*Yoplait*), 6 oz. 190
    ripple (*New Country*), 8 oz. 240
boysenberry (*Dannon*), 8 fl. oz. 260
boysenberry (*Meadow Gold* Swiss Style), 8 oz. 245
cherry:
    (*Colombo* Lite Lowfat), 8 oz. 180
    (*Colombo* Shake), 6 oz. 150
    (*Dannon*), 8 fl. oz. 260
    (*Foremost*), 8 fl. oz. 250
    (*Friendship*), 8 oz. 225
    (*Hood* Swiss Style), 8 oz. 250
    (*Sweet 'N Low*), 8 oz. 150
    (*Yoplait*), 6 oz. 190
    black (*Breyer's*), 8 fl. oz. 270
    black (*Colombo*), 8 oz. 230
    black (*Hood* Firm 'N Fruity), 5 oz. 140
    red (*Colombo* Sundae Style), 5 oz. 140
    supreme (*New Country*), 8 oz. 240
cherry-vanilla (*Colombo*), 8 oz. 250
coffee (*Dannon*), 8 fl. oz. 200
fruit crunch (*New Country*), 8 oz. 240

Yogurt & Yogurt Drinks, continued

Hawaiian delight (*Hood* Firm 'N Fruity), 5 oz. 140
Hawaiian salad (*New Country*), 8 oz. ..,.............240
honey (*Dannon*), 8 fl. oz. 260
honey-banana (*Colombo*), 8 oz. 220
honey and berries (*New Country*), 8 oz. 240
honey-vanilla (*Colombo* Lite Lowfat), 8 oz. 160
honey-vanilla (*Colombo* Sundae Style), 5 oz. 138
lemon:
   (*Dannon*), 8 fl. oz. 200
   (*Foremost*), 8 fl. oz. 250
   (*Hood* Swiss Style), 8 oz. 270
   (*Sweet 'N Low*), 8 oz. 150
   (*Yoplait*), 6 oz. 190
   custard (*Colombo*), 8 oz. 220
   ripple (*New Country*), 8 oz. 240
maple nut (*Hood* Firm 'N Fruity), 5 oz. 140
orange:
   (*Dannon*), 8 fl. oz. 200
   (*Foremost* Mandarin Orange), 8 fl. oz. 250
   (*Meadow Gold* Western Style), 8 oz. 249
   (*Yoplait*), 6 oz. 190
   supreme (*New Country*), 8 oz. 240
peach:
   (*Colombo* Lite Lowfat), 8 oz. 190
   (*Colombo* Sundae Style), 5 oz. 140
   (*Foremost* Lowfat Drink/Liquid), 8 fl. oz. 190
   (*Friendship*), 8 oz. 225
   (*Hood* Firm 'N Fruity), 5 oz. 140
   (*Hood* Swiss Style), 8 oz. 230
   (*Meadow Gold* Western Style), 8 oz. 249
   (*Sweet 'N Low*), 8 oz. 150
   (*Yoplait*), 6 oz. 190
   and cream (*New Country*), 8 oz. 240
   melba (*Colombo*), 8 oz.................................230
   melba (*Hood* Firm 'N Fruity), 5 oz. 150

Yogurt & Yogurt Drinks, continued

pineapple:
   (*Colombo* Lite Lowfat), 8 oz. 190
   (*Colombo* Sundae Style), 5 oz. 130
   (*Foremost*), 8 fl. oz. 250
   (*Meadow Gold* Western Style), 8 oz. 249
pineapple-orange (*Dannon*), 8 fl. oz. 260

raspberry:
   (*Colombo*), 8 oz. 250
   (*Colombo* Lite Lowfat), 8 oz. 190
   (*Colombo* Sundae Style), 5 oz. 140
   (*Foremost*), 8 fl. oz. 250
   (*Foremost* Lowfat Drink/Liquid), 8 fl. oz. 190
   (*Friendship*), 8 oz. 225
   (*Hood* Firm 'N Fruity), 5 oz. 140
   (*Hood* Swiss Style), 8 oz. 250
   (*Meadow Gold* Swiss Style), 8 oz. 245
   (*Meadow Gold* Western Style), 8 oz. 249
   (*Sweet 'N Low*), 8 oz. 150
   red (*Dannon*), 8 fl. oz. 260
   ripple (*New Country*), 8 oz. 240

strawberry:
   (*Breyer's*), 8 fl. oz. 240
   (*Colombo*), 8 oz. 230
   (*Colombo* Lite Lowfat), 8 oz. 190
   (*Colombo* Shake), 6 oz. 150
   (*Colombo* Sundae Style), 5 oz. 140
   (*Dannon*), 8 fl. oz. 260
   (*Foremost*), 8 fl. oz. 250
   (*Foremost* Lowfat Drink/Liquid), 8 fl. oz. 190
   (*Friendship*), 8 oz. 225
   (*Hood* Firm 'N Fruity), 5 oz. 140
   (*Hood* Swiss Style), 8 oz. 250
   (*Meadow Gold* Swiss Style), 8 oz. 245
   (*Meadow Gold* Western Style), 8 oz. 249
   (*Naja*), 8 fl. oz. 240

strawberry, continued

    (*Sweet 'N Low*), 8 oz. 150
    supreme (*New Country*), 8 oz. 240
vanilla:
    (*Dannon*), 8 fl. oz. 200
    (*Yami*), 8 oz. 220
    bean (*Breyer's*), 8 fl. oz. 230
    French, ripple (*New Country*), 8 oz. 240
vanilla-honey (*Colombo*), 8 oz. 220

* *Note variation in sizes*

FROZEN YOGURT, one serving*
See also "Yogurt & Yogurt Drinks"
and "Ice Cream & Frozen Confections"

	CALORIES

boysenberry (*Danny In-A-Cup*), 8 fl. oz. 210
boysenberry, bar, carob-coated
    (*Danny On-A-Stick*), 2½-fl.-oz. bar 140
cherry (*Danny In-A-Cup*), 8 fl. oz. 210
cherry (*Yami Pushups*), 3 fl. oz. 90
(*Danny Parfait*), 4 fl. oz. 160
(*Danny Sampler*), 3 fl. oz. 70
(*Danny-Yo*), 3½ fl. oz. 110
lemon (*Danny In-A-Cup*), 8 fl. oz. 180
lemon-lime (*Yami Pushups*), 3 fl. oz. 90
orange (*Yami Pushups*), 3 fl. oz. 80
peach (*Danny In-A-Cup*) 8 fl. oz. 210
piña colada (*Danny In-A-Cup*), 8 fl. oz. 230
piña colada, bar (*Danny On-A-Stick*), 2½-fl.-oz. bar 70
pineapple-orange (*Danny In-A-Cup*), 8 fl. oz. 210
raspberry:
    (*Yami Pushups*), 3 fl. oz. 90
    red (*Danny In-A-Cup*), 8 fl. oz. 210

raspberry, continued

    red (*Sealtest*), 4 fl. oz. 110
    red, bar, chocolate-coated
        (*Danny On-A-Stick*), 2½-fl.-oz. bar 130
strawberry:
    (*Danny In-A-Cup*), 8 fl. oz. 210
    (*Sealtest*), 4 fl. oz. 110
    (*Yami Pushups*), 3 fl. oz. 80
    bar (*Danny On-A-Stick*), 2½-fl.-oz. bar 70
    bar, chocolate coated
        (*Danny On-A-Stick*), 2½-fl.-oz. bar 130
    with strawberry topping (*Danny Flip*), 5 fl. oz. 180
vanilla:
    (*Danny In-A-Cup*), 8 fl. oz. 180
    (*Sealtest*), 4 fl. oz. 120
    bar (*Danny On-A-Stick*), 2½-fl.-oz. bar 60
    bar, carob coated (*Danny On-A-Stick*), 2½-fl.-oz. bar ..130
    with raspberry topping (*Danny Flip*), 5 fl. oz. 170

* *Note variation in sizes*

CHAPTER 5

CHEESE AND
CHEESE PRODUCTS

CHEESE*, one ounce, except as noted
See also "Cheese Food," "Cheese Spreads,"
"Cottage Cheese" and "Cheese Entrees, Frozen"

	CALORIES
American:	
(*Borden*)	104
(*Dorman's*)	106
(*Hood*)	110
(*Kraft*)	105
(*Kraft Old English*)	105
(*Land O Lakes*)	110
(*Pauly*)	106
(*Saffola*—loaf)	93
(*Saffola*—slices)	96
(*Vera Sharp*)	104
asiago (*Frigo*)	113
blue:	
(*Bordon Blufort*), 1¼-oz. portion	131
(*Borden* Danish)	105
(*Borden Flora Danica*)	105
(*Dorman's* Danish)	100
(*Frigo*)	99
(*Kraft*)	99
(*Pauly* Danish)	100

colby, continued

    (*Pauly* Low-Sodium) 110

    (*Sargento*) 100

cottage, *see "Cottage Cheese," page 69*

cream:

    (*Kraft Philadelphia Brand*) 100

    with chives (*Kraft Philadelphia Brand*) 100

    whipped (*Kraft*) 100

    whipped (*TempTee*) 100

    imitation (*King Smoothee*) 65

Edam:

    (*Dorman's*) 101

    (*House of Gold*) 105

    (*Kraft*) 105

    (*Pauly*) 101

farmer (*Friendship*) 40

farmer (*Wispride*) 100

fontina (*Dorman's*) 110

fontina (*Pauly* Danish) 110

Frankenmuth (*Kraft*) 113

gjetost (*Kraft*) 134

Gouda:

    (*Borden Dutch Maid*) 86

    (*Dorman's*) 101

    (*Kraft*) 107

    (*Pauly*) 101

Gruyère:

    (*Dorman's*) 117

    (*Kraft*) 110

    (*Pauly*) 117

    (*Swiss Knight*) 101

imitation (*Dorman's Lo-Chol*) 100

imitation (*Pauly Lo-Chol*) 100

jack-dry (*Kraft*) 101

jack-fresh (*Kraft*) 95

Jarlsberg (*Dorman's*) 107

Jarlsberg (*Pauly*) 107

Cheese, continued

Leyden (*Kraft*) 80
(*Liederkranz Brand*) 86
Limburger (*Kraft*) 98
Monterey Jack:
  (*Borden*) 103
  (*Dorman's*) 106
  (*Frigo*) 103
  (*Kraft*) 103
  (*Pauly*) 100
  (*Sargento*) 100
Mozzarella:
  (*Borden*) 96
  (*Dorman's*—part skim) 72
  (*Frigo*) 79
  (*Kraft*) 79
  (*Pauly*—part skim) 80
  (*Sargento*) 90
Muenster:
  (*Borden*—natural) 85
  (*Dorman's*) 104
  (*Kraft*) 100
  (*Kraft*—processed) 102
  (*Pauly*) 104
  (*Sargento*) 100
Neufchâtel:
  plain (*Borden*) 73
  plain (*Kraft*) 69
  flavored, *see "Cheese Spreads," page 69*
nuworld (*Kraft*) 104
Parmesan:
  (*Dorman's*) 111
  (*Frigo*) 107
  (*Kraft*) 107
  (*Pauly*) 111
  grated (*Colonna*), ½ oz. 52
  grated (*Frigo*), ½ oz. 65

Cheese, continued

Scamorze (*Kraft*) 100
Skandor (*Dorman's* Swedish) 100
Skandor (*Pauly* Swedish) 100
Swiss:
    (*Borden* Finland Imported) 104
    (*Borden* Switzerland Imported) 104
    (*Dorman's*—natural) 107
    (*Dorman's*—processed) 95
    (*Kraft*—natural) 104
    (*Kraft*—processed, loaves) 93
    (*Kraft*—processed, slices) 95
    (*Pauly*—natural) 107
    (*Pauly*—processed) 95
    (*Pauly* Iceland Baby Swiss) 100
    (*Sargento*) 100
Tilsiter (*Dorman's* Danish) 96
Tilsiter (*Pauly*) 96
washed curd (*Kraft*) 108

* Note: *unless otherwise noted, the figure listed for any cheese above applies to all of the forms in which it may be packaged—slices, loaves, wedges, etc. Be careful not to confuse "real" cheese with a "cheese spread" or "cheese food" that bears the same or a similar name. Generally, it isn't hard to differentiate between cheese and cheese spreads, but cheese foods sometimes pose a problem (especially when they're packaged in slices). Check the label if you're confused about a product; if it is a cheese food, the label will say so.*

CHEESE FOOD, one ounce
See also "Cheese" and "Cheese Spreads"

	CALORIES
American (*Clearfield*)	90
American (*Pauly*)	90
bacon (*Kraft Cheez 'n Bacon*)	101
blue cheese (*Wispride*)	100
Cheddar (*Wispride*)	100

Cheese Food, continued

hickory smoke flavor (*Kraft Smokelle*) 93
(*Kraft Munst-ett*) 101
(*Kraft Superblend*) 92
(*Pauly Sweet Munchee*) 100
pimento (*Borden*) 91
pimento (*Pauly*) 90
pizza (*Kraft Pizzalone*) 90
port wine (*Wispride*) 90
salami (*Kraft*) 94
sharp (*Kraft Nippy Brand*) 93
Swiss:
  (*Kraft*) 91
  (*Pauly*) 90
  (*Wispride*) 100

CHEESE SPREADS, one ounce, except as noted
See also "Cheese" and "Cheese Food"

CALORIES

American:
  (*Hood*) 80
  (*Kraft*) 77
  (*Snack Mate*), 4 tsp. 60
cheddar (*Snack Mate*), 4 tsp. 60
cheddar, sharp (*Wispride*) 80
cheese and bacon (*Snack Mate*), 4 tsp. 60
(*Cheez Whiz*) 76
chive and green onion (*Snack Mate*), 4 tsp. 60
garlic (*Kraft*) 86
Gruyère (*Dorman's*) 90
Gruyère (*Pauly*) 90
hickory smoke flavor (*Kraft Smokelle*) 90
jalapeno pepper (*Cheez Whiz*) 76
(*Land O Lakes Golden Velvet*) 80
(*Laughing Cow*) 74

Cheese Spreads, continued

Neufchâtel cheese:

w/bacon and horseradish (*Kraft Party Snack*) 74

w/chipped beef (*Kraft Party Snack*) 67

w/chives (*Kraft Party Snack*) 69

w/clams (*Kraft Party Snack*) 67

w/onion (*Kraft Party Snack*) 66

w/relish (*Kraft Party Snack*) 72

pimento:

(*Cheez Whiz*) 76

(*Kraft Squeez-a-Snak*) 86

(*Snack Mate*), 4 tsp. 60

sharp (*Kraft Sharpie*) 90

sharp (*Kraft Squeez-a-Snak*) 85

(*Velveeta*) 85

COTTAGE CHEESE, four ounces, except as noted
See also "Cheese"

CALORIES

creamed:

(*Borden*) 120

(*Foremost*), ½ cup 120

(*Friendship* California Style) 120

(*Friendship* Calorie Meter) 100

(*Friendship Calorie Meter*—salt free) 90

(*Hood*) 120

(*Hood* Country Style) 120

(*Kraft*), ½ cup 107

(*Meadow Gold*), ½ cup 117

(*Sealtest*) 120

w/chives (*Hood* Chivier Cottage Cheese) 110

w/fruit salad (*Friendship Calorie Meter*) 120

w/peach-pineapple (*Sealtest*), ½ cup 115

w/pineapple (*Friendship*) 140

Cottage Cheese, continued

creamed partially:

(*Foremost So-Lo*), ½ cup 100
(*Meadow Gold*), ½ cup 102
(*Sealtest Light 'n Lively*), ½ cup 77

uncreamed or low-fat:

(*Friendship* Low Fat) 90
(*Friendship* Pot Style) 100
(*Hood Nuform*) 90
(*Kraft*) 103
(*Sealtest*) 90

CHEESE ENTREES, FROZEN,
one whole package*, except as noted

	CALORIES
cheese blintzes (*Golden*), 1 piece**	213
cheese souflé (*Stouffer's*), 12-oz. pkg.	710
Welsh rarebit (*Green Giant Toast Toppers*), 5-oz. pkg.	220
Welsh rarebit (*Stouffer's*), 10-oz. pkg.	710

 * *Note variations in size*
 ** *As packaged*

CHAPTER 6

FRUIT AND
FRUIT PRODUCTS

FRUIT, CANNED OR IN JARS,
½ cup, except as noted
See also "Fruit, Dried (Uncooked),"
"Fruit, Frozen" and "Fruit Juices"

                                                          CALORIES

applesauce:
   (*Del Monte*) 85
   (*Mott's*) 105
   (*Musselman's*) 97
   (*Seneca*) 93
   (*Seneca* Cinnamon) 90
   (*Seneca* Golden Delicious) 93
   (*Seneca* McIntosh) 90
   (*Stokely-Van Camp*) 90
   sugar-free (*Diet Delight*) 50
   sugar-free (*Featherweight*) 50
   sugar-free (*Mott's* Natural Style), 4 oz. 45
   sugar-free (*Musselman's*) 50
   sugar-free (*S & W Nutradiet*) 55
   sugar-free (*Seneca* 100% Natural) 50
apricots, solids and liquid:
   in juice (*Diet Delight*) 60
   in juice (*Featherweight*) 50
   in juice, halves (*S & W Nutradiet*) 50
   in juice, whole (*S & W Nutradiet*) 40

apricots, solids and liquid, continued

    in syrup, halves (*Ann Page*) 110

    in syrup, halves, unpeeled (*Del Monte*) 100

    in syrup, halves, unpeeled (*Libby's*) 99

    in syrup, halves (*Stokely-Van Camp*) 110

    in syrup, whole (*Ann Page*) 100

    in syrup, whole, peeled (*Del Monte*) 100

    in water (*Diet Delight*) 35

    in water (*Featherweight*) 30

    in water, halves (*S & W Nutradiet*) 35

cherries, solids and liquid:

    in juice (*Diet Delight*) 60

    in syrup, red sour, pitted (*A & P*) 58

    in syrup, red sour, pitted (*Stokely-Van Camp*) 45

    in syrup, Royal Anne (*Del Monte*) 95

    in syrup, sweet, w/pits (*Del Monte*) 90

    in syrup, sweet, pitted (*Del Monte*) 95

    in water, dark sweet (*Featherweight*) 57

    in water, light sweet (*Featherweight*) 48

cranberries, fresh-pack (*Ocean Spray*) 25

cranberry sauce, jellied (*Ocean Spray*), 2 oz. 90

cranberry sauce, whole (*Ocean Spray*), 2 oz. 90

cranberry-orange relish (*Ocean Spray*), 2 oz. 100

figs, in syrup, whole (*Del Monte*) 105

figs, in water (*Featherweight*) 60

fruit cocktail, solids and liquid:

    in juice (*Diet Delight*) 50

    in juice (*Featherweight*) 50

    in juice (*S & W Nutradiet*) 50

    in syrup (*Del Monte*) 85

    in syrup (*Libby's*) 94

    in syrup (*Stokely-Van Camp*) 95

    in extra heavy syrup (*A & P*) 115

    in water (*Diet Delight*) 40

    in water (*Featherweight*) 40

    in water (*Libby's*) 40

    in water (*S & W Nutradiet*) 40

Fruit, Canned or in Jars, continued

fruit for salad, solids and liquid:

    in juice (*Diet Delight*) 60

    in juice (*Featherweight*) 50

    in juice (*S & W Nutradiet*) 60

    in syrup (*A & P*) 100

    in syrup (*Del Monte*) 85

    in syrup (*Libby's*) 90

    in syrup (*Stokely-Van Camp*) 95

    in water (*Featherweight*) 35

    in water (*S & W Nutradiet*) 35

fruit, mixed (*Del Monte Fruit Cup*), 5-oz. can 100

fruit salad, in juice (*Kraft*) 50

fruit salad, tropical, in syrup (*Del Monte*) 100

grapefruit sections, solids and liquid:

    in juice (*Del Monte*) 45

    in juice (*Diet Delight*) 45

    in juice (*Featherweight*) 40

    in juice (*Kraft*) 60

    in juice (*S & W Nutradiet*) 40

    in syrup (*Del Monte*) 70

grapes, in water, light seedless (*Featherweight*) 50

orange sections, in juice (*Kraft*) 60

oranges, Mandarin, solids and liquid:

    in juice (*Diet Delight*) 45

    in syrup (*Del Monte*), 5½ oz. 100

    in water (*Featherweight*), 5¼ oz. 35

    in water (*S & W Nutradiet*) 28

peaches, solids and liquid:

    diced (*Del Monte Fruit Cup*), 5-oz. can 110

    in juice, sling or freestone, halves or slices

        (*Diet Delight*) 50

    in juice, cling or freestone, halves or slices

        (*Featherweight*) 50

    in juice, cling, halves or slices (*S & W Nutradiet*) 60

    in juice, freestone, halves or slices (*S & W Nutradiet*) ...50

    in syrup, cling, halves or slices (*Ann Page*) 95

peaches, solids and liquid, continued

in syrup, halves or slices (*Del Monte*) 85
in syrup, halves (*Libby's*) 95
in syrup, halves (*Stokely-Van Camp*) 95
in syrup, slices (*Libby's*) 92
in syrup, slices (*Stokely-Van Camp*) 90
in syrup, spiced (*Del Monte*), 7¼ oz. 150
in extra heavy syrup, freestone, sliced (*A & P*) 130
in extra heavy syrup, freestone, halves (*A & P*) 130
in water, cling, halves (*Diet Delight*) 30
in water, cling, halves or slices (*Featherweight*) 30
in water, cling, halves or slices (*S & W Nutradiet*) 30
in water, cling, slices (*Diet Delight*) 30
in water, slices (*Libby's*) 29

pears, Bartlett, solids and liquid:

in juice (*Diet Delight*) 60
in juice, halves (*Featherweight*) 57
in juice (*S & W Nutradiet*) 60
in syrup, halves or sliced (*Ann Page*) 95
in syrup (*Del Monte*) 80
in syrup (*Libby's*) 94
in syrup, halves (*Stokely-Van Camp*) 105
in syrup, slices (*Stokely-Van Camp*) 100
in water (*Diet Delight*) 35
in water, halves (*Featherweight*) 37
in water (*Libby's*) 36
in water (*S & W Nutradiet*) 35

pineapple, solids and liquid:

in juice, chunks, crushed or slices (*Ann Page/A & P*) 70
in juice, chunks, slices or tidbits (*Diet Delight*) 70
in juice, chunks, crushed or slices (*Del Monte*) 70
in juice, chunks, crushed, tidbits or slices
    (*Featherweight*) 70
in juice, chunks or crushed (*Dole*) 70
in syrup, chunks (*A & P*) 75
in syrup, crushed, slices or tidbits (*A & P*) 95

pineapple, solids and liquid, continued

    in syrup, chunks, crushed or slices (*Del Monte*) 95
    in syrup, chunks, crushed or slices (*Dole*) 95
    in water, sliced (*Featherweight*) 60
    in water, slices (*S & W Nutradiet*) 60
plums, purple, solids and liquid:
    in juice (*Diet Delight*) 70
    in juice (*Featherweight*) 67
    in juice (*S & W Nutradiet*) 80
    in syrup (*Del Monte*) 95
    in syrup (*Stokely-Van Camp*) 120
    in water (*Featherweight*) 39
prunes, stewed, with pits (*Del Monte*) 115
prunes, stewed, in water (*Featherweight*) ....130⁻

FRUIT, DRIED (UNCOOKED), one ounce,
except as noted
*See also "Fruit, Canned or
In Jars" and "Fruit, Frozen"*

                                     CALORIES

apple fruit roll, sweetened (*Sahadi*) 90
apples, evaporated (*Del Monte*) 70
apples, freeze-dried (*Mountain House*) 100
apricot fruit roll, sweetened (*Sahadi*) 90
apricots (*Del Monte*) 70
apricots (*Sunsweet*), ½ cup 224
banana chips (*Mountain House*) 155
blueberries, freeze-dried (*Mountain House*) 134
cherry fruit roll, sweetened (*Sahadi*) 90
coconut, *see "Sweet Baking Ingredients," page 246*
currants, zante:
    (*Del Monte*), ½ cup 190
    (*Sun•Maid*) 83
    (*Sun•Maid*), ½ cup 206

Fruit, Dried (Uncooked), continued

dates:

    chopped *(Dromedary)* 99

    diced *(Bordo)* 82

    pitted *(Bordo)* 83

    pitted *(Dromedary)* 94

fruit mix, freeze-dried *(Mountain House)*, .66 oz. 70

grape fruit roll, sweetened *(Sahadi)* 90

peaches:

    (Del Monte) 70

    (Sunsweet), ½ cup 210

    freeze-dried *(Mountain House)* 100

pears:

    (Del Monte) 75

    (Sunsweet), ½ cup 208

    freeze-dried *(Mountain House)* 100

pineapple, freeze-dried *(Mountain House)*, .85 oz. 90

plum fruit roll, sweetened *(Sahadi)* 90

plums, freeze-dried *(Mountain House)* 100

prunes:

    w/pits *(Del Monte)* 60

    w/pits *(Del Monte Moist-Pak)* 60

    w/pits *(Sunsweet)* 60

    pitted *(Del Monte)* 70

raisins:

    golden seedless *(Del Monte)* 87

    golden seedless *(Sun•Maid)* 83

    golden seedless *(Sun•Maid)*, ½ cup 250

    muscat *(Del Monte)* 83

    seedless *(Del Monte)* 87

    seedless *(Sun•Maid)* 83

    seedless *(Sun•Maid)*, ½ cup 250

    freeze-dried *(Mountain House)*, .82 oz. 80

raspberry fruit roll, sweetened *(Sahadi)* 90

strawberries, freeze-dried *(Mountain House)* 90

strawberry fruit roll, sweetened *(Sahadi)* 100

FRUIT, FROZEN, five ounces, except as noted
See also "Fruit, Canned or in Jars"
and "Fruit, Dried (Uncooked)"

	CALORIES
apple fritters (*Hanover*), 2 oz.	150
apple fritters (*Mrs. Paul's*), 2 oz. or 1 fritter	120
apples, escalloped (*Stouffer's*), 4 oz.	140
fruit, mixed (*Birds Eye* Quick Thaw)	130
peaches (*Birds Eye* Quick Thaw)	130
red raspberries (*Birds Eye* Quick Thaw)	140
red raspberries, in syrup (*Stokely-Van Camp*)	160
strawberries:	
(*Birds Eye* Quick Thaw)	110
halves (*Birds Eye*), 5.3 oz.	170
halves, in syrup (*Stokely-Van Camp*)	160
whole (*Birds Eye*), 4 oz.	70
whole, without syrup (*Stokely-Van Camp*)	60
whole, in syrup (*Stokely-Van Camp*), 4 oz.	110

FRUIT JUICES, six fluid ounces,
except as noted
See also "Fruit & Fruit-Flavored Drinks"
and "Vegetable Juices"

	CALORIES
apple:	
bottled (*Ann Page*)	90
bottled, from concentrate (*Hood*)	85
bottled (*Red Cheek*)	80
bottled (*Seneca*)	90
canned or bottled (*Mott's*)	80
canned (*Heinz*)	90
canned (*Musselman's*)	80

apple, continued

   canned (*Tree Top*) 75

   frozen* (*Ann Page*) 90

   frozen* (*Seneca*) 90

   frozen* (*Tree Top*) 75

grape:

   bottled (*Seneca*) 120

   bottled (*Welch's*) 120

   canned (*Heinz*) 122

   frozen* (*Minute Maid*) 99

   frozen* (*Seneca*) 100

   frozen, reconstituted 1 + 1 (*Welch's*) 200

   frozen, reconstituted 1 + 3 (*Welch's*) 100

grapefruit:

   bottled (*Ocean Spray*) 70

   canned (*Del Monte*) 70

   canned, sweetened (*Del Monte*) 80

   dairy pack (*Hood*) 70

   dairy pack (*Kraft*) 72

   dairy pack (*Tropicana*) 75

   frozen* (*Minute Maid*) 75

   pink, canned (*Texsun*) 77

lemon:

   fresh (*Sunkist*), 2 tbsp. 8

   bottled (*ReaLemon*), 2 tbsp. 6

   bottled (*Seneca*), 2 tbsp. 8

   frozen, full-strength (*Minute Maid*), 2 tbsp. 7

   reconstituted (*Ann Page*), 2 tbsp. 6

lime, bottled (*ReaLime*), 2 tbsp. 4

lime, bottled, sweetened (*Rose's*), 2 tbsp. 49

orange:

   canned (*Del Monte*) 70

   canned, sweetened (*Del Monte*) 80

   canned (*Featherweight*) 80

   canned (*Texsun*) 83

orange, continued

dairy pack (*Kraft*) 90
dairy pack (*Sunkist*) 78
dairy pack (*Tropicana*) 83
dairy pack, from concentrate (*Hood*) 80
frozen* (*Minute Maid*) 90
frozen* (*Snow Crop*) 90
frozen*, from concentrate (*Minute Maid*) 83

orange-grapefruit:

canned (*Del Monte*) 80
canned, sweetened (*Del Monte*) 80
frozen* (*Minute Maid*) 76
orange-pineapple, canned (*Texsun*) 89
pear apple (*Tree Top*) 75
pear grape (*Tree Top*) 83

pineapple:

canned (*A & P*) 100
canned (*Del Monte*) 100
canned (*Dole*) 100
canned (*Heinz*) 100
canned (*Texsun*) 97
frozen* (*Minute Maid*) 92

pineapple-grapefruit, canned (*Texsun*) 91
pineapple-orange, frozen* (*Minute Maid*) 94
pineapple-pink grapefruit, canned (*Dole*) 100

prune:

bottled or canned (*Ann Page*) 140
bottled or canned (*Mott's*) 140
bottled or canned (*Sunsweet*) 140
canned (*Del Monte*) 120
canned (*Heinz*) 130
with prune pulp, bottled (*Mott's*) 120

tangerine, sweetened, frozen* (*Minute Maid*) 85

* *Reconstituted according to package directions*

FRUIT & FRUIT FLAVORED DRINKS,
six fluid ounces, except as noted
See also "Fruit Juices" and "Soft Drinks & Mixers"

	CALORIES
all flavors, mix* (*Ann Page*)	60
all flavors, mix* (*Funny Face*)	60
all flavors, unsweetened mix, prepared with sugar (*Kool-Aid*)	75
apple:	
canned (*Ann Page*)	90
canned (*Hi-C*)	92
cider, canned (*Ann Page*)	90
apple-cherry, canned (*Musselman's* Breakfast Cocktail)	83
apple-grape, canned or bottled (*Mott's "P.M."*)	90
apple-grape, canned (*Musselman's* Breakfast Cocktail)	83
apricot nectar:	
canned (*Del Monte*)	100
canned (*Heart's Delight*)	100
canned (*Sunsweet*)	105
apricot-pineapple nectar, unsweetened, canned (*S & W Nutradiet*)	35
berry, wild (*Ann Page*)	90
berry, wild, canned (*Hi-C*)	88
cherry:	
canned (*Ann Page*)	90
canned (*Hi-C*)	93
mix* (*Cramores*)	68
mix* (*Hi-C*)	76
mix* (*Kool-Aid*)	75
mix* (*Wyler's*)	68
citrus, canned (*Ann Page* Citrus Cooler)	90
citrus, canned (*Hi-C* Citrus Cooler)	93
cranberry juice cocktail:	
(*Ann Page*)	120

cranberry juice cocktail, continued

   bottled *(Ocean Spray)* 110
   bottled *(Welch's)* 110
   low-calorie, bottled *(Ocean Spray)* 35
cranberry-apple:
   (Ann Page) 140
   bottled *(Ocean Spray Cranapple)* 130
   low-calorie, bottled *(Ocean Spray Cranapple)* 30
cranberry-apricot, bottled *(Ocean Spray Cranicot)* 110
cranberry-prune, bottled *(Ocean Spray Cranprune)* 120
grape:
   (Ann Page) 90
   bottled *(Welch's)* 110
   bottled *(Welchade)* 90
   dairy pack *(Tropicana)* 70
   canned *(Hi-C)* 89
   mix* *(Hi-C)* 76
   mix* *(Kool-Aid)* 68
   mix* *(Tang)* 90
   mix* *(Wyler's)* 68
   red, bottled *(Welchade)* 90
grape-cranberry, bottled *(Ocean Spray Crangrape)* 110
grapefruit:
   (A & P) 80
   dairy pack *(Tropicana)* 70
   mix* *(Tang)* 75
grapefruit-orange, canned
   (Musselman's Breakfast Cocktail) 68
lemonade:
   canned *(Country Time)* 68
   canned(*Lipton Lemon Tree)* 68
   dairy pack *(Hood)* 75
   dairy pack *(Sealtest)* 83
   freeze-dried *(Mountain House)*, 1 serving 80
   frozen* *(Country Time)* 68
   frozen* *(Minute Maid)* 74

Fruit & Fruit Flavored Drinks, continued

orangeade, mix* (*Wyler's*) 68
orangeade, frozen* (*Minute Maid*) 94
orange-apricot, canned (*Ann Page*) 90
orange-apricot, canned (*BC*) 75
orange-apricot, canned (*Musselman's* Breakfast Cocktail) ...75
orange-pineapple:
  canned (*Ann Page*) 90
  canned (*Hi-C*) 94
  canned (*Musselman's* Breakfast Cocktail) 75
peach, canned (*Hi-C*) 90
peach nectar, canned (*Del Monte*) 100
peach nectar, canned (*Heart's Delight*) 100
pear nectar, canned (*Del Monte*) 110
pear nectar, canned (*Heart's Delight*) 100
pineapple-grapefruit, canned (*Del Monte*) 90
pineapple-grapefruit, dairy pack (*Tropicana*) 70
pineapple-orange, canned (*Del Monte*) 90
pineapple-pink grapefruit, canned (*Del Monte*) 90
prune nectar, bottled (*Mott's*) 100
punch:
  all flavors, canned (*Hawaiian Punch*) 90
  all flavors, frozen* (*Hawaiian Punch*) 90
  fruit, bottled (*Welch's*) 100
  fruit, dairy pack (*Hood*) 75
  fruit, dairy pack (*Tropicana*) 70
  fruit, mix* (*Cramores*) 68
  fruit, mix* (*Hi-C*) 76
  fruit, mix* (*Wyler's*) 68
  fruit, Florida, canned (*Hi-C*) 95
  fruit, tropical, canned (*Ann Page*) 90
  fruit, tropical, mix* (*Kool-Aid*) 75
  red, mix* (*Hawaiian Punch*) 75
raspberry, mix* (*Kool Aid*) 68
raspberry, black, mix* (*Cramores*) 68

* Prepared or reconstituted according to package directions

CHAPTER 7

VEGETABLES AND VEGETABLE PRODUCTS

VEGETABLES, CANNED OR IN JARS,
½ cup, except as noted
See also "Vegetables, Dried & Mixes" and
"Vegetables, Frozen"

CALORIES

asparagus:
    (*Diet Delight*) 16
    (*Joan of Arc Pride*), 4 oz.* 24
    (*Musselman's*) 20
    (*S & W Nutradiet*) 17
    spears and tips (*Ann Page*) 18
    spears and tips (*Del Monte*) 18
    spears and cuts (*Green Giant*) 20
    spears, cut (*Featherweight*) 16
    spears, cut (*Kounty Kist/Lindy*) 20
    spears (*Le Sueur*) 20
    spears (*Stokely-Van Camp*) 25
    cuts (*Stokely-Van Camp*) 23
    puree (*Cellu*) 25
bamboo shoots (*La Choy*), 4 oz. 12
bean salad:
    kidney (*Read*) 138
    three-bean (*Green Giant*) 95
    three-bean (*Hanover* Old Fashioned), 4 oz.* 123
    three-bean (*Read*) 103

Vegetables, Canned or in Jars, continued

bean sprouts (*La Choy*) 12

beans, baked, *see "Beans, Baked & Baked-Style," page 106*

beans, black turtle (*Progresso*) 103

beans, butter:

    (*Ann Page*), 4 oz.* 85

    (*Hanover*), 4 oz.* 113

    (*Joan of Arc*) 100

    (*Van Camp*) 85

    w/ham (*Libby's*) 114

beans, cannellini or white kidney (*Progresso*) 95

beans, chili:

    (*Joan of Arc*) 110

    (*Van Camp* Mexican Style) 120

    in chili gravy (*Ann Page*), 4 oz.* 115

beans, fava (*Progresso*) 90

beans, great northern (*Joan of Arc*) 95

beans, green:

    (*Comstock* Blue Lake) 13

    (*Diet Delight*) 20

    whole (*Ann Page*) 20

    whole (*Del Monte*) 18

    whole (*Libby's* Blue Lake) 16

    whole (*Stokely-Van Camp*) 15

    whole, tiny (*Del Monte*) 20

    whole, cut or French style (*Green Giant*) 15

    whole, cut or French style (*Kounty Kist/Lindy*) 20

    cut (*Ann Page*) 23

    cut (*Del Monte*) 20

    cut (*Featherweight*) 20

    cut (*Hanover*), 4 oz.* 20

    cut (*Libby's* Blue Lake) 19

    cut (*S & W Nutradiet*) 20

    cut (*Stokely-Van Camp*) 18

    cut or French style (*Comstock*) 13

    French style (*Ann Page*) 20

beans, green, continued

French style (*Del Monte*) 20
French style (*Featherweight*) 20
French style (*Hanover*), 4 oz.* 19
French style (*Libby's* Blue Lake) 18
sliced (*Stokely-Van Camp*) 18
seasoned (*Del Monte*) 20
puree (*Cellu*) 35
beans, green, and whole potatoes, in ham-flavored sauce
   (*Hanover*), 4 oz.* 33
beans, Italian (*Del Monte*) 30
beans, kidney:
red (*Ann Page*), 4 oz.* 110
red (*Progresso*) 93
red (*Van Camp* New Orleans Style) 100
red, dark (*Hanover*), 4 oz.* 123
red, dark (*Joan of Arc*) 115
red, dark (*Van Camp*) 100
red, light (*Hanover*), 4 oz.* 122
red, light (*Joan of Arc*) 110
red, light (*Van Camp*) 105
salad, *see "bean salad," above*
white, *see "beans, cannellini or white kidney," above*
beans, lima:
(*Del Monte*) 75
(*Libby's*) 87
(*Stokely-Van Camp*) 80
baby (*Ann Page*), 4 oz.* 100
green (*Featherweight*) 73
medium green (*Ann Page*) 85
seasoned (*Del Monte*) 80
beans, pink (*Hanover*), 4 oz.* 115
beans, pinto:
(*Hanover*), 4 oz.* 100
(*Joan of Arc*) 110
(*Progresso*) 83

Vegetables, Canned or in Jars, continued

beans, red:

   (*Ann Page*), 4 oz.* 110

   (*Joan of Arc*) 115

   (*Van Camp*) 110

beans, refried, Mexican style (*Gebhardt*), 4 oz.* 114

beans, Roman (*Progresso*) 105

beans, shellie (*Stokely-Van Camp*) 40

beans, wax:

   whole (*Stokely-Van Camp*) 20

   cut (*Ann Page*) 23

   cut (*Del Monte*) 18

   cut (*Featherweight*) 20

   cut (*Libby's*) 22

   cut (*Stokely-Van Camp*) 20

   cut or French style (*Comstock*) 13

   French style (*Del Monte*) 18

   sliced (*Stokely-Van Camp*) 18

blackeye peas:

   (*Hanover*), 4 oz.* 105

   (*Progresso*) 83

   cook-dried, w/pork (*Ann Page*) 110

beets:

   whole (*Ann Page*) 45

   whole (*Stokely-Van Camp*) 40

   whole, cut or sliced (*Comstock*) 25

   whole, cut or sliced (*Del Monte*) 35

   cut (*Stokely-Van Camp*) 40

   diced (*Stokely-Van Camp*) 35

   shoestring (*Libby's*) 25

   sliced (*Ann Page*) 45

   sliced (*Featherweight*) 40

   sliced (*Libby's*—canned) 35

   sliced (*Libby's*—in jars) 37

   sliced (*S & W Nutradiet*) 35

   sliced (*Stokely-Van Camp*) 40

   Harvard (*Comstock*) 55

beets, continued

  Harvard (*Stokely-Van Camp*) 80
  Harvard, diced (*Libby's*—canned) 84
  Harvard, diced (*Libby's*—in jars) 86
  pickled, whole, tiny (*Libby's*) 84
  pickled, whole (*Stokely-Van Camp*) 100
  pickled, crinkle-cut (*Del Monte*) 75
  pickled, sliced (*Comstock*) 45
  pickled, sliced (*Libby's*) 78
  pickled, sliced (*Stokely-Van Camp*) 95
  puree (*Cellu*) 50
beets, pickled, w/onions (*Comstock*) 45
cabbage:
  red, sweet and sour (*Comstock*) 60
  red, sweet and sour (*Greenwoods*) 60
  sauerkraut, *see "sauerkraut," below*
  stuffed (*Joan of Arc*) 98
carrots:
  diced (*Del Monte*) 30
  diced (*Libby's*) 18
  diced (*Stokely-Van Camp*) 25
  sliced (*Ann Page*) 35
  sliced (*Del Monte*) 30
  sliced (*Featherweight*) 25
  sliced (*Libby's*) 23
  sliced (*S & W Nutradiet*) 30
  sliced (*Stokely-Van Camp*) 23
  puree (*Cellu*) 35
chickpeas or garbanzos:
  (*Hanover*), 4 oz.* 110
  (*Joan of Arc* Ceci Beans) 125
  (*Progresso*) 98
  (*Old El Paso*) 103
corn:
  whole kernel (*A & P*) 85
  whole kernel (*Del Monte* Family Style) 85
  whole kernel (*Del Monte*—vacuum pack) 100

corn, continued

whole kernel (*Diet Delight*) 60
whole kernel (*Featherweight*) 70
whole kernel (*Green Giant*) 80
whole kernel (*Green Giant* Nuggets) 75
whole kernel (*Kounty Kist/Lindy*) 90
whole kernel (*Kounty Kist/Lindy*—vacuum pack) 80
whole kernel (*Le Sueur*) 85
whole kernel (*Libby's*) 80
whole kernel (*S & W Nutradiet*) 80
whole kernel (*Stokely-Van Camp*) 90
whole kernel (*Stokely-Van Camp*—vacuum pack) 115
cream style (*A & P/Ann Page*) 105
cream style (*Del Monte*) 105
cream style (*Featherweight*) 80
cream style (*Green Giant*) 105
cream style (*Kounty Kist/Lindy*) 115
cream style (*Libby's*) 87
cream style (*S & W Nutradiet*) 100
cream style (*Stokely-Van Camp*) 105
white, whole kernel (*Del Monte*) 75
white, whole kernel (*Green Giant*—vacuum pack) 75
white, whole kernel (*Stokely-Van Camp*) 95
white, cream style (*Del Monte*) 95
white, cream style (*Stokely-Van Camp*) 100
corn and peppers (*Del Monte*) 95
corn and peppers (*Green Giant Mexicorn*) 75
garbanzo beans, *see "chickpeas or garbanzos," above*
mushrooms, whole, sliced or pieces and stems
   (*Green Giant*), 2 oz. 14
onions:
   boiled (*O & C*), 1 oz. 8
   French fried (*O & C*), 1 oz. 178
   in cream sauce (*O & C*), 1 oz. 143
peas:
   (*Diet Delight*) 50
   (*Libby's*) 60

peas, continued

early *(Del Monte)* 55
early *(Stokely-Van Camp)* 60
early, small *(A & P)* 65
early, small *(April Showers)* 60
early, small *(Kounty Kist/Lindy)* 70
early, small *(Le Sueur)* 55
early, small *(Minnesota Valley)* 55
sweet *(Featherweight)* 50
sweet *(Green Giant)* 55
sweet *(Kounty Kist/Lindy)* 65
sweet *(S & W Nutradiet)* 40
sweet *(Stokely-Van Camp)* 60
sweet, small *(Del Monte)* 50
sweet, small *(Green Giant Sweetlets)* 50
sweet, small *(Le Sueur)* 50
seasoned *(Del Monte)* 60
puree *(Cellu)* 70
peas, early, w/onions *(Green Giant)* 60
peas, sweet, w/onions *(Green Giant)* 55
peas and carrots:
  (Del Monte) 50
  (Diet Delight) 40
  (Libby's) 52
  (S & W Nutradiet) 35
  (Stokely-Van Camp) 50
peppers:
  chili, whole green *(Old El Paso)*, 4-oz. can 24
  chili, whole Jalapeno *(Old El Paso)*, 10-oz. can 90
  stuffed *(Joan of Arc)* 102
potato salad *(Joan of Arc)* 159
potato salad, German *(Read)*, 4 oz.* 115
potatoes, sweet, *see "sweet potatoes" or "yams," below*
potatoes, white:
  new *(Del Monte)* 45
  whole *(Ann Page)* 45
  whole *(Hanover)*, 4 oz.* 48

potatoes, continued

    whole (*Stokely-Van Camp*) 50
    sliced (*Ann Page*) 45
    sliced (*Hanover*), 4 oz.* 50
potatoes au gratin, w/bacon (*Hormel*), 7½-oz. can 234
potatoes, hashed, w/beef (*Dinty Moore*), 7½-oz. can 255
potatoes, scalloped, w/ham (*Hormel*), 7½-oz. can 253
pumpkin:
    (*A & P*) 40
    (*Del Monte*) 25
    (*Joan of Arc*), 4 oz.* 45
    (*Libby's*) 43
    (*Stokely-Van Camp*) 40
    pie filling, see "Pie Fillings, Canned," page 235
sauerkraut:
    (*Ann Page*) 25
    (*Del Monte*) 25
    (*Libby's—canned*) 21
    (*Libby's—in jars*) 19
    (*Stokely-Van Camp Bavarian Style*) 30
    chopped (*Stokely-Van Camp*) 20
    shredded (*Stokely-Van Camp*) 20
spinach:
    (*Ann Page*) 23
    (*Del Monte*) 23
    (*Featherweight*) 30
    (*Libby's*) 23
    puree (*Cellu*) 50
squash, puree (*Cellu*) 50
succotash:
    whole kernel (*Libby's*) 78
    whole kernel (*Stokely-Van Camp*) 85
    cream style (*Libby's*) 96
sweet potatoes, whole and pieces (*A & P*) 100
tomatoes:
    (*A & P*) 25
    whole, round and pear (*Contadina*), 4 oz.* 25

tomatoes, continued

    whole *(Del Monte)* 25
    whole *(Diet Delight)* 25
    whole *(Featherweight)* 20
    whole *(Hunt's)*, 4 oz.* 25
    whole *(Libby's)* 23
    whole *(S & W Nutradiet)* 25
    whole *(Stokely-Van Camp)* 25
    crushed *(Red Pack)* 45
    sliced, baby *(Contadina)*, 4 oz.* 35
    stewed *(Ann Page)* 35
    stewed *(Contadina)*, 4 oz.* 35
    stewed *(Del Monte)* 35
    stewed *(Featherweight)* 35
    stewed *(Hunt's)*, 4 oz.* 30
    stewed *(Libby's)* 32
    stewed *(Stokely-Van Camp)* 35
    wedges *(Del Monte)* 30
tomato paste, *see "Tomato Paste & Puree," page 107*
tomato puree, *see "Tomato Paste & Puree," page 108*
tomato sauce, *see "Sauces," page 189*
turnip greens, chopped *(Stokely-Van Camp)* 18
vegetables, mixed:
    (Ann Page) 45
    (Del Monte) 40
    (Featherweight) 35
    (Hanover), 4 oz.* 45
    (Libby's) 41
    (Stokely-Van Camp) 40
    Chinese, *see "Oriental & Oriental-Style Foods," page 168*
vegetable salad, garden *(Hanover)*, 4 oz.* 65
vegetable salad, sweet and sour *(Hanover)*, 4 oz.* 83
vegetable stew *(Dinty Moore)*, 7½-oz. can 162
water chestnuts *(La Choy)*, 4 oz. 33
yams:
    whole or cut, in syrup *(Ann Page)* 115
    whole, in heavy syrup *(Royal Prince)*, 4 oz. 147

yams, continued

    cut, in light syrup *(Princella)*, 4 oz.* 105
    in orange-pineapple sauce *(Royal Prince)*, 4 oz.* 180
zucchini, in tomato sauce *(Del Monte)* 30

* *Approximately ½ cup*

VEGETABLES, DRIED & MIXES
*See also "Vegetables, Canned or in Jars" and
"Vegetables, Frozen"*

CALORIES

beans, green, freeze-dried *(Mountain House)*, ⅓ oz. dry ...40
carrots, freeze-dried *(Mountain House)*, ⅓ oz. dry 35
corn, freeze-dried *(Mountain House)*, ¾ oz. dry 90
mushrooms, freeze-dried *(Mountain House)*, ⅓ oz. dry 25
onions, dehydrated *(Mountain House)*, .71 oz. 80
peas, green, freeze-dried *(Mountain House)*, ¾ oz. dry 90
potato pancakes, mix*
    (French's Big Tate), 1 oz. or 3″ cake 43
potato pancakes, mix* *(Tato Mix)*, 2¾-oz. serving 132
potatoes, hash brown, freeze-dried
    (Mountain House), 1½-oz. dry 150
potatoes, mashed *(Borden Country Store)*, ⅓ cup flakes ...70
potatoes, mashed, freeze-dried
    (Mountain House), .63 oz. dry 70
potatoes, mix*:
    au gratin *(A & P)*, ½ cup 90
    au gratin *(Betty Crocker)*, ½ cup 150
    au gratin *(French's Big Tate* Casserole), ½ cup 190
    creamed *(Betty Crocker*—oven method), ½ cup 160
    creamed *(Betty Crocker*—oven method), ½ cup 160
    creamed *(Betty Crocker*—saucepan method), ½ cup ...160
    creamed *(Betty Crocker* Potatoes 'N Cream), ½ cup ...140
    hash brown *(Betty Crocker)*, ½ cup 130
    hash brown *(French's Big Tate)*, ½ cup 165

potatoes, mix*, continued

  julienne (*Betty Crocker*), ½ cup 150
  mashed (*American Beauty*), ½ cup 140
  mashed (*Betty Crocker* Potato Buds), ½ cup 130
  mashed (*French's Big Tate*), ½ cup 140
  mashed (*French's* Idaho), ½ cup 120
  mashed (*Hungry Jack* Flakes), ½ cup 140
  scalloped (*A & P*), ½ cup 90
  scalloped (*Betty Crocker*), ½ cup 150
  scalloped (*French's Big Tate*), ½ cup 190
  w/sour cream and chives (*Betty Crocker*), ½ cup 140
soup greens (*Durkee*), 2½-oz. jar 216
spinach, freeze-dried (*Mountain House*), ¼ oz. dry 35
squash, freeze-dried (*Mountain House*), ¼ oz. dry 40
yams, instant flakes (*Royal Prince*), 2 oz. dry 222

* Prepared according to package directions

VEGETABLES, FROZEN
See also "Vegetable Entrees, Frozen," "Vegetables, Canned or in Jars" and "Vegetables, Dried & Mixes"

                                                    CALORIES
artichoke hearts (*Birds Eye*), 3 oz. 20
asparagus:
  spears or cut spears (*Birds Eye*), 3.3 oz. 25
  spears or cut spears (*Seabrook Farms*), 3.3 oz. 25
  spears (*Stokely-Van Camp*), 4 oz. 30
  cut spears (*Stokely-Van Camp*), 4 oz. 35
  cut spears in butter sauce (*Green Giant*), ½ cup 45
bean combination
  (*Hanover* Romano Bean Medley), 3.2 oz. 30
beans, butter:
  baby (*Birds Eye*), 3.3 oz. 140
  baby (*Seabrook Farms*), 3.3 oz. 140

beans, butter, continued

baby (*Stokely-Van Camp*), 3.3 oz. 140
speckled (*Green Giant*), ½ cup 140
speckled (*Seabrook Farms*), 3.3 oz. 130
speckled (*Southland*), 3.3 oz. 110

beans, green:

whole (*Birds Eye*), 3 oz. 25
whole (*Hanover* Blue Lake), 3.2 oz. 25
whole (*Seabrook Farms*), 3 oz. 30
whole (*Southland*), 3.3 oz. 25
cut (*Birds Eye*), 3 oz. 25
cut (*Hanover* Blue Lake), 3.2 oz. 28
cut (*Kounty Kist*), ½ cup 15
cut (*Southland*), 3.2 oz. 28
cut (*Stokely-Van Camp*), 3 oz. 30
French style (*Birds Eye*), 3 oz. 30
French style (*Hanover* Blue Lake), 3.2 oz. 25
French style (*Seabrook Farms*), 3 oz. 30
French style (*Southland*), 3.3 oz. 25
French style (*Stokely-Van Camp*), 3.3 oz. 30
Italian style (*Birds Eye*), 3 oz. 30
Italian style (*Hanover*), 3.2 oz. 40
Italian style (*Seabrook Farms*), 3 oz. 35
French style in butter sauce (*Green Giant*), ½ cup 35
French style in cheese sauce (*Birds Eye*), 5 oz. 150

beans, green, and mushroom casserole
    (*Stouffer's*), 4¾ oz. 150
beans, green, and pearl onions (*Bird's Eye*), 3 oz. 35
beans, green, French style, w/onions and bacon bits
    (*Green Giant*), ½ cup 40
beans, green, French style, w/sliced mushrooms
    (*Birds Eye*), 3 oz. 30
beans, green, French style, w/toasted almonds
    (*Birds Eye*), 3 oz. 50
beans, green, and spaetzle
    (*Birds Eye* Bavarian Style), 3.3 oz. 70

Vegetables, Frozen, continued

beans, lima:

  baby (*Birds Eye*), 3.3 oz. 120

  baby (*Green Giant*), ½ cup 75

  baby (*Hanover*), 3.2 oz. 115

  baby (*Kounty Kist*), ½ cup 95

  baby (*Seabrook Farms*), 3.3 oz. 130

  baby (*Stokely-Van Camp*), 3.3 oz. 120

  Fordhook (*Birds Eye*), 3.3 oz. 100

  Fordhook (*Hanover*), 3.2 oz. 100

  Fordhook (*Seabrook Farms*), 3.3 oz. 100

  Fordhook (*Stokely-Van Camp*), 3.3 oz. 100

  baby, in butter sauce (*Green Giant*), ½ cup 110

beans, wax, cut (*Birds Eye*), 3 oz. 30

blackeye peas:

  (*Birds Eye*), 3.3 oz. 130

  (*Green Giant*), ½ cup 140

  (*Seabrook Farms*), 3.3 oz. 130

  (*Southland*), 3.3 oz. 120

broccoli:

  florettes (*Hanover*), 3.2 oz. 35

  spears (*Birds Eye*), 3.3 oz. 25

  spears (*Seabrook Farms*), 3.3 oz. 30

  spears (*Stokely-Van Camp*), 3.3 oz. 30

  cut (*Green Giant*), ½ cup 15

  cut (*Hanover*), 3.2 oz. 25

  cut (*Kounty Kist*), ½ cup 15

  cut (*Stokely-Van Camp*), 3 oz. 25

  chopped (*Birds Eye*), 3.3 oz. 25

  chopped (*Seabrook Farms*), 3.3 oz. 25

  chopped (*Stokely-Van Camp*), 3.3 oz. 25

  au gratin (*Stouffer's*), 5 oz. 170

  light batter-fried, and cheese (*Mrs. Paul's*), 2½ oz. 150

  w/butter sauce (*Green Giant*), ½ cup 45

  w/cheese sauce (*Birds Eye*), 3.3 oz. 110

  w/cheese sauce (*Green Giant*), ½ cup 65

broccoli, continued

w/cheese sauce (*Green Giant* Bake 'n Serve), ½ cup ..130
w/hollandaise sauce (*Birds Eye*), 3.3 oz. 100
broccoli and cauliflower (*Hanover*), 3.2 oz. 15
broccoli, cauliflower and carrots
  (*Kounty Kist* California Blend), ½ cup 15
broccoli, cauliflower and carrots, with cheese sauce
  (*Green Giant*), ½ cup 70
broccoli Florentine (*Stokely-Van Camp*), 3.3 oz. 30
Brussels sprouts:
  (*Birds Eye*), 3.3 oz. 30
  (*Green Giant*), ½ cup 25
  (*Hanover*), 3.2 oz. 38
  (*Kounty Kist*), ½ cup 25
  (*Stokely-Van Camp*), 3.3 oz. 40
  baby (*Birds Eye*), 3.3 oz. 35
  au gratin (*Stouffer's*), 5 7/16 oz. 180
  halves, w/cheese sauce (*Green Giant*), ½ cup 85
  w/butter sauce (*Green Giant*), ½ cup 55
carrots:
  whole (*Seabrook Farms*), 3.3 oz. 40
  cut (*Stokely-Van Camp*), 3.3 oz. 35
  sliced (*Hanover*), 3.2 oz. 35
  w/brown sugar glaze (*Birds Eye*), 3.3 oz. 80
  nuggets, w/butter sauce (*Green Giant*), ½ cup 50
cauliflower:
  (*Birds Eye*), 3.3 oz. 25
  (*Green Giant*), ½ cup 13
  (*Kounty Kist*), ½ cup 13
  (*Seabrook Farms*), 3.3 oz. 25
  (*Stokely-Van Camp*), 3.3 oz. 25
  flowerettes or cut (*Hanover*), 3.2 oz. 20
  au gratin (*Stouffer's*), 5 oz. 155
  and cheese, light batter-fried (*Mrs. Paul's*), 2.6 oz. 120
  w/cheese sauce (*Birds Eye*), 3.3 oz. 110
  w/cheese sauce (*Green Giant*), ½ cup 65
  w/cheese sauce (*Green Giant* Bake 'n Serve), ½ cup ..110

Vegetables, Frozen, continued

collard greens:

    chopped (*Birds Eye*), 3.3 oz. 25

    chopped (*Seabrook Farms*), 3.3 oz. 25

    chopped (*Southland*), 3.3 oz. 30

corn:

    on cob (*Birds Eye*), 1 ear 130

    on cob (*Green Giant*), 5½" ear 160

    on cob (*Ore-Ida*), 6" ear 150

    on cob (*Seabrook Farms*), 5" ear 140

    on cob, small (*Birds Eye Little Ears*), 2 ears 140

    on cob, small (*Green Giant Nibblers*), 2 ears 180

    whole kernel (*Birds Eye*), 3.3 oz. 70

    whole kernel (*Green Giant*), ½ cup 65

    whole kernel (*Hanover*), 3.2 oz. 85

    whole kernel (*Kounty Kist*), ½ cup 70

    whole kernel (*Ore-Ida*), ½ cup 100

    whole kernel (*Seabrook Farms*), 3.3 oz. 90

    whole kernel (*Stokely-Van Camp*), 3.3 oz. 90

    cream style (*Green Giant*), ½ cup 90

    cream style (*Stokely-Van Camp*), 3.3 oz. 90

    white, whole kernel (*Green Giant*), ½ cup 65

    white, whole kernel (*Hanover* Shoepeg Corn), 3.2 oz. ...90

    white, whole kernel (*Kounty Kist*), ½ cup 70

    w/butter sauce (*Green Giant Niblets*), ½ cup 95

    white, w/butter sauce (*Green Giant*), ½ cup 95

corn, combination (*Birds Eye Corn Jubilee*), 3.3 oz. 120

corn, combination

    (*Stokely-Van Camp* Chuckwagon Corn), 3.3 oz. 90

corn w/cut green beans (*Hanover* Shoepeg Corn), 3.2 oz. ...60

corn fritters (*Hanover*), 2 oz. 140

corn fritters (*Mrs. Paul's*), 2 oz. or 1 fritter 130

corn w/fordhook lima beans

    (*Hanover* Shoepeg Corn), 3.2 oz. 90

corn soufflé, *see "Vegetable Entrees, Frozen," page 106*

eggplant:

    fried slices (*Mrs. Paul's*), 3 oz. 230

eggplant, continued

    fried sticks (*Mrs. Paul's*), 3.5 oz. 260

    Parmesan (*Mrs. Paul's*), 5.5 oz. 250

    Parmigiana, *see "Vegetable Entrees, Frozen," page 106*

kale:

    leaf (*Southland*), 3.3 oz. 30

    chopped (*Birds Eye*), 3.3 oz. 25

    chopped (*Seabrook Farms*), 3.3 oz. 30

    chopped (*Southland*), 3.3 oz. 30

mixed vegetables, *see "vegetables, mixed," below*

mushrooms w/butter sauce (*Green Giant*), 2 oz. 30

mushrooms, cocktail, *see "Appetizers, Hors d'Oeuvres & Snacks, Canned, Dried or in Jars," page 126*

mustard greens:

    chopped (*Birds Eye*), 3.3 oz. 20

    chopped (*Seabrook Farms*), 3.3 oz. 25

    chopped (*Southland*), 3.3 oz. 20

okra:

    whole (*Birds Eye*), 3.3 oz. 30

    whole (*Hanover*), 3.2 oz. 35

    whole (*Seabrook Farms*), 3.3 oz. 35

    whole (*Southland*), 3.3 oz. 35

    cut (*Birds Eye*), 3.3 oz. 25

    cut (*Hanover*), 3.2 oz. 25

    cut (*Seabrook Farms*), 3.3 oz. 30

    cut (*Southland*), 3.3 oz. 25

    okra gumbo (*Green Giant*), ½ cup 110

onions:

    whole, small (*Birds Eye*), 4 oz. 40

    chopped (*Birds Eye*), 1 oz. 8

    chopped (*Ore-Ida*), ¼ cup 10

    chopped (*Southland*), 1 oz. 10

    small, w/cream sauce (*Birds Eye*), 3 oz. 100

    in creamy cheese flavor sauce (*Green Giant*), ½ cup 70

    fried rings (*Mrs. Paul's*), 2.5 oz. 150

    fried rings (*Mrs. Paul's* Family), 3 oz. 180

onions, continued

fried rings (*Mrs. Paul's* Party-Pak), 4 oz. 240
fried rings (*Ore-Ida* Onion Ringers), 4 rings 147
peas, blackeye, *see "blackeye peas," above*
peas, crowder (*Southland*), 3.3 oz. 120
peas, field, w/snap peas (*Southland*), 3.3 oz. 120
peas, green:
  (*Kounty Kist*), ½ cup 60
  (*Seabrook Farms*), 3.3 oz. 80
  (*Stokely-Van Camp*), 3.3 oz. 70
  early, small (*Green Giant*), ½ cup 50
  small (*Birds Eye* Tender Tiny Peas), 3.3 oz. 60
  small (*Hanover* Petit Pois), 3.2 oz. 65
  small (*Seabrook Farms* Petite), 3.3 oz. 60
  early, in butter sauce (*Le Sueur*), ½ cup 75
  sweet, in butter sauce (*Green Giant*), ½ cup 75
  w/cream sauce (*Birds Eye*), 3.3 oz. 130
peas and carrots:
  (*Birds Eye*), 3.3 oz. 50
  (*Kounty Kist*), ½ cup 45
  (*Stokely-Van Camp*), 3.3 oz. 50
  peas and cauliflower w/cream sauce
    (*Birds Eye*), 3.3 oz. 120
  peas, onions and carrots in butter sauce
    (*Le Sueur*), ½ cup 80
  peas, pea pods and water chestnuts in sauce
    (*Le Sueur*), ½ cup 90
  peas and potatoes in cream sauce (*Birds Eye*), 3.3 oz. ...140
  peas w/sliced mushrooms (*Birds Eye*), 3.3 oz. 70
peppers, sweet:
  green, diced (*Southland*), 2 oz. 10
  green, and onions (*Southland*), 2 oz. 15
  red and green, cut (*Southland*), 2 oz. 15
  red and green, and onions (*Southland*), 2 oz. 20
potato pancakes (*Golden*), 1⅝-oz. pancake 85
potato pirogen (*Golden*), 1¾-oz. pirogen 61

Vegetables, Frozen, continued

potatoes:

whole, small, boiled (*Seabrook Farms*), 3.5 oz. ....7(

whole, small, peeled (*Birds Eye*), 3.2 oz. ....6(

whole, small, peeled (*Ore-Ida*), 3 average 4:

au gratin (*Green Giant* Bake 'n Serve), ½ cup 19

au gratin (*Stouffer's*), 3-13/16 oz. 13:

bites (*Birds Eye Tiny Taters*), 3.2 oz. ....20(

in butter sauce (*Ore-Ida* Southern Style), ½ cup ....7(

in butter sauce, shoestring (*Green Giant*), ½ cup ......15!

in butter sauce, sliced (*Green Giant*), ½ cup ....10!

in butter sauce, w/onion

   (*Ore-Ida* Southern Style), ½ cup 71

fried (*Heinz* Self-Sizzling Fries), 17 pieces 156

fried (*Ore-Ida* Crispers), 17 pieces ....24!

fried (*Ore-Ida* Country Style Dinner Fries), 10 pieces ..145

fried (*Ore-Ida* Golden Fries), 17 pieces ....10(

fried, cottage fries (*Birds Eye*), 2.8 oz. 120

fried, cottage fries (*Ore-Ida*), 17 pieces 136

fried, crinkle cut (*Birds Eye*), 3 oz. 110

fried, crinkle cut (*Heinz* Self-Sizzling), 17 pieces 163

fried, crinkle cut (*Ore-Ida* Golden Crinkles), 17 pieces ..107

fried, crinkle cut (*Ore-Ida* Pixie Crinkles), 25 pieces 74

fried, crinkle cut (*Stokely-Van Camp*), 3 oz. 120

fried, French (*Birds Eye*), 3 oz. 110

fried, French (*Birds Eye Tasti Fries*), 2.5 oz. 140

fried, shoestring (*Birds Eye*), 3.3 oz. 140

fried, shoestring (*Hanover* Julienne), 3.2 oz. 130

fried, shoestring (*Heinz* Self-Sizzling), 25 pieces 104

fried, shoestring (*Ore-Ida*), 25 pieces 73

fried, steak fries (*Birds Eye*), 3 oz. 110

hash brown (*Birds Eye*), 4 oz. 70

hash brown (*Hanover*), 3.2 oz. 100

hash brown (*Hanover* Potato Medley), 3.2 oz. 90

hash brown O'Brien (*Birds Eye*), 4 oz. 60

hash brown O'Brien (*Ore-Ida*), ½ cup 41

hash brown, shredded (*Birds Eye*), 3 oz. 60

potatoes, continued

hash brown, shredded (*Ore-Ida*), ½ patty 63

hash brown (*Ore-Ida* Southern Style), ½ cup 50

puffs (*Birds Eye Tasti Puffs*), 2.5 oz. 190

puffs (*Ore-Ida Tater Tots*), 10 pieces 168

puffs, bacon flavor (*Ore-Ida Tater Tots*), 10 pieces 159

puffs, onion flavor (*Ore-Ida Tater Tots*), 10 pieces 163

scalloped (*Stouffer's*), 4 oz. 126

potatoes, stuffed, w/cheese flavor topping

(*Green Giant* Entree), 5 oz. 240

potatoes, stuffed, w/sour cream and chives

(*Green Giant* Entree), 5 oz. 230

potatoes, sweet (yams):

candied, orange or yellow (*Mrs. Paul's*), 4 oz. 180

candied, w/apples

(*Mrs. Paul's* Sweets 'n Apples), 4 oz. 160

glazed (*Green Giant*), ½ cup 170

rutabagas (*Southland*), 4 oz. 50

spinach:

leaf or chopped (*Birds Eye*), 3.3 oz. 20

leaf or chopped (*Seabrook Farms*), 3.3 oz. 25

leaf or chopped (*Stokely-Van Camp*), 3.3 oz. 25

in butter sauce (*Green Giant*), ½ cup 45

creamed (*Birds Eye*), 3 oz. 60

creamed (*Green Giant*), ½ cup 95

spinach soufflé, *see "Vegetable Entrees, Frozen," page 106*

squash:

(*Stokely-Van Camp*), 3 oz. 30

cooked (*Birds Eye*), 4 oz. 50

butternut (*Southland*), 4 oz. 60

crookneck (*Seabrook Farms*), 3.3 oz. 20

crookneck (*Southland*), 3.3 oz. 20

crookneck, w/onions (*Southland*), 3.2 oz. 20

summer, sliced (*Birds Eye*), 3.3 oz. 18

summer, in cheese sauce (*Green Giant*), ½ cup 60

zucchini, *see "zucchini," below*

Vegetables, Frozen, continued

succotash:

    (*Birds Eye*), 3.3 oz. 80

    (*Hanover*), 3.2 oz. 95

    (*Stokely-Van Camp*), 3.3 oz. 60

stew vegetables, *see "vegetables, mixed," below*

turnip greens:

    chopped (*Birds Eye*), 3.3 oz. 20

    chopped (*Seabrook Farms*), 3.3 oz. 20

    chopped (*Southland*), 3.3 oz. 20

    w/turnip roots (*Southland*), 3.3 oz. 20

    w/diced turnips (*Birds Eye*), 3.3 oz. 20

turnip roots, diced (*Seabrook Farms*), 3.3 oz. 4

turnips, chopped (*Southland*), 3.3 oz. 20

vegetables, mixed:

    (*Birds Eye Americana* New England Style), 3.3 oz. 70

    (*Birds Eye Americana*

      New Orleans Creole Style), 3.3 oz. 70

    (*Birds Eye Americana*

      Pennsylvania Dutch Style), 3.3 oz. 45

    (*Birds Eye Americana* San Francisco Style), 3.3 oz. 50

    (*Birds Eye Americana*

      Wisconsin Country Style), 3.3 oz. 45

    (*Green Giant*), ½ cup 45

    (*Hanover*), 3.2 oz. 45

    (*Hanover* Country Mixed Vegetables), 3.2 oz. 75

    (*Hanover* Garden Fiesta), 3.2 oz. 47

    (*Hanover* Garden Medley), 3.2 oz. 29

    (*Hanover* Harvest Vegetables), 3.2 oz. 70

    (*Hanover* Summer Vegetables), 3.2 oz. 38

    (*Kounty Kist*), ½ cup 45

    (*Stokely-Van Camp*), 3.3 oz. 60

    stew (*Ore-Ida*), 1½-lb. pkg. 442

    stew (*Ore-Ida*), 4 oz. 74

    stew (*Stokely-Van Camp*), 4 oz. 60

    in butter sauce (*Green Giant*), ½ cup 65

Vegetables, Frozen, continued

vegetables, mixed, international:

   (*Stokely-Van Camp* Vegetables Del Sol), 3.2 oz. 25

   (*Stokely-Van Camp* Vegetables Grande), 3.2 oz. 50

   (*Stokely-Van Camp* Vegetables La Cariba), 3.2 oz. 20

   Cantonese style (*Birds Eye* Stir-Fry), 3.3 oz. 50

   Chinese style (*Birds Eye*), 3.3 oz. 25

   Chinese style (*Birds Eye* Stir-Fry), 3.3 oz. 30

   Chinese style (*Green Giant*), ½ cup 65

   Danish style (*Birds Eye*), 3.3 oz. 45

   Hawaiian style (*Birds Eye*), 3.3 oz. 50

   Hawaiian style (*Green Giant*), ½ cup 100

   Italian style (*Birds Eye*), 3.3 oz. 60

   Italian style

      (*Stokely-Van Camp* Vegetables Milano), 3.2 oz. 45

   Italian style

      (*Stokely-Van Camp* Vegetables Romano), 3.2 oz. 40

   Japanese style (*Birds Eye*), 3.3 oz. 40

   Japanese style (*Birds Eye* Stir-Fry), 3.3 oz. 30

   Japanese style (*Green Giant*), ½ cup 65

   Japanese style (*Stokely-Van Camp*), 3.2 oz. 25

   Mandarin style (*Birds Eye* Stir-Fry), 3.3 oz. 25

   Oriental style

      (*Stokely-Van Camp* Vegetables Orient), 3.2 oz. 30

   Parisian style (*Birds Eye*), 3.3 oz. 30

   Parisian Style (*Stokely-Van Camp*), 3.2 oz. 40

yams, *see "potatoes, sweet," above*

zucchini:

   (*Birds Eye*), 3.3 oz. 16

   (*Seabrook Farms*), 3.5 oz. 18

   sliced (*Southland*), 3.2 oz. 15

   sticks, light batter-fried (*Mrs. Paul's*), 3 oz. 180

VEGETABLE ENTREES, FROZEN,
one whole package*
See also "Vegetables, Frozen"

	CALORIES
asparagus soufflé (*Stouffer's*), 12-oz. pkg.	345
cabbage rolls, stuffed, in tomato sauce (*Green Giant Baked Entree*), 7-oz. pkg.	220
corn soufflé (*Stouffer's*), 12-oz. pkg.	465
eggplant Parmigiana (*Buitoni*), 12-oz. pkg.	624
eggplant Parmigiana (*Weight Watchers*), 13-oz. pkg.	280

green pepper, stuffed:
   in creole sauce

	CALORIES
(*Green Giant* Baked Entree), 7-oz. pkg.	200
w/beef, in tomato sauce (*Stouffer's*), 15½-oz. pkg.	450
w/veal, in sauce (*Weight Watchers*), 13-oz. pkg.	320
mushroom crepes (*Stouffer's*), 6¼-oz. pkg.	255
spinach soufflé (*Stouffer's*), 12-oz. pkg.	405

* Pay attention to package sizes

BEANS, BAKED & BAKED-STYLE,
one cup, except as noted

	CALORIES
(*Campbell's* Home Style), 8 oz.	300
(*Howard Johnson's*)	340
(*Van Camp Beanee Weenee*)	340
(*Van Camp* October Beans)	230
w/bacon (*Hormel*), 7½-oz. can	339
barbecue (*Campbell's*), 8 oz.	280

in brown sugar sauce:

	CALORIES
(*Van Camp*)	330
pea beans (*B & M*)	336
red kidney beans (*B & M*)	360
yellow eye (*B & M*)	360

Beans, Baked & Baked-Style, continued

w/frankfurters:

    (*Hormel* Beans 'n Wieners), 7½-oz. can 286

    in tomato sauce (*Heinz*), 8¾-oz. can 399

    in tomato sauce & molasses (*Campbell's*), 8 oz. 370

w/ham (*Hormel*), 7½-oz. can 367

in molasses sauce:

    (*Heinz*) 284

    (*Libby's*) 279

    and brown sugar (*Campbell's* Old Fashioned), 8 oz. 290

pea beans (*Homemaker's*) 320

w/pork:

    (*Hanover*), 8 oz. 273

    (*Van Camp*) 250

    in molasses sauce, Boston-style (*Ann Page*), 8 oz. 290

    in tomato sauce (*Campbell's*), 8 oz. 260

    in tomato sauce (*Ann Page*), 8 oz. 240

    in tomato sauce (*Heinz*) 262

    in tomato sauce (*Joan of Arc*) 280

    in tomato sauce (*Libby's*) 274

red kidney beans (*Homemaker's*) 336

vegetarian:

    (*Hanover*), 8 oz. 270

    (*Van Camp's*) 260

    in tomato sauce (*Ann Page*) 230

    in tomato sauce (*Libby's*) 266

TOMATO PASTE & PUREE, six ounces,
except as noted
See also "Sauces"

                                                         CALORIES

tomato paste:

    (*Ann Page*) 160

    (*Contadina*) 150

    (*Del Monte*) 150

tomato sauce, continued
  (*Featherweight*) 150
  (*Hunt's*) 140
tomato puree:
  (*Ann Page*) 68
  (*Cellu*), 1 cup 80
  heavy (*Contadina*) 75

PICKLES & RELISH
See also "Olives" and "Condiments & Seasonings"

CALORIES

cauliflower, sweet (*Heinz*), 1 bud 9
onions, sour, cocktail (*Crosse & Blackwell*), 1 tbsp. 9
onions, sour, cocktail (*Heinz*), 1 onion ....tr.
onions, spiced (*Heinz*), 1 onion 2
pickles, dill and sour:
  whole (*Bond's Flavor-Pack Dills*), 1 pickle* 1
  whole (*Bond's Fresh-Pack Dills*), 1 pickle* 2
  whole (*Bond's* Fresh-Pack Kosher Dills), 1 pickle* 2
  whole (*Heinz* Fresh Kosher Baby Dills), 1 pickle* 2
  whole (*Heinz* Fresh Kosher Dills), 1 pickle* 5
  whole (*Heinz* Genuine Dills), 1 pickle* 10
  whole (*Heinz* Processed Dills), 1 pickle* 2
  whole (*Heinz* Sour Gherkins), 1 pickle* 4
  whole (*L & S Dills*), 1 pickle* 1
  whole (*L & S* Fresh-Pack Kosher Dills), 1 pickle* 2
  whole, unsalted (*Featherweight*), 1 oz. 12
  whole, unsalted (*Featherweight* Dills), 1 oz. 5
  whole, unsalted (*Featherweight* Kosher Dills), 1 oz. 5
  spears (*Bond's* Fresh-Pack Dills), 1 piece* 2
  spears (*Bond's* Fresh-Pack Kosher Dills), 1 piece* 2
  slices (*Crosse & Blackwell* Kosher Dills), 1 tbsp. 2
  slices (*Heinz* Hamburger), 3 slices* 1
  slices, unsalted (*Featherweight*), 1 oz. 12

Pickles & Relish, continued

pickles, sweet:

  whole (*Bond's Gherkins*), 1 pickle* 19

  whole (*Heinz Gherkins*), 1 pickle* 20

  whole (*Heinz* Midget Gherkins), 1 pickle* 5

  whole (*Heinz* Sweet Pickles), 1 pickle* 40

  whole (*L & S* Sweet Pickles), 1 pickle* 19

  pieces (*Heinz* Mixed), 3 pieces* 23

  slices (*Crosse & Blackwell*

    Fresh Cucumber Slices), 1 tbsp. 15

  slices (*Crosse & Blackwell* Sweet Chips), 1 tbsp. 17

  slices (*Fannings* Bread & Butter Pickles), 1 oz. 13

  slices (*Heinz* Candied Krink-L-Chips), 3 pieces* 33

  slices (*Heinz* Fresh Cucumber Slices), 3 pieces* 12

  slices (*Heinz* Sweet Pickle Chips), 3 pieces* 15

  spears (*Crosse & Blackwell*

    Fresh Cucumber Spears), 1 piece* 28

  spears (*Heinz* Sweet Pickle Spears), 1 piece* 16

  sticks (*Heinz* Sweet Pickle Sticks), 1 piece* 16

  strips (*Heinz* Candied Dill Strips), 1 piece* 30

relishes:

  barbecue (*Crosse & Blackwell*), 1 tbsp. 22

  barbecue (*Heinz*), 1 tbsp. 32

  corn (*Crosse & Blackwell*), 1 tbsp. 15

  cucumber (*Featherweight*), 1 oz. 11

  hamburger (*Crosse & Blackwell*), 1 tbsp. 20

  hamburger (*Heinz*), 1 tbsp. 17

  hot dog (*Crosse & Blackwell*), 1 tbsp. 22

  hot dog (*Heinz*), 1 tbsp. 22

  hot pepper (*Crosse & Blackwell*), 1 tbsp. 22

  Indian (*Crosse & Blackwell*), 1 tbsp. 26

  India (*Heinz*), 1 tbsp. 28

  mustard (*Crosse & Blackwell* Chow Chow), 1 tbsp. 6

  piccalilli (*Crosse & Blackwell*), 1 tbsp. 26

  piccalilli, green tomato (*Heinz*), 1 tbsp. 19

relishes, continued
   sweet (*Crosse & Blackwell*), 1 tbsp. 26
   sweet (*Heinz*), 1 tbsp. 20
watermelon rind, pickled (*Crosse & Blackwell*), 1 tbsp. 38

* *Average-size piece, as packed*

OLIVES, one piece*

                                          CALORIES

green:
   Manzanilla (*Grandee*), 1 medium 4
   Manzanilla, pimento-stuffed (*Grandee*), 1 queen-size 14
ripe:
   (*Lindsay*), 1 large 5
   (*Lindsay*), 1 extra large 5
   (*Lindsay*), 1 giant 8
   (*Lindsay*), 1 jumbo 10
   (*Lindsay*), 1 colossal 13
   (*Lindsay*), 1 super-colossal 16
   (*Lindsay*), 1 super-supreme 18

* *As packaged; note variations in size*

VEGETABLE JUICES, six fluid ounces,
except as noted
See also "Fruit Juices"

                                          CALORIES

clam- and tomato-flavored cocktail (*Mott's Clamato*) 80
tomato juice:
   (*Ann Page*) 30
   (*Campbell's*) 35
   (*Del Monte*) 35
   (*Diet Delight*) 35
   (*Featherweight*), 12-oz. can 35

CHAPTER 8

VEGETARIAN PROTEIN FOODS AND MEATLESS "MEATS"

VEGETARIAN FOODS, CANNED & DRY
See also "Vegetarian Foods, Frozen"

                                                                CALORIES

"beef," sliced (*Worthington*), 2 oz. or 2 slices 110
bits (*Loma Linda Tender Bits*), approximately 4 pieces 100
bits (*Worthington Veja-Bits*), approximately ½ cup 70
burgers and burger granules:
    (*Loma Linda Redi Burger*), ½" slice 129
    (*Loma Linda VegeBurger*), ½ cup 110
    (*Loma Linda VegeBurger* NSA), ½ cup 120
    (*Worthington Vegetarian Burger*), ⅓ cup 130
    chunks (*Loma Linda VitaBurger*), ¼ cup 70
    granules (*Loma Linda VitaBurger*), 3 tbsp. 70
    granules (*Worthington Granburger*), 3 tbsp. 65
"chicken":
    diced (*Worthington Soyameat*), ¼ cup 120
    fried (*Worthington Fri-Chik Soyameat*), 2 pieces 190
    fried, w/gravy (*Loma Linda*), 2 pieces 210
    sliced (*Worthington Soyameat*), 2 slices 130
chili (*Worthington*), ½ cup 190
chops (*Worthington Choplets*), 2 slices 100
cold cuts:
    (*Loma Linda Nuteena*), ½" slice 162
    (*Loma Linda Proteena*), ½" slice 144

cold cuts, continued

   (*Loma Linda Vegelona*), ½" slice 100
   (*Worthington Numete*), ½" slice 160
   (*Worthington Protose*), ½" slice 190
cutlets (*Worthington Cutlets*), 1½" slice 94
franks (*Loma Linda Big Franks*), 1 frank 100
franks (*Loma Linda Sizzle Franks*), 2 franks 190
(*Loma Linda Dinner Cuts*), 2 cuts 100
(*Loma Linda Savorex*), 1 tbsp. 32
(*Loma Linda Soyagen*, All Purpose),
   ¼ cup = 1 cup reconstituted 140
(*Loma Linda Soyagen*, Carob),
   ¼ cup = 1 cup reconstituted 140
(*Loma Linda Soyagen*, No Sucrose),
   ¼ cup = 1 cup reconstituted 140
links:
   (*Loma Linda Linketts*), 2 links 180
   (*Loma Linda Little Links*), 2 links 90
   (*Worthington Saucettes*), 2 links 130
   (*Worthington Super Links*), 1 link 120
   (*Worthington Veja-Links*), 2 links 140
"meat" balls (*Loma Linda Tender Rounds*), 3 pieces 140
"meat" balls (*Worthington Non-Meat Balls*), 3 pieces 120
sandwich spread (*Loma Linda*), 3 tbsp. 70
sandwich spread (*Worthington*), 2½ oz. 120
"scallops" (*Worthington Vegetable Skallops*),
   ½ cup drained 70
soy "milk," dry:
   (*Worthington Soyamel*—Regular), 1 oz. 140
   (*Worthington Soyamel*—Fortified), 1 oz. 140
   (*Worthington Soyamel*—Lowfat), 1 oz. 110
stew (*Loma Linda Stew Pac*), 2 oz. 70
"turkey" (*Worthington 209*), 2 slices 150

VEGETARIAN FOODS, FROZEN

See also "Vegetarian Foods, Canned & Dry"

CALORIES

"bacon" strips (*Worthington Stripples*), 4 pieces 100
"beef":
  corned, *see "corned 'beef' roll" or "slices," below*
  roast (*Loma Linda*), 2 slices 140
  roll (*Worthington*), 2½ oz. 140
  slices (*Worthington Luncheon Slices*), 2 slices 120
  smoked, roll (*Worthington*), 2½ oz. 170
  smoked, slices (*Worthington Luncheon Slices*), 6 slices . .130
"beef" pot pie (*Worthington*), 8 oz. pie 470
"bologna" (*Loma Linda*), 2 slices 140
"bologna" (*Worthington Bolono*), 2 slices 70
burger (*Loma Linda Sizzle Burger*), 1 piece 200
burger (*Worthington FriPats*), 1 piece 180
"chicken":
  (*Loma Linda*), 2½ oz. 140
  (*Worthington Chic-Ketts*), ½ cup 180
  fried (*Loma Linda*), 1 piece 190
  roll (*Worthington*), 2½ oz. 170
  slices (*Worthington*), 2 slices 140
"chicken" pot pie (*Worthington*), 8-oz. pie 450
corned "beef," roll (*Worthington*), 2½ oz. 190
corned "beef," slices
  (*Worthington Luncheon Slices*), 4 slices 160
croquettes (*Worthington Croquettes*), 2 pieces 150
"fish" fillets
  (*Worthington Vegetarian Fillets*), 2 pieces 215
"ham," roll (*Worthington Wham*), 2½ oz. 140
"ham," slices (*Worthington Wham*), 3 slices 140
"meat" balls (*Loma Linda*), 4 pieces 190
"salami" (*Loma Linda*), 2 slices 140
"salami" (*Worthington*), 2 slices 100

Vegetarian Foods, Frozen, continued

"sausage," breakfast style:

    (*Loma Linda*), 3 oz. 210

    links (*Worthington Prosage*), 3 links 180

    patties (*Worthington Prosage*), 2 pieces 200

    roll (*Worthington Prosage*), ⅜" slice 90

"steak" (*Worthington Stakelets*), 1 piece 180

"tuna" (*Worthington Tuno*), 2 oz. 90

"tuna" pot pie (*Worthington*), 8-oz. pie 460

"turkey":

    (*Loma Linda*), 2 slices 120

    smoked, roll (*Worthington*), 2½ oz. 180

    smoked, slices (*Worthington Luncheon Slices*), 4 slices ..200

CHAPTER 9

SOUPS, BROTHS AND CHOWDERS

SOUPS, CANNED
See also "Soups, Mixes"

Soups are listed below either by the full can, a half can, or an average serving of one cup (eight fluid ounces). Note the variations in size. Also, if "condensed" (cond.) or "semicondensed" (semicond.) is not indicated, this means that the soup is ready to eat.

	CALORIES
asparagus, cream of, cond.* (*Campbell's*), 10 oz.	100
asparagus, cream of, cond.** (*Campbell's*), 10 oz.	200
bean:	
w/bacon, cond.* (*Ann Page*), 1 cup	140
w/ bacon, cond. (*Campbell's*), 10 oz.	190
w/ham, old fashioned (*Campbell's* Chunky), 9½ oz.	260
w/ham, old fashioned	
(*Campbell's* Chunky—Individual), 11-oz. can	300
w/hot dog, cond.* (*Campbell's*), 10 oz.	210
old fashioned, semicond.***	
(*Campbell's* Soup for One), 11⅝ oz.	210
bean, black, cond.* (*Campbell's*), 10 oz.	130
bean, black, w/sherry (*Crosse & Blackwell*), 13-oz. can	160
beef:	
(*Campbell's* Chunky), 9½ oz.	190
(*Campbell's* Chunky—Individual), 10¾-oz. can	220
(*Campbell's* Chunky—Low-Sodium), 7¼-oz. can	170

beef, continued

    cond.* (*Campbell's*), 10 oz. 100

    broth or bouillon, cond.* (*Campbell's*), 10 oz. 35

    broth (*College Inn*), 1 cup 18

    broth (*Swanson*), 6¾ oz. 20

    cabbage (*Manischewitz*), 8 oz. 125

    consommé, cond.* (*Campbell's*), 10 oz. 45

    noodle, cond.* (*Campbell's*), 10 oz. 90

borscht:

    (*Manischewitz*), 8 oz. 72

    (*Mother's*), 1 cup 90

    egg-enriched (*Mother's*), 1 cup 124

    low-calorie (*Manischewitz*), 8 oz. 25

celery, cream of:

    cond.* (*Ann Page*), 1 cup 60

    cond.* (*Campbell's*), 10 oz. 110

    cond.** (*Campbell's*), 10 oz. 210

cheddar cheese, cond.* (*Campbell's*), 10 oz. 180

chicken:

    (*Campbell's* Chunky), 9½ oz. 200

    (*Campbell's* Chunky—Individual), 10¾-oz. can 230

    (*Campbell's* Chunky—Low-Sodium), 7¼-oz. can 170

    (*Progresso Chickarina*), 1 cup 100

    alphabet, cond.* (*Campbell's*), 10 oz. 110

    barley (*Manischewitz*), 8 oz. 168

    broth (*College Inn*), 1 cup 35

    broth (*Swanson*), 6¾ oz. 25

    broth, cond.* (*Campbell's*), 10 oz. 50

    broth, low-calorie, cond.* (*Dia-Mel*), 8 oz. 18

    cream of, cond.* (*Ann Page*), 1 cup 90

    cream of, cond.* (*Campbell's*), 10 oz. 140

    cream of, cond.** (*Campbell's*), 10 oz. 240

    and dumplings, cond.* (*Campbell's*), 10 oz. 120

    gumbo, cond.* (*Campbell's*), 10 oz. 70

    golden, and noodles, semicond.***

        (*Campbell's* Soup for One), 11⅝ oz. 120

    noodle (*Manischewitz*), 8 oz. 91

chicken, continued

noodle, cond.* (*Ann Page*), 1 cup 70
noodle, cond.* (*Campbell's*), 10 oz. 90
noodle, O-shape, cond.* (*Ann Page*), 1 cup 70
noodle, O-shape, cond.*   —
   (*Campbell's* NoodleO's), 10 oz. 90
noodle stars, cond.* (*Ann Page*), 1 cup 60
noodle stars, cond. (*Campbell's*), 10 oz. 80
rice (*Campbell's* Chunky), 9½ oz. 160
rice (*Manischewitz*), 8 oz. 95
rice, cond.* (*Ann Page*), 1 cup 50
rice, cond.* (*Campbell's*), 10 oz. 80
vegetable (*Campbell's* Chunky), 9½ oz. 190
vegetable (*Manischewitz*), 8 oz. 109
vegetable, cond.* (*Ann Page*), 1 cup 70
vegetable, cond.* (*Campbell's*), 10 oz. 90

chili beef:
  (*Campbell's* Chunky), 9¾ oz. 260
  (*Campbell's* Chunky—Individual), 11-oz. can 300
  cond.* (*Campbell's*), 10 oz. 190

clam chowder:
  (*Progresso*), 1 cup 100
  Manhattan (*Campbell's* Chunky), 9½ oz. 160
  Manhattan (*Crosse & Blackwell*), 13-oz. can 100
  Manhattan, cond.* (*Campbell's*), 10 oz. 100
  Manhattan, cond.* (*Doxsee*), 6 oz. 48
  Manhattan, cond.* (*Snow's*), 7½ oz. 70
  New England (*Crosse & Blackwell*), 13-oz. can 180
  New England, cond.* (*Campbell's*), 10 oz. 100
  New England, cond.** (*Campbell's*), 10 oz. 200
  New England, cond.** (*Snow's*), 7½ oz. 130
  New England, semicond.***
    (*Campbell's* Soup for One), 11⅝ oz. 125
  New England, semicond.†
    (*Campbell's* Soup for One), 11⅝ oz. 200
crab, à la Maryland (*Crosse & Blackwell*), 13-oz. can 100
escarole, in chicken broth (*Progresso*), 1 cup 25

Soups, Canned, continued

gazpacho (*Crosse & Blackwell*), 13-oz. can 60

green pea, *see "pea," below*

lentil (*Progresso*), 1 cup 150

lentil, w/ham (*Crosse & Blackwell*), 13-oz. can 160

Madrilene consommé, clear
   (*Crosse & Blackwell*), 13-oz. can 50

Madrilene consommé, red
   (*Crosse & Blackwell*), 13-oz. can 60

meatball alphabet, cond.* (*Campbell's*), 10 oz. 140

minestrone:
   (*Campbell's* Chunky), 9½ oz. 160
   (*Crosse & Blackwell*), 13-oz. can 180
   cond.* (*Campbell's*), 10 oz. 110
   w/beef stock, cond. (*Ann Page*), 1 cup 80

mushroom:
   barley (*Manischewitz*), 8 oz. 145
   cream of (*Campbell's—Low-Sodium*), 7¼-oz. can 140
   cream of (*Featherweight*), 8-oz. can 120
   cream of, bisque (*Crosse & Blackwell*), 13-oz. can 180
   cream of, cond.* (*Ann Page*), 1 cup 120
   cream of, cond.* (*Campbell's*), 10 oz. 150
   cream of, cond.** (*Campbell's*), 10 oz. 250
   cream of, w/wine, semicond.***
     (*Campbell's* Soup for One), 11¼ oz. 160
   golden, cond.* (*Campbell's*), 10 oz. 110

noodles and ground beef, cond.* (*Campbell's*), 10 oz. 110

noodle, curly, w/chicken, cond.* (*Campbell's*), 10 oz. 100

onion, cond.* (*Campbell's*), 10 oz. 80

onion, cream of, cond.†† (*Campbell's*), 10 oz. 180

oyster stew:
   (*Chicken of the Sea*), 8 oz. 163
   cond.* (*Campbell's*), 10 oz. 70
   cond.** (*Campbell's*), 10 oz. 170

pea:
   green (*Campbell's—Low-Sodium*), 7½-oz. can 150
   green (*Featherweight*), 8-oz. can 180

pea, continued

    green, cond.* (*Campbell's*), 10 oz. 180

    split (*Manischewitz*), 8 oz. 265

    split, w/ham (*Campbell's* Chunky), 9½ oz. 220

    split, w/ham, cond.* (*Ann Page*), 1 cup 60

    split, w/ham and bacon, cond.*

       (*Campbell's*), 10 oz. 210

pepperpot, cond.* (*Campbell's*), 10 oz. 130

potato, cream of:

    cond.* (*Campbell's*), 10 oz. 90

    cond.** (*Campbell's*), 10 oz. 190

    cond.†† (*Campbell's*), 10 oz. 140

shav (*Manischewitz*), 8 oz. 11

Scotch broth, cond.* (*Campbell's*), 10 oz. 100

shrimp, cream of:

    (*Crosse & Blackwell*), 13-oz. can 180

    cond.* (*Campbell's*), 10 oz. 110

    cond.** (*Campbell's*), 10 oz. 210

sirloin burger (*Campbell's* Chunky), 9½ oz. 210

sirloin burger

    (*Campbell's* Chunky—Individual), 10¾-oz. can 230

steak and potato (*Campbell's* Chunky), 9½ oz. 190

tomato:

    (*Campbell's*—Low-Sodium), 7¼-oz. can 130

    (*Featherweight*), 8-oz. can 120

    (*Manischewitz*), 8 oz. 127

    (*Progresso*), 1 cup 110

    cond.* (*Ann Page*), 1 cup 80

    cond.* (*Campbell's*), 10 oz. 110

    cond.** (*Campbell's*), 10 oz. 210

    semicond.*** (*Campbell's* Royale

      Soup for One), 11⅝ oz. 180

    beef, noodle, O-shaped, cond.*

      (*Campbell's* NoodleO's), 10 oz. 160

    bisque, cond.* (*Campbell's*), 10 oz. 140

    rice, cond.* (*Ann Page*), 1 cup 90

    rice, old fashioned, cond.* (*Campbell's*), 10 oz. 130

Soups, Canned, continued

turkey:

    (*Campbell's* Chunky), 9¼ oz. 160

    noodle (*Campbell's*—Low-Sodium), 7¼-oz. can 60

    noodle, cond.* (*Ann Page*), 1 cup 70

    noodle, cond.* (*Campbell's*), 10 oz. 80

    vegetable, cond.* (*Ann Page*), 1 cup 60

    vegetable, cond.* (*Campbell's*), 10 oz. 90

turtle, mock (*Stegner's*), 10½-oz. can 212

turtle, mock (*Stegner's*), 15-oz. can 302

vegetable:

    (*Campbell's* Chunky), 9½ oz. 140

    (*Campbell's* Chunky—Individual), 10¾ oz. can 150

    (*Campbell's*—Low-Sodium), 7¼-oz. can 90

    (*Manischewitz*), 8 oz. 125

    cond.* (*Campbell's*), 10 oz. 100

    semicond.***

        (*Campbell's* Old World Soup for One), 11⅝ oz. 125

    low-calorie, cond.* (*Dia-Mel*), 8 oz. 60

    and beef, stockpot, cond.* (*Campbell's*), 10 oz. 120

    and beef stock, cond.* (*Ann Page*), 1 cup 70

    beef (*Campbell's*—Low-Sodium), 7¼-oz. can 80

    beef, cond.* (*Ann Page*), 1 cup 80

    beef, cond.* (*Campbell's*), 10 oz. 90

    beef, low-calorie, cond.* (*Dia-Mel*), 8 oz. 80

    beef, old fashioned (*Campbell's* Chunky), 9½ oz. 160

    golden, w/O-shaped noodles, cond.*

        (*Campbell's* NoodleO's), 10 oz. 90

    old fashioned, cond.* (*Campbell's*), 10 oz. 90

    vegetarian, cond.* (*Ann Page*), 1 cup 70

    vegetarian, cond.* (*Campbell's*), 10 oz. 90

vichyssoise, cream of (*Crosse & Blackwell*), 13-oz. can 140

  * *Prepared with 5 oz. soup and 5 oz. water*
  ** *Prepared with 5 oz. soup and 5 oz. whole milk*
  *** *Prepared with 7¾ oz. soup and 3⅞ oz. water*
  † *Prepared with 7¾ oz. soup and 3⅞ oz. whole milk*
  †† *Prepared with 5 oz. soup, 2½ oz. water and 2½ oz. whole milk*

SOUPS, MIXES*, six-ounce cup,
except as noted
See also "Soups, Canned"

	CALORIES
alphabet (*Golden Grain*), 8-oz. cup	55
asparagus (*Knorr*)	45
beef and beef flavor:	
barley (*Knorr*)	45
bouillon, *see "bouillon," below*	
broth, *see "broth," below*	
mushroom (*Lipton*), 8-oz. can	45
noodle (*Knorr Swiss*)	25
noodle (*Lipton Cup-a-Soup*)	35
noodle (*Nestlé Souptime*)	30
noodle, beef flavor, *see "noodle," below*	
onion (*Lipton*), 8-oz. cup	30
bouillon:	
beef (*Herb-Ox*), 1 cube	7
beef (*Maggi*), 1 cube	6
beef (*Steero*), 1 cube or 1 tsp	10
chicken (*Herb-Ox*), 1 cube	7
chicken (*Maggi*), 1 cube	7
chicken (*Steero*), 1 cube or 1 tsp.	10
vegetable (*Herb-Ox*), 1 cube	7
vegetable (*Steero*), 1 cube or 1 tsp.	10
broth:	
beef (*Carmel*), 1 tsp.	12
beef (*Herb-Ox*)	8
beef (*Maggi* Broth & Seasoning), 1 tsp.	27
beef (*MBT*)	14
beef (*Weight Watchers*)	10
chicken (*Carmel*), 1 tsp.	12
chicken (*Lipton Cup-a-Broth*)	25
chicken (*Maggi* Broth & Seasoning), 1 tsp.	29
chicken (*MBT*)	12

broth, *continued*

chicken (*Weight Watchers*) 10

onion (*Carmel*), 1 tsp 12

onion (*Maggi* Broth & Seasoning), 1 tsp. 28

onion (*MBT*) 16

onion (*Weight Watchers*) 10

vegetable (*Maggi* Broth & Seasoning), 1 tsp. 27

vegetable (*MBT*) 12

chicken and chicken flavor:

  bouillon, *see "bouillon," above*

  broth, *see "broth," above*

  cream of (*Knorr* Swiss) 80

  cream of (*Lipton Cup-a-Soup*) 80

  cream of (*Nestlé Souptime*) 100

  creamy (*Hain* Old Fashion Naturals), 8-oz. cup 224

  noodle (*Golden Grain*) 34

  noodle (*Knorr*) 45

  noodle (*Knorr Swiss*) 20

  noodle (*Nestlé Souptime*) 30

  noodle, chicken flavor, *see "noodle," below*

  noodle, w/white meat (*Lipton*), 8-oz. cup 70

  noodle, w/white meat (*Lipton Cup-a-Soup*) 45

  noodle ripples (*Lipton*), 8-oz. cup 80

  rice (*Lipton*), 8-oz. cup 60

  rice, w/white meat (*Lipton Cup-a-Soup*) 50

  vegetable, w/white meat (*Lipton Cup-a-Soup*) 40

green pea, *see "pea," below*

leek (*Knorr*) 50

minestrone (*Golden Grain*), 8-oz. cup 66

minestrone (*Knorr*) 50

mushroom:

  (*Carmel*), 1 tsp. 12

  (*Knorr*) 50

  (*Nestlé Souptime*) 80

  cream of (*Hain* Old Fashion Naturals), 8-oz. cup 275

  cream of (*Lipton Cup-a-Soup*) 80

Napoli (*Knorr*) 40

Soups, Mixes, continued

tomato:
   (*Knorr Swiss*) 70
   (*Lipton Cup-a-Soup*) 70
   (*Nestlé Souptime*) 70
   tangy (*Hain* Old Fashion Naturals), 8-oz. cup 264

vegetable:
   (*Knorr*) 25
   (*Knorr Swiss*) 75
   alphabet (*Lipton*), 8-oz. cup 40
   beef (*Lipton*), 8-oz. cup 60
   beef (*Lipton Cup-a-Soup*) 60
   bouillon, *see "bouillon," above*
   broth, *see "broth," above*
   cream of (*Nestlé Souptime*) 80
   hearty (*Hain* Old Fashion Naturals), 8-oz. cup 147
   spring vegetable (*Lipton Cup-a-Soup*) 45

  * *Prepared according to package directions, except as noted*
 ** *Unprepared dry mix*

CHAPTER 10

DIPS, APPETIZERS
AND HORS D'OEUVRES

APPETIZERS, HORS D'OEUVRES & SNACKS, CANNED, DRIED OR IN JARS

See also "Appetizers, Hors d'Oeuvres & Snacks, Frozen," "Fish, Smoked" and "Meat, Fish & Poultry Spreads"

	CALORIES
anchovies, flat (*Reese*), 2-oz. can	100
caviar:	
black sturgeon (*Northland Queen*), 1 oz.	74
black sturgeon (*Romanoff Iranian*), 1 oz.	74
red salmon (*Romanoff*), 1 oz.	68
red salmon (*Romar Brand*), 1 oz.	68
chicken livers, chopped (*Reese*), 1 oz.	47
clam cocktail, w/sauce (*Sau-Sea*), 4-oz. jar	99
crab cocktail, w/sauce (*Sau-Sea*), 4-oz. jar	107
fish balls (*King Oscar*), 14-oz. can	137
frankfurters, cocktail (*Vienna*), 1 oz.	88
gefilte fish balls, cocktail (*Manischewitz Fishlets*), 1 oz.	30
herring snacks, kippered (*King Oscar Kippered Snacks*), 3¾ oz. can	205
herring, pickled, kippered or salad, see "Fish & Shellfish, Canned or in Jars," page 156	
mushrooms, cocktail (*Reese* Buttons), 4-oz. jar, drained	25
paté:	
liver (*Hormel*), 1 tbsp.	33
liver (*Sell's*), 1 tbsp.	45
liver, w/herbs (*Le Parfait*), 1 oz.	73
liver, w/truffles (*Le Parfait*), 1 oz.	73

Appetizers, Hors d'Oeuvres & Snacks, continued

salami, cocktail, Danish (*Reese* Sticks), 1 oz. 128
sardines, *see "Fish & Shellfish, Canned or in Jars," page 157*
sausage rolls, dried:

    (*Cow-Boy Jo's* Beef Jerky), ¼-oz. pkg. 24
    (*Cow-Boy Jo's* Beef Sausage), ⅝-oz. pkg. 81
    (*Cow-Boy Jo's Smok-O-Roni* Beef Sausage), ¼-oz. pkg. ..42
    (*Frito-Lay's* Smoked Beef Polish Sausage), 1-oz. pkg. 70
    (*Lowrey's* Pickled Hot Sausage), 1¼-oz. pkg. 110
    (*Lowrey's* Pickled Polish Sausage), ⅝-oz. pkg. 50
sausages, Vienna:

    (*Armour Star*), 3 sausages* 150
    (*Wilson's Certified*), 3 sausages* 144
    barbecue (*Libby's*), 3 sausages* 154
    beef broth (*Libby's*), 3 sausages* 138
shrimp cocktail, w/sauce (*Sau-Sea*), 4-oz. jar 112
shrimp cocktail, w/sauce (*Sau-Sea*), 6-oz. jar 121

* *As packaged*

APPETIZERS, HORS D'OEUVRES
& SNACKS, FROZEN, one piece*,
except as noted
*See also "Appetizers, Hors d'Oeuvres & Snacks,
Canned, Dried or in Jars"*

CALORIES

cheese straws (*Durkee*), 1 piece 29
crab, deviled, miniatures (*Mrs. Paul's*), 1 oz. 63
dim sum:

  turkey-vegetable
    (*Royal Dragon—Potsticker*), 1-oz. piece 45
  turkey-shrimp-vegetable
    (*Royal Dragon—Shaomai*), .6-oz. 27
  shrimp-bamboo shoot
    (*Royal Dragon—Hargow*), ½-oz. piece 27

Appetizers, Hors d'Oeuvres & Snacks, continued

egg rolls:

    chicken (*Chun King*), ½-oz. roll 28

    chicken (*La Choy*), .45-oz. roll 30

    chicken and mushroom (*Mow Sang*), 1-oz. roll 69

    lobster (*La Choy*), .45-oz. roll 27

    meat and lobster (*Chun King*), ½-oz. roll 26

    meat and shrimp (*Chun King*), ½-oz. roll 29

    meat and shrimp (*Chun King*), 1-oz. roll 46

    meat and shrimp (*La Choy*), .45-oz. roll 27

    meat and shrimp (*La Choy*), ¼-oz. roll 17

    pork, barbecue (*Mow Sang*), 1-oz. roll 74

    shrimp (*Chun King*), ½-oz. roll 24

    shrimp (*Chun King*), 2½-oz. roll 145

    shrimp (*La Choy*), .45-oz. roll 26

    shrimp (*La Choy*), 2½-oz. roll 108

    shrimp (*Mow Sang*), 1-oz. roll 64

    vegetable (*Mow Sang*), 1-oz. roll 66

fish miniatures, light batter-fried (*Mrs. Paul's*), 1 oz. 51

franks in pastry (*Durkee Franks-N-Blankets*), 1 piece 45

pizza rolls:

    cheeseburger (*Jeno's*), ½-oz. roll 45

    pepperoni and cheese (*Jeno's*), ½-oz. roll 43

    sausage and cheese (*Jeno's*), ½-oz. roll 43

    shrimp and cheese (*Jeno's*), ½-oz. roll 37

puff-pastry, stuffed:

    beef (*Durkee*), 1 piece 47

    cheese (*Durkee*), 1 piece 59

    chicken (*Durkee*), 1 piece 49

    chicken liver (*Durkee*), 1 piece 48

    shrimp (*Durkee*), 1 piece 44

spring roll (*Royal Dragon*), 1½-oz. roll 106

spring roll, cocktail (*Royal Dragon*), ½-oz. roll 40

wontons (*Royal Dragon*), ⅓-oz. piece 30

---

* *As packaged; note variations in size*

DIPS, READY TO SERVE,
eight-ounce container, except as noted
See also "Dip Mixes" and "Cheese Spreads"

CALORIES

bacon and horseradish (*Kraft Teez* Dip)	456
blue cheese (*Kraft Ready* Dip)	552
clam (*Kraft Teez* Dip)	360
clam and lobster (*Borden*), 4-oz. container	240
dill pickle (*Kraft Ready* Dip)	536
enchilada (*Fritos*), 3⅛-oz. serving	120
garden spice (*Borden*), 4-oz. container	264
garlic (*Kraft Teez* Dip)	376
green goddess (*Kraft Teez* Dip)	368
jalapeno:	
(*Fritos*), 3⅛-oz. serving	110
(*Gebhardt*)	240
(*Old El Paso*), 7½-oz. container	263
onion (*Kraft Ready* Dip)	544
onion, French (*Kraft Teez* Dip)	344

DIP MIXES, one packet
See also "Dips, Ready to Serve"

CALORIES

garlic and onion (*McCormick/Schiller*), 1¼ oz.	158
horseradish w/imitation bacon bits	
(*McCormick/Schiller*), 1¼ oz.	153
onion (*Ann Page* Soup/Dip), .27 oz.	25
onion, toasted (*McCormick/Schiller*), 1¼ oz.	103

CHAPTER 11

FROZEN DINNERS AND POT PIES

FROZEN DINNERS, one complete dinner*
See also "Frozen Pot Pies," "Meat & Poultry Entrees, Frozen" and "Fish & Shellfish, Frozen"

CALORIES

beans and beef patties (*Swanson TV Brand*), 11-oz. pkg. ...500
beans and franks:
    (*Banquet*), 10¼-oz. pkg. 528
    (*Morton*), 10¾-oz. pkg. 530
    (*Swanson TV Brand*), 11¼-oz. pkg. 550
beef:
    (*Banquet*), 11-oz. pkg. 312
    (*Morton*), 10-oz. pkg. 260
    (*Swanson*), 15-oz. pkg. 490
    (*Swanson TV Brand*), 11½-oz. pkg. 370
    Chinese (*La Choy*), 11-oz. pkg.......................242
    chopped (*Banquet*), 11-oz. pkg. 443
    chopped, beefsteak
      (*Swanson Hungry-Man*), 18-oz. pkg. 730
    chopped sirloin (*Morton Steak House*), 9½-oz. pkg. 760
    chopped sirloin (*Swanson TV Brand*), 10-oz. pkg. 460
    low-calorie, beefsteak (*Weight Watchers*), 10-oz. pkg. ..390
    pepper, Oriental (*Chun King*), 1 dinner** 430
    rib eye (*Morton Steak House*), 9-oz. pkg. 820
    sliced (*Morton Country Table*), 15-oz. pkg. 510

beef, continued

    sliced (*Swanson Hungry-Man*), 17-oz. pkg. 540

    sirloin strip (*Morton Steak House*), 9½-oz. pkg. 760

    tenderloin (*Morton Steak House*), 9½-oz. pkg. 890

chicken:

    boneless (*Morton*), 10-oz. pkg. 230

    boneless (*Morton* King Size), 17-oz. pkg. 530

    boneless (*Swanson Hungry-Man*), 19-oz. pkg. 730

    Chinese (*La Choy*), 11-oz. pkg. 354

    chow mein, *see "chicken chow mein," below*

    croquette (*Morton*), 10¼-oz. pkg. 410

    fried (*Banquet*), 11-oz. pkg. 530

    fried (*Banquet Man Pleasers*), 17-oz. pkg. 916

    fried (*Morton*), 11-oz. pkg. 460

    fried (*Morton Country Table*), 15-oz. pkg. 710

    fried (*Morton* King Size), 17-oz. pkg. 860

    fried (*Swanson*), 15-oz. pkg. 630

    fried (*Swanson Hungry-Man*), 15¾-oz. pkg. 910

    fried (*Swanson TV Brand*), 11½-oz. pkg. 570

    fried, barbecue flavor

      (*Swanson Hungry-Man*), 16½-oz. pkg. 760

    fried, barbecue flavor

      (*Swanson TV Brand*), 11¼-oz. pkg. 530

    fried, crispy (*Swanson TV Brand*), 10¾-oz. pkg. 650

    and dumplings (*Morton*), 11-oz. pkg. 280

    and noodles (*Morton*), 10.3-oz. pkg. 260

chicken chow mein (*Chun King*), 1 dinner** 330

chicken chow mein/sweet and sour pork

    (*Chun King*), 1 dinner** 390

clams, fried (*Taste O'Sea Platter*), 6½-oz. pkg. 540

cod, batter-fried

    (*Taste O'Sea Batter Dipt*), 8¾-oz. pkg. 500

corned beef hash (*Banquet*), 10-oz. pkg. 372

enchilada:

    beef (*Banquet*), 12-oz. pkg. 479

    beef (*Morton*), 12-oz. pkg. 350

enchilada, continued

   beef (*Swanson TV Brand*), 15-oz. pkg. 570
   beef (*Van de Kamp's*), 12-oz. pkg. 420
   cheese (*Banquet*), 12-oz. pkg. 459
   cheese (*Van de Kamp's*), 12-oz. pkg. 430
fish:
   (*Banquet*), 8¾-oz. pkg. 282
   (*Morton*), 9-oz. pkg. 260
   and chips (*Swanson Hungry-Man*), 15¾-oz. pkg. 760
   and chips (*Swanson TV Brand*), 10¼-oz. pkg. 450
fish, batter-fried (*Van de Kamp's*), 11-oz. pkg. 540
fish cake, fried (*Taste O' Sea*), 8-oz. pkg. 380
fish fillet:
   (*Van de Kamp's*), 12-oz. pkg. 300
   low-calorie (*Weight Watchers*), 16-oz. pkg. 290
   low-calorie, w/peas, mushrooms and sauce
     (*Weight Watchers*), 9½-oz. pkg. 210
fish, fried (*Taste O' Sea Moby Dick*), 9-oz. pkg. 430
fish, fried, pollock (*Taste O' Sea*), 1 dinner** 390
flounder:
   fried (*Taste O' Sea*), 9-oz. pkg. 350
   low-calorie (*Weight Watchers*), 8½-oz. pkg. 160
   low-calorie, w/lobster sauce
     (*Weight Watchers*), 16-oz. pkg. 240
German style (*Swanson TV Brand*), 11¾-oz. pkg. 430
haddock:
   fried (*Taste O' Sea*), 9-oz. pkg. 380
   low-calorie (*Weight Watchers*), 16-oz. pkg. 250
   low-calorie, w/stuffing and chopped spinach
     (*Weight Watchers*), 8¾-oz. pkg. 180
ham:
   (*Banquet*), 10-oz. pkg. 369
   (*Morton*), 10-oz. pkg. 440
   (*Swanson TV Brand*), 10¼-oz. pkg. 380
Italian style (*Banquet*), 11-oz. pkg. 446
Italian style (*Swanson TV Brand*), 13-oz. pkg. 420
lasagna w/meat (*Swanson Hungry-Man*), 17¾-oz. pkg. ...740

Frozen Dinners, continued

macaroni:

    and beef (*Morton*), 10-oz. pkg. 260

    and beef (*Swanson TV Brand*), 12-oz. pkg. 400

    and cheese (*Morton*), 11-oz. pkg. 320

    and cheese (*Swanson TV Brand*), 12½-oz. pkg. 390

meat loaf:

    (*Banquet*), 11-oz. pkg. 412

    (*Banquet Man Pleaser*), 19-oz. pkg. 916

    (*Morton*), 11-oz. pkg. 340

    (*Morton Country Table*), 15-oz. pkg. 480

    (*Swanson TV Brand*), 10¾-oz. pkg. 530

meat balls (*Swanson TV Brand*), 11¾-oz. pkg. 400

Mexican style:

    (*Banquet*), 12-oz. pkg. 608

    (*Morton*), 12-oz. pkg. 410

    (*Van de Kamp's*), 12-oz. pkg. 480

    combination (*Banquet*), 12-oz. pkg. 571

    combination (*Swanson TV Brand*), 16-oz. pkg. 600

    combination (*Van de Kamp's*), 11-oz. pkg. 420

noodles and chicken (*Swanson TV Brand*), 10¼-oz. pkg. ..390

ocean perch, *see "perch," below*

pepper Oriental (*La Choy*), 11-oz. pkg. 349

perch:

    fried (*Taste O' Sea*), 9-oz. pkg. 400

    ocean, low-calorie (*Weight Watchers*), 16-oz. pkg. 320

    ocean, low-calorie, w/chopped broccoli and breadcrumbs

    (*Weight Watchers*), 8-oz. pkg. 310

Polynesian style (*Swanson TV Brand*), 13-oz. pkg. 490

pork, loin of (*Swanson TV Brand*), 11¼-oz. pkg. 470

salisbury steak:

    (*Banquet*), 11-oz. pkg. 390

    (*Banquet Man Pleaser*), 19-oz. pkg. 873

    (*Morton*), 11-oz. pkg. 290

    (*Morton Country Table*), 15-oz. pkg. 500

    (*Morton* King Size), 19-oz. pkg. 780

    (*Swanson*), 16-oz. pkg. 490

salisbury steak, continued

    (*Swanson Hungry-Man*), 17-oz. pkg. 870

    (*Swanson TV Brand*), 11½-oz. pkg. 500

scallops, fried (*Taste O' Sea*), 8-oz. pkg. 380

scrod, batter-fried

    (*Taste O' Sea Batter Dipt*), 8¾-oz. pkg. 500

seafood platter (*Taste O' Sea*), 9-oz. pkg. 520

shrimp:

    (*Van de Kamp's*), 10-oz. pkg. 370

    Chinese (*La Choy*), 11-oz. pkg. 325

    chow mein, *see "shrimp chow mein," below*

    fried (*Taste O' Sea*), 7-oz. pkg. 350

    patty, fried (*Taste O' Sea*), 1 dinner** 390

shrimp chow mein/beef pepper Oriental

    (*Chun King*), 1 dinner** 360

sole:

    fried (*Taste O' Sea*), 9-oz. pkg. 330

    low-calorie (*Weight Watchers*), 16-oz. pkg. 240

    low-calorie, w/peas, mushrooms and sauce

      (*Weight Watchers*), 9½-oz. pkg. 200

spaghetti and meatballs:

    (*Morton*), 11-oz. pkg. 360

    (*Swanson Hungry-Man*), 18½-oz. pkg. 660

    (*Swanson TV Brand*), 12½-oz. pkg. 410

Swiss Steak (*Swanson TV Brand*), 10-oz. pkg. 350

turbot, Greenland, low-calorie, w/stuffing

    (*Weight Watchers*), 16-oz. pkg. 420

turbot, Greenland, low-calorie, w/peas, carrots, and

    breadcrumbs (*Weight Watchers*), 8-oz. pkg. 310

turkey:

    (*Banquet*), 11-oz. pkg. 293

    (*Banquet Man Pleaser*), 19-oz. pkg. 620

    (*Morton*), 11-oz. pkg. 340

    (*Morton Country Table*), 15-oz. pkg. 550

    (*Morton* King Size), 19-oz. pkg. 580

    (*Swanson*), 16-oz. pkg. 520

    (*Swanson Hungry-Man*), 19-oz. pkg. 740

urkey, continued
    (*Swanson TV Brand*), 11½-oz. pkg. 360
eal Parmigiana:
    (*Banquet*), 11-oz. pkg. 421
    (*Morton*), 11-oz. pkg. 250
    (*Morton* King Size), 20-oz. pkg. 600
    (*Swanson Hungry-Man*), 20½-oz. pkg. 910
    (*Swanson TV Brand*), 12¼-oz. pkg. 520
Western style:
    (*Banquet*), 11-oz. pkg. 399
    (*Morton*), 11.8-oz. pkg. 400
    (*Swanson Hungry-Man*), 17¾-oz. pkg. 890
    (*Swanson TV Brand*), 11¾-oz. pkg. 460

* *Pay attention to package sizes*
** *As packaged*

FROZEN POT PIES, one whole pie*
See also "Frozen Dinners," "Meat & Poultry Entrees, Frozen" and "Fish & Shellfish, Frozen"

                                                              CALORIES

eef:
    (*Banquet*), 8-oz. pie 400
    (*Morton*), 8-oz. pie 320
    (*Stouffer's*), 10-oz. pie 550
    (*Swanson*), 8-oz. pie 430
    (*Swanson Hungry-Man*), 16-oz. pie 770
    sirloin burger (*Swanson Hungry-Man*), 16-oz. pie 800
hicken:
    (*Banquet*), 8-oz. pie 427
    (*Morton*), 8-oz. pie 350
    (*Stouffer's*), 10-oz. pie 500
    (*Swanson*), 8-oz. pie 450
    (*Swanson Hungry-Man*), 16-oz. pie 780
    (*Van de Kamp's*), 7½-oz. pie 520

* *Pay attention to package sizes*

CHAPTER 12

MEAT, FISH AND POULTRY

MEAT & POULTRY ENTREES, CANNED OR REFRIGERATED

See also "Meat & Poultry Entrees, Frozen,"
"Frankfurters, Luncheon Meats & Sausages" and
"Meat, Fish and Poultry, Freeze-Dried"

CALORIES

beef:

    chopped (*Armour Star*), 12-oz. can 1190

    dried, creamed (*Hormel* Short Order), 7½-oz. can 157

    goulash (*Heinz*), 7½-oz. can 253

    goulash (*Hormel* Short Order), 7½-oz. can 229

    roast (*Wilson Certified Tender Made*), 8 oz. 267

    roast, w/gravy (*Armour Star*), 8 oz. 290

    sliced, and gravy

        (*Morton House* Heat 'n Serve), 6¼ oz. 190

    stew, *see "stew," below*

    top round (*Vienna Choice*), 3½ oz. 216

    top round (*Vienna Top Ten*), 3½ oz. 101

chicken:

    à la king (*Swanson*), 5¼ oz. 190

    boned (*Hormel Tender Chunk*), 6¾-oz. can 256

    boned (*Swanson*), 5 oz. 110

    boned, chunk (*Chicken Ready*), 6½-oz. can 273

    boned, chunk (*Swanson*), 5 oz. 110

chicken, continued

    breast, oven-roasted

        (*Chef's Gourmet Norwestern*), 8 oz. 200

    and dumplings (*Swanson*), 7½ oz. 230

    and noodles (*Heinz*), 7½-oz. can 160

    roll, boneless cooked (*Swift Premium*), 3½ oz. 180

    stew, *see "stew," below*

    whole (*Ranch Table*), 8 oz. 443

chili con carne, *see "Mexican & Mexican-Style Foods," page 164*

corned beef, *see "Frankfurters, Luncheon Meats & Sausage," page 145*

corned beef hash, *see "hash," below*

ham:

    (*Armour Star*), 8 oz. 416

    (*Armour Star Golden*), 8 oz. 304

    (*Armour Star Parti Style*), 8 oz. 336

    (*Hormel*—3-lb. can), 8 oz. 255

    (*Hormel* Bone-In), 8 oz. 418

    (*Hormel Cure-81*), 8 oz. 388

    (*Hormel Curemaster*), 8 oz. 274

    (*Hormel Holiday Glaze*), 8 oz. 279

    (*Hormel Tender Chunk*), 6¾-oz. can 314

    (*Oscar Mayer Jubilee*), 8 oz. 280

    (*Swift Premium*), 8 oz. 499

    (*Swift Premium Hostess*), 8 oz. 318

    (*Swift Premium Hostess*—Boneless), 8 oz. 340

    (*Wilson Certified*—3- or 5-lb. can), 8 oz. 386

    (*Wilson Certified* Boneless), 8 oz. 382

    (*Wilson Corn King*—3- or 5-lb. can), 8 oz. 386

    (*Wilson Corn King* Boneless), 8 oz. 382

    (*Wilson Masterpiece*—3-lb. can), 8 oz. 250

    (*Wilson Masterpiece* Boneless), 8 oz. 250

    (*Wilson Tender Made*), 8 oz. 344

    patties (*Wilson Certified*), 2 oz. 146

    steak (*Oscar Mayer Jubilee*), 2-oz. slice 70

ham luncheon meat, *see "Frankfurters, Luncheon Meats & Sausages," page 148*

Meat & Poultry Entrees, Canned or Refrigerated, continued

hash:

corned beef (*Armour Star*), 8-oz. 435

corned beef (*Mary Kitchen*), 7½ oz. 398

corned beef (*Mary Kitchen* Short Order), 7½ oz. can ..366

roast beef (*Mary Kitchen*), 7½ oz. 395

roast beef (*Mary Kitchen* Short Order), 7½-oz. can 366

lamb stew, *see "stew," below*

liver, sliced (*Swift's Tru Tender*), 2.6 oz. 140

pork:

roast (*Wilson Tender Made*), 8 oz. 354

shoulder (*Wilson Certified*), 8 oz. 558

shoulder (*Wilson Corn King*), 8 oz. 558

sliced, and gravy

   (*Morton House* Heat 'n Serve), 6¼ oz. 190

Salisbury steak, and mushroom gravy

   (*Morton House* Heat 'n Serve), 4⅙ oz. 160

sausages, *see "Frankfurters, Luncheon Meats & Sausages," page 145*

Sloppy Joe:

   (*Hormel* Short Order), 7½-oz. can 344

   (*Morton House*), 5 oz. 240

   beef (*Libby's*), 8 oz. 370

   pork (*Libby's*), 8 oz. 315

stew:

   beef (*Armour Star*), 8 oz. 200

   beef (*Dinty Moore*), 7½ oz. 183

   beef (*Dinty Moore* Short Order), 7½-oz. can 173

   beef (*Featherweight*), 7¼-oz. can 210

   beef (*Heinz*), 7½-oz. can 200

   beef (*Libby's*), 8 oz. 206

   beef (*Morton House*), 8 oz. 240

   beef (*Swanson*), 7½ oz. 190

   chicken (*Featherweight*), 7¼-oz. can 160

   chicken (*Swanson*), 7½ oz. 180

   chicken, w/dumplings (*Heinz*), 7½-oz. can 202

   chicken, w/dumplings (*Libby's*), 8 oz. 199

stew, continued

    lamb (*Featherweight*), 7¼-oz. can 2

    meatball (*Dinty Moore*), 7½ oz. 2

    meatball (*Libby's*), 8 oz. 2

    meatball (*Morton House*), 8 oz. 2

    Mulligan (*Dinty Moore's* Short Order), 7½-oz. can 2

tripe (*Libby's*), 5 oz. 2

turkey:

    boned (*Hormel Tender Chunk*), 6¾-oz. can 2

    boned (*Swanson*), 5 oz. 2

    boned, breast, roasted

        (*Chef's Gourmet Norwestern*), 8 oz. 2

    boned, roll, roasted

        (*Chef's Gourmet Norwestern*), 8 oz. 2

    roast (*Wilson Certified*), 8 oz. 2

    roasted (*Swift Premium Deep Basted Butterball*

        Young Turkey*), 3½ oz. 2

    roasted, dark meat

        (*Swift Premium Deep Basted Butterball*), 3½ oz. 2

    roasted, light meat

        (*Swift Premium Deep Basted Butterball*), 3½ oz. 1

MEAT & POULTRY ENTREES, FROZEN,
one whole package*, except as noted
See also "Meat & Poultry Entrees, Canned or Refrigerated,"
"Frozen Dinners" and "Meat, Fish & Poultry, Freeze-Dried"

CALORI

beef:

    breaded, with American cheese food

        (*Pierre Golddiggers*), 3½ oz. 3

    chipped, creamed (*Banquet Cookin' Bags*), 5-oz. pkg. ..1

    chipped, creamed (*Stouffer's*), 11-oz. pkg. 4

    chop suey, *see "Oriental & Oriental-Style Foods," page 166*

    corned beef, *see "Frankfurters, Luncheon Meat & Sausages,*
        page 145*

beef, continued

enchiladas, tamales, *see "Mexican & Mexican-Style Foods,"*
   page 164

hamburger steaks (*Pierre* 100% Beef), 3½ oz. 248

patties (*Pierre Beef Patties*), 3½ oz. 247

patties, breaded (*Pierre*), 3½ oz. 319

patties, breaded (*Pierre Chuckwagon*), 3½ oz. 297

patties, hoagie (*Pierre* Hoagie Beef Patties), 3½ oz. 246

patties, w/red and green pepper
   (*Pierre* Zesty Hoagie Beef Patties), 3½ oz. 226

short ribs, boneless, w/vegetable gravy
   (*Stouffer's*), 11½-oz. pkg. 700

sirloin (*Weight Watchers*), 16-oz. pkg. 560

sliced, barbecue sauce w/
   (*Banquet Cookin' Bags*), 5-oz. pkg. 120

sliced, gravy and (*Banquet Cookin' Bags*), 5-oz. pkg. ...105

sliced, gravy and (*Banquet Buffet Suppers*), 32-oz. pkg. ...589

sliced, gravy and
   (*Green Giant Toast Toppers*), 5-oz. pkg. 130

sliced, w/gravy and whipped potatoes
   (*Swanson TV Brand* Entree), 8-oz. pkg. 190

sliced (*Swanson Hungry-Man* Entree), 12¼-oz. pkg.....330

steaks, breaded (*Hormel*), 4 oz. 373

stew, *see "stew," below*

stroganoff, w/parsley noodles (*Stouffer's*), 9¾-oz. pkg. ...390

teriyaki, *see "Oriental & Oriental-Style Foods," page 166*

chili con carne, *see "Mexican & Mexican-Style Foods," page 164*

chicken:

à la king (*Banquet Cookin' Bags*), 5-oz. pkg. 137

à la king (*Green Giant Toast Toppers*), 5-oz. pkg. 170

à la king, w/rice (*Stouffer's*), 9½-oz. pkg. 330

baked breast (*Stouffer's*), 16-oz. pkg. 770

and biscuits (*Green Giant* Baked Entree), 7-oz. pkg. 200

breast Parmigiana (*Weight Watchers*), 9-oz. pkg. 200

cacciatore, w/spaghetti (*Stouffer's*), 11¼-oz. pkg. 310

chow mein, *see "Oriental & Oriental-Style Foods," page 166*

chicken, continued

creamed (*Stouffer's*), 6½-oz. pkg. 300
croquettes, w/fricassee sauce
  (*Howard Johnson's*), 12-oz. pkg. 505
divan (*Stouffer's*), 8-oz. pkg. 335
and dumplings (*Banquet Buffet Suppers*), 32-oz. pkg. ...990
escalloped, and noodles (*Stouffer's*), 11½-oz. pkg. 500
fillets (*Buitoni*), 15-oz. pkg. 546
fried (*Banquet Buffet Suppers*), 32-oz. pkg. 2591
fried (*Morton*), 32-oz. pkg. 1500
fried (*Morton Country Table* Entree), 12-oz. pkg. 600
fried (*Swanson Hungry-Man* Entree), 12-oz. pkg. 620
fried, assorted pieces (*Swanson* Chicken Parts), 3.2-oz. ...260
fried, barbecue flavor
  (*Swanson Hungry-Man* Entree), 12-oz. pkg. 550
fried, breast (*Morton*), 22-oz. pkg. 1320
fried, breast (*Swanson* Chicken Parts), 3.2 oz. 250
fried, nibbles (*Swanson* Chicken Parts), 3.2 oz. 290
fried, nibbles, w/French fries
  (*Swanson TV Brand* Entree), 6-oz. pkg. 370
fried, thighs and drumsticks
  (*Swanson* Chicken Parts), 3.2 oz. 260
fried, w/whipped potatoes
  (*Swanson TV Brand* Entree), 7-oz. pkg. 360
and noodles (*Banquet Buffet Suppers*), 32-oz. pkg. 764
and noodles (*Green Giant* Entree), 9-oz. pkg. 250
paprikash, w/egg noodles (*Stouffer's*), 10½-oz. pkg. 385
w/peas, onions and sauce
  (*Weight Watchers*), 9-oz. pkg. 270
sliced, breast of (*Weight Watchers*), 15-oz. pkg. 330
chicken livers and onions
  (*Weight Watchers*), 10½-oz. pkg. 220
crepes:
beef burgundy (*Stouffer's*), 6¼-oz. pkg. 335
chicken w/mushroom sauce (*Stouffer's*), 8¼-oz. pkg.....390
ham and asparagus (*Stouffer's*), 6¼-oz. pkg...........325

crepes, continued

frankfurters, *see "Frankfurters, Luncheon Meats &
Sausages," page 145*

frankfurters, batter-wrapped
(*Hormel Corn Dogs*), 1 wiener* 231

frankfurters, batter-wrapped
(*Hormel Tater Dogs*), 1 wiener* 187

hash, roast beef (*Stouffer's*), 11½-oz. pkg. 530

lasagna, *see "Pasta Entrees, Frozen," page 175*

meatballs, w/brown gravy and whipped potatoes
(*Swanson TV Brand* Entree), 9¼-oz. pkg. 330

meatballs, Swedish, w/parsley noodles
(*Stouffer's*), 11-oz. pkg. 475

meat loaf:
w/tomato sauce (*Banquet Cookin' Bags*), 5-oz. pkg. 232
w/tomato sauce
(*Banquet Buffet Suppers*), 32-oz. pkg. 1325
w/tomato sauce and whipped potatoes
(*Swanson TV Brand* Entree), 9-oz. pkg. 330

pork steaks, breaded (*Hormel*), 3 oz. 223

salisbury steak:
(*Howard Johnson's*), 4½ oz. 273
(*Morton Country Table* Entree), 10¼-oz. pkg. 500
(*Swanson Hungry-Man* Entree), 12½-oz. pkg. 640
w/crinkle cut potatoes
(*Swanson TV Brand* Entree), 5½-oz. pkg. 370
w/gravy (*Banquet Cookin' Bags*), 5-oz. pkg. 210
gravy and (*Banquet Buffet Suppers*), 32-oz. pkg. 1386
w/gravy (*Green Giant* Baked Entree), 7-oz. pkg. 290
w/onion gravy (*Stouffer's*), 12-oz. pkg. 500
w/tomato sauce (*Green Giant* Entree), 9-oz. pkg. 390

sausage, *see "Frankfurters, Luncheon Meat & Sausages,"
page 145*

sausage and peppers (*Buitoni*), 15-oz. pkg. 618

sloppy Joe, seasoned w/tomato sauce and beef
(*Green Giant Toast Toppers*), 5-oz. pkg. 160

Meat & Poultry Entrees, Frozen, continued

spaghetti and meatballs, *see "Pasta Entrees, Frozen," page 176*

steak, green pepper, w/rice (*Stouffer's*), 10½-oz. pkg. 350

stew:

   beef (*Banquet Buffet Suppers*), 32-oz. pkg. 700

   beef (*Green Giant* Entree), 9-oz. pkg. 160

   beef (*Stouffer's*), 10-oz. pkg. 310

   beef, and biscuits

      (*Green Giant* Baked Entree), 7-oz. pkg. 190

turkey:

   (*Swanson Hungry-Man* Entree), 13¼-oz. pkg. 380

   w/gravy, dressing and whipped potatoes

      (*Swanson TV Brand* Entree), 8¾-oz. pkg. 260

   sliced (*Morton Country Table* Entree), 12.3-oz. pkg. 370

   sliced, breast of (*Weight Watchers*), 16-oz. pkg. 400

   sliced, gravy and (*Banquet Cookin' Bags*), 5-oz. pkg. ...133

   sliced, gravy and (*Banquet Buffet Suppers*), 32-oz. pkg. ..534

   sliced, gravy and

      (*Green Giant Toast Toppers*), 5-oz. pkg. 100

   tetrazzini (*Stouffer's*), 12-oz. pkg. 480

   tetrazzini (*Weight Watchers*), 13-oz. pkg. 380

veal:

   breaded, patties (*Pierre*), 3½ oz. 274

   breaded, w/Italian sauce and Provolone cheese

      (*Pierre Veal Golddiggers*), 3.7 oz. 271

   breaded, and spaghetti in tomato sauce

      (*Swanson TV Brand* Entree), 8¼-oz. pkg. 290

   Parmigiana (*Banquet Cookin' Bags*), 5-oz. pkg. 228

   Parmigiana (*Buitoni*), 19-oz. pkg. 767

   Parmigiana (*Green Giant* Baked Entree), 7-oz. pkg. 310

   Parmigiana (*Weight Watchers*), 9½-oz. pkg. 230

   Parmigiana, w/tomato sauce

      (*Banquet Buffet Suppers*), 32-oz. pkg. 1563

   steaks (*Hormel*), 4 oz. 131

   steaks, breaded (*Hormel*), 4 oz. 242

* *As packaged*

FRANKFURTERS, LUNCHEON MEATS & SAUSAGES

See also "Meat & Poultry Entrees, Canned or Refrigerated"
and "Meat, Fish & Poultry Spreads"

CALORIES

bacon, *see "Bacon," page 152*
banquet loaf, beef (*Eckrich*), 1 slice* 75
banquet loaf, beef (*Eckrich Smorgas Pac*), 1 slice* 55
barbecue loaf:
   (*Hormel BBQ*), 1-oz. slice 47
   (*Oscar Mayer Bar-B-Q*), 1 slice* 50
beef:
   (*Danola* Thin Sliced), 1 oz. 35
   (*Eckrich* Slender Sliced), 1 slice* 40
   (*Kahn's*), 1 oz. 90
   bologna, *see "bologna," below*
   corned (*A & P*), 1 oz. 40
   corned (*Danola* Thin Sliced), 1 oz. 35
   corned (*Eckrich* Slender Sliced), 1 slice* 40
   corned (*Hormel* Loaf), .8-oz. slice 37
   corned, brisket (*Vienna*), 3½ oz. 305
   corned, brisket (*Wilson Certified Tender Made*), 8 oz. ..361
   corned, flats (*Vienna*), 3½ oz. 171
   corned, jellied loaf (*Oscar Mayer*), 1-oz. slice 39
   dried (*Armour Star*), 5-oz. jar 234
   dried (*Swift Premium*), 3-oz. pkg. 140
   frankfurters, *see "frankfurters and wieners," below*
   jellied loaf (*Hormel*), 1.2-oz. slice 32
   pastrami, *see "pastrami," below*
   peppered (*Vienna*), 3½ oz. 176
   sausages, *see "sausage, beef," below*
   sausage, smoked, *see "smoked links and sausages," below*
   smoked (*A & P*), 1 oz. 35
   smoked (*Oscar Mayer* Thin Sliced), 3-oz. pkg. 118
   spicy (*A & P*), 1 oz. 45

Frankfurters, Luncheon Meats & Sausages, continued

bologna:

    (*Armour Star*), 1 oz. 90

    (*Eckrich*), 1 slice* 95

    (*Eckrich* Thick Sliced—12-oz. pkg.), 1 slice* 160

    (*Eckrich* Thick Sliced—1-lb. pkg.), 1 slice* 170

    (*Eckrich Smorgas Pac*), 1 slice* 90

    (*Kahn's* Jumbo), 1 oz. 87

    (*Oscar Mayer German*), .8-oz. slice 75

    (*Swift Premium*), 1-oz. slice 95

    (*Wilson Certified*), 1 slice* 90

    (*Wilson Corn King*), 1 slice* 90

    beef (*Eckrich*), 1-oz. slice 95

    beef (*Eckrich Smorgas Pac*), 1 slice* 70

    beef (*Hormel*), 1-oz. slice 82

    beef (*Kahn's*), 1-oz. slice 88

    beef (*Oscar Mayer Lebanon*), .8-oz slice 75

    beef (*Vienna*), 3½ oz. 296

    beef (*Wilson Certified*), 1 slice* 90

    beef (*Wilson Corn King*), 1 slice* 90

    beef-garlic (*Oscar Mayer*), .8-oz. slice 75

    garlic (*Eckrich*), 1 slice* 95

    meat (*Hormel*), 1-oz. slice 84

    meat (*Wilson Certified*), 1 oz. 87

    meat (*Wilson Corn King*), 1 oz. 87

    ring (*Eckrich*), 1 oz. 100

    ring (*Hormel*—coarse ground), 1 oz. 76

    ring (*Hormel*—fine ground), 1 oz. 82

    ring (*Oscar Mayer Wisconsin*—coarse ground), 1 oz. 82

    ring (*Oscar Mayer Wisconsin*—fine ground), 1 oz. 88

    ring, garlic (*Eckrich*), 1 oz. 95

bologna and cheese (*Oscar Mayer*), .8-oz. slice 73

bratwurst:

    (*Kahn's*), 2-oz. link 180

    (*Kahn's Lauderdale* Jumbo), 1 link* 178

    cured (*Oscar Mayer*), 3-oz. link 277

Frankfurters, Luncheon Meats & Sausages, continued

braunschweiger:
    (*Oscar Mayer*—sliced), 1-oz. slice 103
    (*Oscar Mayer*—tube), 1 oz. 100
    (*Wilson Certified*), 8-oz. pkg. 716
breakfast sausage, *see "pork sausage," below*
buffet loaf (*Hormel*), 1-oz. slice 52
cervelat, *see "summer sausage," below*
chicken:
    (*A & P*), 1 oz. 60
    (*Danola* Thin Sliced), 1 oz. 45
    (*Eckrich* Slender Sliced), 1 slice* 47
    breast of (*Eckrich*), 6-oz. pkg. 193
chicken franks (*Longacre*), 1 frank* 120
cocktail loaf (*Oscar Mayer*), 1-oz. slice 65
corned beef, *see "beef, corned," above*
frankfurters and wieners:
    (*Armour Star* Hot Dogs), 1 link* 142
    (*Eckrich*), 1 link* 120
    (*Eckrich* Jumbo), 1 link* 190
    (*Eckrich* Skinless), 1 link* 150
    (*Kahn's* Wieners), 1 link* 150
    (*Kahn's* Jumbo Wieners), 1 link* 187
    (*Kahn's Lauderdale* Jumbo Wieners), 1 link* 184
    (*Oscar Mayer* Wieners), 1 link* 140
    (*Oscar Mayer* Wieners—Imperial Size), 1 link* 177
    (*Wilson Certified* Skinless), 1-lb. pkg. 1398
    (*Wilson* Western Style), 1-lb. pkg. 1400
    beef (*Eckrich*), 1 link* 150
    beef (*Eckrich* Jumbo), 1 link* 190
    beef (*Hormel*—12-oz. pkg.), 1 link* 104
    beef (*Hormel*—1-lb. pkg.), 1 link* 139
    beef (*Kahn's*), 1 link* 148
    beef (*Kahn's* Jumbo), 1 link* 185
    beef (*Oscar Mayer*—1-lb. pkg.), 1 link* 140
    beef (*Oscar Mayer* Machiaeh), 1 link* 180

frankfurters and wieners, continued

   beef (*Vienna*), 3½ oz. 311

   beef (*Wilson Certified*), 1-lb. pkg. 1358

   beef (*Wilson Certified* Skinless), 1-lb. pkg. 1400

   beef (*Wilson Corn King*), 1-lb. pkg. 1358

   chicken, *see "chicken franks," above*

   cocktail, *see "Appetizers & Hors d'Oeuvres," pages 126 and 128*

   meat (*Hormel—12-oz. pkg.*), 1 link* 106

   meat (*Hormel—1-lb. pkg.*), 1 link* 142

   meat (*Wilson Certified*), 1-lb. pkg. 1398

   meat (*Wilson Corn King*), 1-lb. pkg. 1398

   smoked, *see "smoked links and sausages," below*

   turkey, *see "turkey franks," below*

gourmet loaf (*Eckrich—8-oz. pkg.*), 1-oz. slice 40

gourmet loaf (*Eckrich Smorgas Pac*), 1 slice* 30

ham:

   (*Oscar Mayer* Thin Sliced), 3-oz. bag 113

   chopped (*Oscar Mayer*), 1-oz. slice 65

   chopped, canned (*Armour Star*), 12-oz. can 1004

   chopped, canned (*Hormel*), 12-oz. can 917

   cooked (*Danola*), 1 oz. 56

   cooked (*Eckrich*), 1 slice* 40

   cooked (*Hormel*), .8-oz. slice 28

   cooked (*Oscar Mayer*), ¾-oz. slice 30

   cured, whole or steaks, *see "Meat & Poultry Entrees, Canned or Refrigerated," page 138*

   minced (*Oscar Mayer*), .8-oz. slice 56

   sausage roll (*Oscar Mayer*), .8-oz. slice 36

   smoked (*A & P*), 1 oz. 50

   smoked (*Eckrich*), 1 slice* 40

ham and cheese loaf (*Hormel*), 1-oz. slice 77

ham and cheese loaf (*Oscar Mayer*), 1-oz. slice 70

head cheese (*Oscar Mayer*), 1-oz. slice 52

honey loaf (*Eckrich*), 1 slice* 45

honey loaf (*Oscar Mayer*), 1-oz. slice 35

honey roll sausage (*Oscar Mayer*), .8-oz. slice 40

Frankfurters, Luncheon Meats & Sausages, continued

kielbasa:

(*Eckrich* Polska), 1 oz. 100

(*Eckrich* Polska Skinless), 2-oz. link 190

(*Hormel* Kolbase), 1 oz. 81

(*Kahn's* Polska), 1 oz. 92

(*Vienna*), 3½ oz. 290

knockwurst (*Oscar Mayer Chubbies*), 2.4-oz. link 214

liver cheese (*Oscar Mayer*), 1.3-oz. slice 115

liver loaf (*Hormel*), 1-oz. slice 80

luncheon meat:

(*Oscar Mayer*), 1-oz. slice 95

(*Spam*), 12-oz. can 1055

(*Treet*), 12-oz. can 1014

(*Wilson Certified*), 12-oz. can 1060

(*Wilson Corn King*), 12-oz. can 1060

w/cheese chunks (*Spam*), 12-oz. can 1044

smoked (*Spam*), 12-oz. can 1051

spiced (*Hormel*), 1-oz. slice 76

luxury loaf (*Oscar Mayer*), 1-oz. slice 38

minced roll sausage (*Oscar Mayer*), 1-oz. slice 68

New England loaf (*Hormel*), 1-oz. slice 55

New England sausage

(*Oscar Mayer New England*), .8-oz. slice 35

old fashioned loaf (*Eckrich*), 1-oz. slice 75

old fashioned loaf (*Oscar Mayer*), 1-oz. slice 65

olive loaf (*Hormel*), 1-oz. slice 75

olive loaf (*Oscar Mayer*), 1-oz. slice 65

pastrami:

(*A & P*), 1 oz. 40

(*Danola* Thin Sliced), 1 oz. 35

(*Eckrich* Slender Sliced), 1 slice* 35

(*Vienna*), 3½ oz. 303

peppered loaf (*Oscar Mayer*), 1 oz. slice 46

pepperoni (*Hormel*), 1 oz. 150

pepperoni (*Swift*), 1 oz. 150

Frankfurters, Luncheon Meats & Sausages, continued

pickle loaf:

    (*Eckrich*), 1-oz. slice 85

    (*Eckrich Smorgas Pac*), 1 slice* 85

    (*Hormel*), 1-oz. slice 71

    beef (*Eckrich Smorgas Pac*), 1 slice* 65

pickle and pimento loaf (*Oscar Mayer*), 1-oz. slice 65

picnic loaf (*Oscar Mayer*), 1-oz. slice 62

Polish sausage, *see "kielbasa," above*

pork loin, smoked (*Eckrich* Slender Smoked), 1 slice* 47

pork sausage:

    (*Hormel* Brown 'n Serve), 1 sausage* 78

    (*Hormel Little Sizzlers*), 1 sausage*, cooked 67

    (*Oscar Mayer Little Friers*), 1 sausage*, cooked 60

    (*Swift Premium* Brown 'N Serve), 1 sausage*, cooked ...75

    (*Swift Bacon 'N Sausage*), 1 sausage*, cooked 70

    (*Swift Kountry Kured*), 1 sausage*, cooked 85

    (*Wilson Certified*), 1-lb. pkg. 2100

    (*Wilson Corn King*), 1-lb. pkg. 2100

    (*Wilson* Western Style), 1 patty* 140

    roll (*Oscar Mayer*), 1 oz.*, cooked 109

    smoked, roll, (*Hormel*), 1 oz. 98

salami:

    Beef (*Vienna*), 3½ oz. 278

    beer (*Oscar Mayer*), .8-oz. slice 50

    cotto (*Hormel*), 1-oz. slice 66

    cotto (*Oscar Mayer*), .8-oz. slice 55

    cotto, beef (*Oscar Mayer*), .8-oz. slice 50

    hard (*Hormel*), 1 oz. or about 5 slices 117

    hard (*Oscar Mayer*), 1 oz. or about 3 slices 105

    hard (*Swift*), 1 oz. 110

    Genoa (*Hormel*), 1 oz. or about 5 slices 126

    Genoa (*Swift*), 1 oz. 120

    party (*Hormel*), 1 oz. or about 4 slices 94

sausage, beef (*Swift Premium*), 1 sausage*, cooked 85

sausage, beef, Polish (*Vienna*), 3½ oz. 280

Frankfurters, Luncheon Meats & Sausages, continued

smoked links & sausages:

    (*Eckrich* Skinless Links—12-oz. pkg.), 1 link* 115

    (*Eckrich* Skinless Links—1-lb. pkg.), 1 link* 190

    (*Eckrich Smok-Y-Links*), 1 link* 85

    (*Eckrich* Smoked Sausage), 1 oz. 105

    (*Hormel Range Brand Wranglers*), 1 link* 175

    (*Hormel* Smokies), 1 link* 93

    (*Kahn's Big Red Smoky*), 1 link* 175

    (*Kahn's* Smoked Sausage), 1 oz. 91

    (*Oscar Mayer* Little Smokies), ⅓-oz. link 32

    (*Oscar Mayer* Smoked Breakfast Sausages), .7-oz. link ...68

    (*Oscar Mayer* Smokie Links), 1½-oz. link 135

    (*Vienna*), 3½ oz. 276

    (*Wilson Certified*), 1-lb. pkg. 1525

    (*Wilson Corn King*), 1-lb. pkg. 1525

    beef (*Eckrich Smok-Y-Links*), 1 link* 75

    beef (*Eckrich* Smoked Sausage), 1 oz. 95

    beef (*Hormel Wranglers*), 1 link* 156

    cheese (*Oscar Mayer* Cheese Smokies), 1½-oz. link 136

summer sausage:

    (*Hormel* Buffet Thuringer), 1 oz. or about 4 slices 95

    (*Hormel Old Smokehouse* Thuringer),

      1 oz. or about 4 slices 99

    (*Hormel* Summer Sausage), 1-oz. slice* 90

    (*Oscar Mayer* Summer Sausage), .8-oz. slice 75

    (*Swift*), 1 oz. 90

    beef (*Oscar Mayer* Summer Sausage), .8-oz. slice 68

thuringer, *see "summer sausage," above*

turkey:

    (*Danola* Thin Sliced), 1 oz. 50

    breast (*Hormel*), .8-oz. slice 24

    breast (*Longacre*), 1 slice* 25

    breast (*Norbest* Oven Roasted), 1 slice* 30

    breast (*Oscar Mayer*), .8-oz. slice 23

    breast, smoked (*Norbest* Hickory Smoked), 1-oz. slice ...30

    smoked (*A & P*), 1 oz. 50

turkey, continued

turkey bologna (*Norbest*), 1-oz. slice 65

turkey franks (*Longacre*), 1 link* 128

turkey ham:

    (*Longacre*—chub), 1 oz. 37

    (*Longacre*—sliced), 1 slice* 20

    (*Norbest*), 1-oz. slice 40

turkey pastrami (*Norbest*), 1-oz. slice 40

turkey salami (*Norbest*), 1-oz. slice 40

Vienna sausage, *see "Appetizers & Hors d'Oeuvres, Canned or in Jars," page 127*

* *As packaged*

BACON, one slice* cooked, except as noted

                                     CALORIES

beef (*Vienna*) 36

bits, *see "Condiments & Seasonings," page 194*

breakfast strips (*Sizzlean*) 50

Canadian:

    (*Festival*) 32

    (*Hormel*), 1 oz. or about 1½ slices 50

    (*Oscar Mayer*), 1 oz. 40

cured:

    (*Hormel Black Label*) 33

    (*Hormel Range Brand*) 46

    (*Hormel Red Label*) 38

    (*Lazy Maple*) 40

    (*Oscar Mayer*) 35

    (*Swift Premium*) 40

    (*Wilson Certified*) 40

    (*Wilson Corn King*) 40

    thick-sliced (*Oscar Mayer*) 64

    thin-sliced (*Oscar Mayer*) 29

* *As packaged*

MEAT, FISH & POULTRY SPREADS,
one tablespoon, except as noted

CALORIES

anchovy paste (*Crosse & Blackwell*) 20
braunschweiger (*Oscar Mayer*), ½ oz.* 50
chicken salad (*Longacre*), ½ oz.* 32
chicken salad (*The Spreadables*), ½ oz.* 31
chicken spread:
   (*Chicken Ready*), ½ oz.* 36
   (*Swanson*), ½ oz.* 35
   (*Underwood*) 31
chili con carne (*Gebhardt* Chili Meat) 37
corned-beef spread (*Underwood*) 27
ham, deviled:
   (*Armour Star*) 48
   (*Hormel*) 33
   (*Libby's*), ½ oz.* 42
   (*Underwood*) 47
ham and cheese spread (*Oscar Mayer*), ½ oz.* 36
ham salad (*Oscar Mayer*), ½ oz.* 30
ham salad (*The Spreadables*), ½ oz.* 26
liver sausage, see "braunschweiger," above
liverwurst spread (*Underwood*) 45
luncheon meat, deviled (Deviled *Spam*) 36
luncheon meat, deviled (Deviled *Treet*) 44
meat, potted:
   (*Armour Star*) 35
   (*Hormel*) 29
   (*Libby's*), ½ oz.* 29
paté, see "Appetizers, Hors d'Oeuvres & Snacks,
   Canned or in Jars," page 126
sandwich spread (*Oscar Mayer*), ½ oz.* 30
tuna salad (*Longacre*), ½ oz.* 24
tuna salad (*The Spreadables*), ½ oz.* 27
turkey salad (*The Spreadables*), ½ oz.* 29

* Approximately 1 tablespoon

MEAT, FISH & POULTRY, FREEZE-DRIED,
one serving*

	CALORIES
bacon bar** (*Mountain House*), 1.5 oz.	280

beef:
- almondine (*Mountain House*), 1.65 oz. 230
- chop suey (*Mountain House*), 1.7 oz. 220
- diced, cooked (*Mountain House*), 1 oz. 150
- patties, raw (*Mountain House*), .85 oz. 160
- w/rice and onions (*Mountain House*), 2.4 oz. 330
- steaks (*Mountain House*), 1.5 oz. 250
- stew (*Mountain House*), 1.87 oz. 260
- stroganoff (*Mountain House*), 1.8 oz. 270

chicken:
- à la king (*Mountain House*), .85 oz. —#10 can 100
- chop suey (*Mountain House*), 1.7 oz. 220
- diced, cooked (*Mountain House*), 1.2 oz. 180
- pilaf (*Mountain House*), 2.37 oz. 330
- and rice (*Mountain House*), 1.85 oz. 240
- salad (*Mountain House*), .68 oz. 90
- stew (*Mountain House*), 1.8 oz. 230

fish steaks (*Mountain House*), .75 oz. —#10 can 100
ham (*Mountain House*), 1.26 oz. —#10 can 250
noodles and chicken, *see "Dinner & Side Dish Mixes," page 178*
pork chops (*Mountain House*), 1.2 oz. 180
rice and chicken (*Mountain House*), 2.4 oz. 400
sausage patties (*Mountain House*), 1.37 oz. 240

shrimp:
- (*Mountain House*), .8 oz. —#10 can 100
- cocktail (*Mountain House*), .87 oz. 100
- creole (*Mountain House*), 1.9 oz. 250

tuna:
- à la neptune (*Mountain House*), 1.8 oz. 240

tuna, continued

 cooked (*Mountain House*), .9 oz. —#10 can 170
 salad (*Mountain House*), .68 oz. 110
turkey, cooked (*Mountain House*), 1.4 oz. —#10 can 210
turkey tetrazzini (*Mountain House*), 1.6 oz. 200

 * *Dry weight, based on ½ of two-serving foil pouch (or one serving from #10 can if indicated)*
** *Compressed—not freeze-dried*

FISH & SHELLFISH, CANNED OR IN JARS
See also "Fish & Shellfish, Frozen," "Fish, Smoked" and "Frozen Dinners"

                 CALORIES

caviar, *see "Appetizers, Hors d'Oeuvres & Snacks, Canned or in Jars," page 126*
clam cocktail, *see "Appetizers, Hors d'Oeuvres & Snacks, Canned or in Jars," page 126*
clams:
 whole, meat only (*Doxsee*), 1 cup 194
 whole, half meat/half liquid (*Doxsee*), 1 cup 116
 chopped or minced, meat only (*Doxsee*), 1 cup 196
 chopped or minced, half meat/half liquid
  (*Doxsee*), 1 cup 118
 chopped or minced, w/liquid (*Snow's*), 1 cup 120
crab cocktail, *see "Appetizers, Hors d'Oeuvres & Snacks, Canned or in Jars," page 126*
fish balls, *see "Appetizers, Hors d'Oeuvres & Snacks, Canned or in Jars," page 126*
gefilte fish, 1 piece*
 (*Manischewitz*—4 piece/12-oz. jar) 53
 (*Manischewitz*—8 piece/24-oz. jar) 53
 (*Manischewitz*—24 piece/4-lb. jar) 48
 (*Manischewitz* Homestyle—4 piece/12-oz. jar) 55

gefilte fish, continued

(*Manischewitz* Homestyle—8 piece/24-oz. jar) 55
(*Manischewitz* Homestyle—24 piece/4-lb. jar) 50
(*Mother's*—4 piece/12-oz. jar) 41
(*Mother's*—6 piece/15-oz. jar) 34
(*Mother's*—4 piece/1-lb. jar) 55
(*Mother's*—6 piece/1-lb. jar) 37
(*Mother's*—6 piece/24-oz. jar) 55
(*Mother's*—8 piece/24-oz. jar) 41
(*Mother's*—5 piece/27-oz. jar) 74
(*Mother's*—8 piece/2-lb. jar) 55
(*Mother's*—12 piece/2-lb. jar) 37
sweet (*Manischewitz*—4 piece/12-oz. jar) 65
sweet (*Manischewitz*—8 piece/24-oz. jar) 65
sweet (*Manischewitz*—24 piece/2-lb. jar) 59
sweet, whitefish and pike
    (*Manischewitz*—4 piece/12-oz. jar) 64
sweet, whitefish and pike
    (*Manischewitz*—8 piece/24-oz. jar) 64
sweet, whitefish and pike
    (*Manischewitz*—24 piece/2-lb. jar) 58
whitefish and pike (*Manischewitz*—4 piece/12-oz. jar) ...49
whitefish and pike (*Manischewitz*—8 piece/24-oz. jar) ...49
whitefish and pike (*Manischewitz*—24 piece/2-lb. jar) ...44
miniature, *see "Appetizers, Hors d'Oeuvres & Snacks,*
    Canned or in Jars," page 126
herring, kippered (*King Oscar*), 8-oz. can 480
herring, kippered, snacks, *see "Appetizers, Hors d'Oeuvres &*
    Snacks, Canned or in Jars," page 126
herring, pickled:
Bismarck (*Vita*), 5-oz. jar 210
cocktail (*Vita*), 8-oz. jar 350
lunch (*Vita*), 8-oz. jar 326
party snacks (*Vita*), 8-oz. jar 361
roll mops (*Vita*), 8-oz. jar 242
schmaltz, old fashioned (*Vita*), 16-oz. jar 630

herring, pickled, continued

in sour cream (*Danola*), 2 oz. 140

in sour cream (*Vita*), 8-oz. jar 415

tastee bits (*Vita*), 8-oz. jar 340

in wine sauce (*Danola*), 2 oz. 90

herring salad, pickled (*Vita*), 7½-oz. jar 493

oysters (*High Sea*), 4 oz. 100

oysters, whole (*Bumble Bee*), 1 cup 160

salmon:

blueback (*Icy Point*), 3¾-oz. can 181

blueback (*Icy Point*), 7¾-oz. can 376

coho steak (*Icy Point*), 3¾-oz. can 162

pink (*Del Monte*), 7¾-oz. can 310

pink (*Icy Point*), 7¾-oz. can 310

pink (*Pink Beauty*), 7¾-oz. can 310

red (*Icy Point*), 15½-oz. can 775

red sockeye (*Del Monte*), 7¾-oz. can 340

red sockeye (*Pillar Rock*), 3¾-oz. can 181

red sockeye (*Pillar Rock*), 7¾-oz. can 376

red sockeye (*Pillar Rock*), 15½-oz. can 775

low-sodium (*S & W Nutradiet*), 1 cup 176

sardines:

in mustard sauce (*Underwood*), 3¾-oz. can 197

in oil (*Crown*), 3¾-oz. can, drained 192

in oil (*King Oscar*), 3¾-oz. can, drained 205

in oil (*Underwood*), 3¾-oz. can, drained 233

in tomato sauce (*Del Monte*), 7½-oz. can 330

in tomato sauce (*Underwood*), 3¾-oz. can 169

shrimp (*Blue Gulf/High Sea/Louisiana*), 4 oz. 116

shrimp cocktail, *see "Appetizers, Hors d'Oeuvres & Snacks, Canned or in Jars," page 127*

tuna:

chunk light, in oil (*Bumble Bee*), 1 cup 460

chunk light, in oil (*Chicken of the Sea*), 6½-oz. can 480

chunk light, in oil (*Del Monte*), 6½-oz. can 450

chunk light, in oil (*Icy Point*), 5 oz., drained 278

tuna, continued

chunk light, in oil (*Pillar Rock*), 5 oz., drained 278
chunk light, in oil (*Snow Mist*), 5 oz., drained 278
chunk light, in water (*Chicken of the Sea*), 6½-oz. can..200
chunk light, in water (*Bumble Bee*), 1 cup 220
chunk white, in oil (*Chicken of the Sea*), 6½-oz. can ...500
chunk white, in water, low-sodium
    (*Chicken of the Sea*), 6½-oz. can 220
solid light, in oil (*Chicken of the Sea*), 6½-oz. can 460
solid white, in oil (*Bumble Bee*), 1 cup 500
solid white, in oil (*Chicken of the Sea*), 6½-oz. can 490
solid white, in oil (*Icy Point*), 5¼ oz., drained 290
solid white, in oil (*Pillar Rock*), 5¼ oz., drained 290
solid white, in water (*Bumble Bee*), 1 cup 240
solid white, in water (*Chicken of the Sea*), 6½-oz. can..240

* *As packaged*

FISH & SHELLFISH, FROZEN
See also "Fish & Shellfish, Canned or in Jars,"
"Fish & Shellfish, Smoked" and "Frozen Dinners"

CALORIES

catfish:
    (*Taste O' Sea* Calorie Watchers), 1 portion* 70
    breaded (*Taste O' Sea*), 1 portion* 90
    fillets (*Taste O' Sea*), 16-oz. pkg. 400
clam crepes (*Mrs. Paul's*), 5½-oz. crepe 280
clams:
    cake thins (*Mrs. Paul's*), 5 oz. or 2 cakes 310
    cakes, deviled (*Mrs. Paul's*), 3-oz. cake 180
    fried (*Howard Johnson's*), 5-oz. pkg. 395
    fried (*Mrs. Paul's*), 5-oz. pkg. 540
    fried (*Mrs. Paul's*), 8-oz. pkg. 880
    fritters, batter-fried (*Mrs. Paul's*), 7¾ oz. pkg. 520

clams, continued

sticks, fried
   (*Mrs. Paul's*—8-oz. pkg.), 4 oz. or 5 sticks 240
sticks, fried
   (*Mrs. Paul's*—12-oz. pkg.), 3 oz. or 4 sticks 200
cod:
   (*Taste O' Sea* Calorie Watchers), 1 portion* 60
   breaded (*Taste O' Sea*), 1 porton* 80
   fillets (*Gorton*), 4 oz. 90
   fillets (*Taste O' Sea*), 16-oz. pkg. 320
   sticks, fried (*Taste O' Sea*), 4 sticks* 230
   w/butter sauce (*Gorton*), 6-oz. pkg. 170
   w/cheese sauce (*Gorton*), 6-oz. pkg. 180
crab:
   cake thins (*Mrs. Paul's*), 5 oz. or 2 cakes 320
   cakes, deviled (*Mrs. Paul's*), 3-oz. cake 160
   deviled, miniatures (*Mrs. Paul's*), 7-oz. pkg. 440
crab crepes (*Mrs. Paul's*), 5½-oz. crepe 240
fish:
   portions, batter-fried (*Gorton*), 3 oz. 240
   portions, beer batter-fried (*Booth*), 3 oz. 250
   portions, buttermilk French-fried (*Booth*), 3 oz. 218
   portions, fried (*Booth*), 3 oz. 171
   portions, w/shrimp stuffing (*Gorton*), 3 oz. or 1 portion..250
   ocean snacks, batter-fried (*Gorton*), 3 oz. 270
fish and chips:
   (*Swanson TV Brand*), 5-oz. pkg. 290
   batter-fried (*Mrs. Paul's*), 7-oz. 370
   batter-fried (*Van de Kamp's*), 8 oz. 500
fish au gratin:
   (*Mrs. Paul's*), 10-oz. pkg. 500
   (*Mrs. Paul's*), 16-oz. pkg. 800
   (*Mrs. Paul's*), 32-oz. pkg. 1600
fish cakes:
   (*A & P*), 4 oz. 250
   (*Gorton*), 4 oz. or 2 cakes 250
   (*Mrs. Paul's*), 4 oz. or 2 cakes 210

fish cakes, continued

(*Mrs. Paul's Beach Haven*), 4 oz. or 2 cakes 220
thins (*Mrs. Paul's*), 4 oz. or 2 cakes 320

fish fillets:

batter-fried (*Mrs. Paul's*), 4½ oz. or 2 fillets 280
batter-fried (*Mrs. Paul's* Supreme), 3⅝-oz. fillet 220
batter-fried (*Van de Kamp's*), 3-oz. fillet 220
batter-fried, miniatures (*Mrs. Paul's*), 9-oz. pkg. 450
buttered (*Mrs. Paul's*), 5 oz. or 2 fillets 310
country seasoned (*Van de Kamp's*),
    4¾ oz. or 2 fillets 360
fried (*Gorton*), 3.6 oz. or 2 fillets 220
fried (*Mrs. Paul's*), 4 oz. or 2 fillets 220

fish kabobs:

batter-fried (*Mrs. Paul's* Supreme), ⅓ of 10-oz. pkg. ...200
batter-fried (*Van de Kamp's*), 4 oz. or 10 pieces 260
country seasoned (*Van de Kamp's*), 4 oz. or 10 pieces ..290

fish parmesan (*Mrs. Paul's*), 10-oz. pkg. 440
fish parmesan (*Mrs. Paul's*), 16-oz. pkg. 720

fish sticks:

(*A & P*), 4 oz. 240
(*Booth*), 4 oz. or 4 sticks 216
(*Gorton*), 3.2 oz. or 4 sticks 180
(*Mrs. Paul's*), 3 oz. or 4 sticks 150
(*Van de Kamp's*), 5 oz. or 5 sticks 310
batter-fried (*A & P*), 4.4 oz. 250
batter-fried (*Booth*), 3.6 oz. or 2 sticks 305
batter-fried (*Gorton*), 2 oz. 160
batter-fried (*Gorton*), 3 oz. 230
batter-fried (*Mrs. Paul's*), 3½ oz. or 4 sticks 230
fried (*Taste O' Sea*), 4 sticks* 254
w/shrimp stuffing (*Gorton*), 3 oz. 240

fishburgers (*Booth*), 3 oz. 137

flounder:

(*A & P*), 3 oz. 110
(*Taste O' Sea* Calorie Watchers), 1 portion* 60

flounder, continued

breaded (*Taste O' Sea*), 1 portion* 90

fillets (*Taste O' Sea*), 16-oz. pkg. 360

fillets, fried (*Mrs. Paul's*), 4 oz. or 2 fillets 220

w/lemon butter (*Mrs. Paul's*), 9-oz. pkg. 300

flounder almandine (*Gorton*), ½ pkg. 210

haddock:

(*A & P*), 3 oz. 100

(*Taste O' Sea* Calorie Watchers), 1 portion* 70

batter-fried (*Van de Kamp's*), 4¾ oz. or 2 pieces 330

breaded (*Taste O' Sea*), 1 portion* 80

fillets (*Taste O' Sea*), 16-oz. pkg. 400

fillets, fried (*Mrs. Paul's*), 4 oz. or 2 fillets 230

sticks, fried (*Taste O' Sea*), 4 sticks* 230

in lemon butter (*Gorton*), ½ pkg. 180

haddock au gratin (*Howard Johnson's*), 10-oz. pkg. 318

halibut, batter-fried (*Van de Kamp's*), 4 oz. or 3 pieces ...270

ocean perch, *see "perch," below*

perch:

(*Taste O' Sea* Calorie Watchers), 1 portion* 100

batter-fried (*Van de Kamp's*), 4¾ oz. or 2 pieces 290

breaded (*Taste O' Sea*), 1 portion* 100

ocean (*A & P*), 3 oz. 130

ocean, fillets (*Taste O' Sea*), 16-oz. pkg. 400

ocean, fillets, fried (*Mrs. Paul's*), 4 oz. or 2 fillets 250

pollock fillets (*Taste O' Sea*), 16-oz. pkg. 360

scallop crepes (*Mrs. Paul's*), 5½-oz. crepe 220

scallops:

batter-fried (*Mrs. Paul's*), 7-oz. pkg. 400

country seasoned (*Van de Kamp's*), 3½ oz. 270

fried (*Mrs. Paul's*), 7-oz. pkg. 420

fried (*Mrs. Paul's*), 12-oz. pkg. 720

w/butter and cheese (*Mrs. Paul's*), 7-oz. pkg. 260

scallops and shrimp Mariner, w/rice

(*Stouffer's*), 10¼-oz. pkg. 400

scrod, baked, stuffed (*Gorton*), 9½-oz. pkg. 420

seafood croquettes (*Mrs. Paul's*), 3-oz. cake 180
seafood platter, combination (*Mrs. Paul's*), 9-oz. pkg. 510
shrimp:
   batter-fried (*Booth*), 3 oz. or 5–6 shrimp 193
   batter-fried (*Booth*—Heat 'n Serve),
     3 oz. or 5–7 shrimp 265
   breaded (*Booth*—Heat 'n Serve), 4 oz. or 7–9 shrimp ..296
   breaded (*Booth*—Ready to Fry), 4 oz. or 7–9 shrimp ...160
   breaded (*Gorton 1836*), 4 oz. 190
   cakes (*Mrs. Paul's*), 3-oz. cake 150
   crispy (*A & P*), 3 oz. 230
   croquettes, w/Newburg sauce
     (*Howard Johnson's*), 12-oz. pkg. 478
   fried (*Mrs. Paul's*), 6-oz. pkg. 340
   fritters, batter-fried (*Mrs. Paul's*), 7¾-oz. pkg. 480
   sticks (*Gorton*), 5 sticks* 200
   sticks, batter-fried (*Booth*), 3¼ oz. or 4 sticks 210
   sticks, fried (*Mrs. Paul's*), 3.2 oz. or 4 sticks 190
   sticks, fried
     (*Mrs. Paul's*—Family Size), 3 oz. or 4 sticks 190
shrimp crepes (*Mrs. Paul's*), 5½-oz. crepe 250
shrimp Marinara (*Buitoni*), 17-oz. pkg. 486
shrimp scampi (*Gorton*), ½ pkg. 200
sole:
   (*Taste O' Sea* Calorie Watchers), 1 portion* 70
   batter fried (*Van de Kamp's*), 4¾ oz. or 2 pieces 280
   fillets (*Taste O' Sea*), 16-oz. pkg. 360
   w/lemon butter (*Gorton*), ½ pkg. 200
   w/lemon butter (*Mrs. Paul's*), 9-oz. pkg. 320
tuna:
   creamed, w/peas
     (*Green Giant Toast Toppers*), 5-oz. pkg. 140
   fritters, batter-fried (*Mrs. Paul's*), 7¾-oz. pkg. 540
   pot pie, *see "Frozen Pot Pies," page 136*
tuna noodle casserole (*Stouffer's*), 11½-oz. pkg. 400

Fish & Shellfish, Frozen, continued

turbot fillets (*Taste O' Sea*), 16-oz. pkg. 400
whiting fillets (*Taste O' Sea*), 16-oz. pkg. 320
whiting, breaded (*Taste O' Sea*), 1 portion* 90

* *As packaged*

FISH, SMOKED, two ounces
See also "Fish & Shellfish, Canned or in Jars"

	CALORIES
chubs, flesh only (*Vita*) 108
eel, flesh only (*Vita*) 186
lake herring (*Vita*) 88
lake trout, flesh only (*Vita*) 178
lox, Nova (*Vita*) 122
lox, regular (*Vita*) 112
sable, flesh only (*Vita*) 74
salmon, flesh only (*Vita*) 100
whiting, flesh only (*Vita*) 96

CHAPTER 13

MEXICAN AND ORIENTAL FOODS

MEXICAN & MEXICAN-STYLE FOODS
See also "Frozen Dinners"

CALORIES

beans, Mexican, *see "Vegetables, Canned or in Jars," page 88*
burrito, beef, frozen (*Hormel*), 1 burrito* 220
chili con carne, without beans:
    canned (*Armour Star*), 7¾ oz. 424
    canned (*Austex*), 1 cup 390
    canned (*Gebhardt*), 8 oz. 427
    canned (*Gebhardt* Chunky Beef), 8 oz. 492
    canned (*Gebhardt* Longhorn), 8 oz. 452
    canned (*Hormel*), 7½ oz. 344
    canned (*Hormel* Short Order), 7½-oz. can 368
    canned (*Libby's*), 1 cup 379
    canned (*Morton House*), 7½ oz. 340
    canned (*Old El Paso*), 8 oz. 402
    canned (*Stokely-Van Camp*), 1 cup 430
chili con carne, with beans:
    canned (*A & P*), 8 oz. 440
    canned (*Armour Star*), 7¾ oz. 347
    canned (*Austex*), 1 cup 353
    canned (*Gebhardt*), 8 oz. 493
    canned (*Gebhardt* Instant), 8 oz. 493
    canned (*Gebhardt* Longhorn), 8 oz. 452
    canned (*Heinz*), 1 cup ..:.........................340

chili con carne, with beans, continued

    canned (*Hormel*), 7½ oz. 321

    canned (*Hormel* Short Order), 7½-oz. can 300

    canned (*Libby's*), 1 cup 276

    canned (*Morton House*), 7½ oz. 340

    canned (*Old El Paso*), 1 cup 420

    canned (*Stokely-Van Camp*), 1 cup 390

    canned (*Stokely-Van Camp Chilee Weenee*), 1 cup 330

    canned (*Swanson*), 7¾ oz. 310

    dietetic, canned (*Dia-Mel*), 8-oz. can 360

    dietetic, canned (*Featherweight*), 8-oz. can 300

    hot, canned (*Hormel* Short Order), 7½-oz. can 300

    frozen (*Stouffer's*), 8¾-oz. pkg. 270

chili mac, canned (*Hormel* Short Order), 7½-oz. can 201

chili peppers, *see "Vegetables, Canned or in Jars," page 91*

chili sauce, *see "Condiments & Seasonings," page 195 or*
    "Sauces," page 190

enchilada sauce, *see "Sauces," page 190*

enchiladas, beef:

    canned (*Old El Paso*), 2.4-oz. enchilada 119

    w/chili gravy, frozen

        (*Banquet Buffet Suppers*), 32-oz. pkg. 1369

    w/sauce, frozen (*Banquet Cookin' Bags*), 7-oz. pkg. 273

taco sauce, *see "Condiments & Seasonings," page 197*

taco shell (*Ortega*), 1 shell* 50

tamales:

    canned (*Austex*), 2-oz. tamale 112

    canned (*Gebhardt*), 2-oz. tamale 134

    canned (*Hormel*—5-oz. can) 1 tamale* 72

    canned (*Hormel* Short Order), 7½-oz. can 271

    canned (*Old El Paso*), 2-oz. tamale 117

    in jars (*Armour Star*), 1 tamale* 92

    beef, w/sauce, in jars (*Derby*), 2.2-oz. tamale 92

tortillas, canned (*Old El Paso*), 5" diam. tortilla 40

* *As packaged*

ORIENTAL & ORIENTAL-STYLE FOODS
See also "Frozen Dinners"

CALORIES

bamboo shoots, *see "Vegetables, Canned or in Jars," page 85*
bean sprouts, *see "Vegetables, Canned or in Jars," page 86*
brown gravy sauce, *see "Condiments & Seasonings," page 195*
chop suey:
    frozen (*Banquet Cookin' Bag*), 7-oz. pkg. 93
    beef w/rice, frozen (*Stouffer's*), 12-oz. pkg. 355
    beef, freeze-dried (*Mountain House*), 1.7 oz. dry 220
    vegetables, canned (*La Choy*), 1 cup 53
chow mein, canned:
    beef (*Chun King*—Divider-Pak), ¼ of pkg.* 120
    beef (*La Choy*—1-lb. can), 1 cup 72
    beef (*La Choy*—Bi-Pack), 1 cup* 83
    chicken (*Chun King*—Divider-Pak), ¼ of pkg.* 100
    chicken (*La Choy*—1-lb. can), 1 cup 68
    chicken (*La Choy*—50-oz. can), 1 cup 93
    chicken (*La Choy*—Bi-Pack), 1 cup* 101
    meatless (*La Choy*—1-lb. can), 1 cup 47
    meatless (*La Choy*—50-oz. can) 46
    mushroom (*La Choy*—Bi-Pack), 1 cup* 85
    pork (*Chun King*—Divider-Pak), ¼ of pkg.* 130
    pork (*La Choy*—Bi-Pack), 1 cup* 120
    shrimp (*Chun King*—Divider-Pak), ¼ of pkg. 100
    shrimp (*La Choy*—1-lb. can), 1 cup 61
    shrimp (*La Choy*—Bi-Pack), 1 cup* 110
chow mein, frozen:
    (*Banquet Cookin' Bag*), 7-oz. pkg. 89
    beef (*La Choy*), 16-oz. pkg. 194
    chicken (*Chun King* Pouched Entree), 1 pkg. 260
    chicken (*Green Giant Entree*), 9-oz. pkg. 130
    chicken (*La Choy*), 16-oz. pkg. 216
    chicken (*Stouffer's*), 8-oz. pkg. 145
    shrimp (*Chun King* Pouched Entree), 1 pkg. 220
    shrimp (*La Choy*), 16-oz. pkg. 146

Oriental & Oriental-Style Foods, continued

dim sum, *see "Appetizers, Hors d'Oeuvres & Snacks, Frozen,"*
  page 127
egg foo yung (*Chun King* Stir Fry), ⅕ of pkg. 200
egg rolls, *see "Appetizers, Hors d'Oeuvres & Snacks, Frozen,"*
  page 128
noodles:
  chow mein, canned (*Chun King*), ½ cup 106
  chow mein, canned (*La Choy*), 1 oz. or ½ cup 153
  chow mein, wide, canned (*La Choy*), 1 oz. or ½ cup ...149
  rice, canned (*La Choy*), 1 oz. or ½ cup 130
pepper Oriental:
  canned (*Chun King*—Divider-Pak), ¼ of pkg.* 130
  canned (*La Choy*—1-lb. can), 1 cup 89
  canned (*La Choy*—Bi-Pack), 1 cup* 89
  frozen (*La Choy*), 1 cup 110
  frozen, beef (*Chun King* Pouched Entree), ½ of pkg. ..210
pepper steak, frozen:
  w/chuck steak (*Chun King* Stir Fry), ⅕ of pkg.* 240
  w/flank steak (*Chun King* Stir Fry), ⅕ of pkg.* 250
  w/lean ground (*Chun King* Stir Fry), ⅕ of pkg.* 250
  w/round steak (*Chun King* Stir Fry), ⅕ of pkg.* 280
rice, fried, *see "Rice, Flavored," page 180*
soy sauce, *see "Condiments & Seasonings," page 197*
sukiyaki, w/flank steak (*Chun King* Stir Fry), ⅕ of pkg.* ..280
sukiyaki, w/round steak (*Chun King* Stir Fry),
  ⅕ of pkg.* 220
sweet and sour, frozen:
  (*Chun King* Pouched Entree), ½ of pkg. 250
  w/ham (*Chun King* Stir Fry), ⅕ of pkg.* 440
  w/lean pork (*Chun King* Stir Fry), ⅕ of pkg.* 460
  pork (*La Choy*), 1 cup 245
sweet and sour sauce, *see "Sauces," page 191*
teriyaki, beef w/rice and vegetables, frozen
  (*Stouffer's*), 10-oz. pkg. 365
teriyaki sauce, *see "Condiments & Seasonings," page 198*
vegetables, chop suey, canned (*La Choy*), 1 cup 53

Oriental & Oriental-Style Foods, continued

vegetables, *see "Vegetables, Canned or in Jars," page 85, and "Vegetables, Frozen," page 95*

water chestnuts, *see "Vegetables, Canned or in Jars," page 93*

wontons, *see "Appetizers, Hors d'Oeuvres & Snacks, Frozen," page 128*

* *Prepared according to package directions*

CHAPTER 14

PIZZA, PASTA, NOODLES AND RICE

PIZZA, FROZEN, one whole pie or package*
See also "Pizza, Dry Mix"

	CALORIES
Canadian bacon (*Totino's* Party Pizza), 1 pie**	740

cheese:

(*Buitoni*), 14-oz. pie	896
(*Buitoni* Instant Pizza), 12-oz. pkg.	830
(*Celeste*), 7-oz. pie	490
(*Celeste*), 19-oz. pie	1280
(*Celeste* Sicilian Style), 20-oz. pie	1316
(*Jeno's*), 13-oz. pie	840
(*Jeno's* Deluxe), 20-oz. pie	1470
(*La Pizzeria*), 10¾-oz. pie	624
(*La Pizzeria*), 20-oz. pie	1160
(*La Pizzeria* Thick Crust), 18½-oz. pie	1223
(*Totino's* Classic), 1 pie**	1500
(*Totino's* Extra Cheese), 1 pie**	1120
(*Totino's* Party Pizza), 1 pie**	740
(*Weight Watchers*), 6-oz. pie	380
on bagel (*Lender's*), 2-oz. piece	140
on French bread (*Stouffer's*), 10¼-oz. pkg.	660

combination:

(*Celeste* Deluxe), 9-oz. pie	596
(*Celeste* Deluxe), 23½-oz. pie	1468
(*Celeste* Deluxe Sicilian Style), 26-oz. pie	1700
(*Jeno's* Deluxe), 23-oz. pie	1680

combination, continued

   (*La Pizzeria*), 13½-oz. pie 834
   (*La Pizzeria*), 24½-oz. pie 1526
   (*Van de Kamp's*), 23½-oz. pie 1240
   on bagel (*Lender's Works*), 2¾-oz. piece 170
   on French bread (*Stouffer's* Deluxe), 12⅜-oz. pkg. 800
hamburger:
   (*Jeno's*), 13½-oz. pie 880
   (*Totino's* Party Pizza), 1 pie** 880
   on French bread (*Stouffer's*), 12¼-oz. pkg. 800
mushroom, on bagel (*Lender's*), 2⅕-oz. piece 150
onion, on bagel (*Lender's*), 2⅕-oz. piece 140
pepperoni:
   (*Celeste*), 7¼-oz. pie 528
   (*Celeste*), 20-oz. pie 1424
   (*Jeno's*), 13-oz. pie 900
   (*La Pizzeria*), 21-oz. pie 1308
   (*Totino's* Deep Crust), 1 pie** 1800
   (*Totino's* Extra Pepperoni), 1 pie** 1080
   (*Totino's* Party Pizza), 1 pie** 860
   (*Van de Kamp's*), 22-oz. pie 1480
   on French bread (*Stouffer's*), 11¼-oz. pkg. 820
   pepperoni and mushroom (*Totino's* Classic), 1 pie** ..1530
   pizza rolls, *see "Appetizers, Hors d'Oeuvres, & Snacks,
     Frozen," page 128*
sausage:
   (*Celeste*), 8-oz. pie 562
   (*Celeste*), 22-oz. pie 1500
   (*Celeste* Sicilian Style), 24-oz. pie 1596
   (*Jeno's*), 13½-oz. pie 900
   (*Jeno's* Deluxe), 21-oz. pie 1500
   (*La Pizzeria*), 13-oz. pie 860
   (*La Pizzeria*), 23-oz. pie 1507
   (*Totino's* Extra Sausage), 1 pie** 1140
   (*Totino's* Party Pizza), 1 pie** 880
   on French bread (*Stouffer's*), 12-oz. pkg. 840
sausage and cheese (*Weight Watchers*), 7-oz. pie 390

Pizza, Frozen, continued

sausage and mushroom:
   (*Celeste*), 9-oz. pie 570
   (*Celeste*), 24-oz. pie 1516
   (*Totino's* Classic), 1 pie** 1530
   (*Totino's* Deep Crust), 1 pie** 1800
   on French bread (*Stouffer's*), 12½-oz. pkg. 790
sausage and pepperoni:
   (*Totino's* Classic), 1 pie** 1590
   (*Totino's* Deep Crust), 1 pie** 1740
   (*Totino's* Extra Sausage and Pepperoni), 1 pie** 1160

* *Note variation in sizes*
** *As packaged*

PIZZA, DRY MIX, one serving
See also "Pizza, Frozen"

	CALORIES
regular (*Jeno's*), 6¾ oz.	420
cheese (*Jeno's*), 7⅛ oz.	420
pepperoni (*Jeno's*), 8 oz.	530
sausage (*Jeno's*), 7⅛ oz.	510

MACARONI, NOODLES & PASTA, PLAIN, two ounces*
See also "Rice, Plain"

	CALORIES
macaroni:	
(*American Beauty*)	210
(*Ann Page*)	210
(*La Rosa*)	210
noodles, egg:	
(*American Beauty*)	220
(*Ann Page*)	220

noodles, egg, continued
   (*La Rosa*) 220
   (*Pennsylvania Dutch*) 210
pasta**:
   (*American Beauty*) 210
   (*Ann Page*) 210
   (*Buitoni*—High Protein Brand) 210
   (*Buitoni*—Pasta Romana Brand) 210
   (*La Rosa*) 210

  * *Uncooked weight*
 ** *Includes spaghetti, vermicelli, linguine, etc.*

MACARONI ENTREES, CANNED
*See also "Macaroni Entrees, Frozen" and "Dinner &
Side Dish Mixes"*

                                      CALORIES
macaroni and beef, w/tomato sauce
   (*Franco-American* Beefy Mac), 7½ oz. 220
macaroni and cheese:
   (*Franco-American*), 7¼ oz. 180
   (*Hormel* Short Order), 7½-oz. can 169
   w/cheese sauce (*Heinz*), 1 cup 180
macaroni and meatballs, w/tomato sauce
   (*Franco-American* Beefy Mac), 7½ oz. 220

MACARONI ENTREES, FROZEN,
one whole package*
*See also "Macaroni Entrees, Canned" and "Dinner &
Side Dish Mixes"*

                                      CALORIES
macaroni and beef, w/tomato sauce
   (*Green Giant* Entree), 9-oz. pkg. 240
macaroni and beef, w/tomato sauce
   (*Stouffer's*), 11½-oz. pkg. 380

Macaroni Entrees, Frozen, continued

macaroni and cheese:

    (*Banquet Cookin' Bag*), 8-oz. pkg. 291

    (*Banquet Buffet Supper*), 32-oz. pkg. 1155

    (*Green Giant* Entree), 9-oz. pkg. 380

    (*Green Giant* Baked Entree), 8-oz. pkg. 290

    (*Howard Johnson's*), 10-oz. pkg. 542

    (*Howard Johnson's*), 19-oz. pkg. 1029

    (*Stouffer's*), 12-oz. pkg. 520

    casserole (*Banquet*), 8-oz. pkg. 279

    casserole (*Morton*), 8-oz. pkg. 270

    pot pie, *see "Frozen Pot Pies," page 136*

macaroni and eggplant casserole

    (*Ronzoni* Single Serving), 8-oz. pkg. 260

* *Note variation in package sizes*

NOODLE ENTREES, CANNED & FROZEN
See also "Dinner & Side Dish Mixes"

                               CALORIES

(*Stokley-Van Camp Noodle Weenee*), 1 cup 250

noodles and beef:

    canned (*Hormel* Short Order), 7½-oz. can 229

    w/sauce, canned (*Heinz*), 8½-oz. can 171

    w/gravy, frozen (*Banquet Buffet Supper*), 32-oz. pkg. ..754

noodles and chicken, canned

    (*Dinty Moore* Short Order), 7½-oz. can 205

noodles and chicken, in gravy, canned

    (*Heinz*), 8½-oz. can 186

noodles Romanoff, frozen (*Stouffer's*), 12-oz. pkg. 510

PASTA ENTREES, CANNED

See also "Pasta Entrees, Frozen," "Dinner & Side Dish Mixes," "Macaroni Entrees, Canned" and "Noodle Entrees, Canned & Frozen"

CALORIES

lasagna (*Hormel* Short Order), 7½-oz. can 262
ravioli:
  (*Dia-Mel*), 8-oz. can 230
  beef (*Featherweight*), 8-oz. can 230
  beef, in meat sauce (*Franco-American*), 7½ oz. 220
  cheese (*Buitoni*), 15-oz. can 408
  meat (*Buitoni*), 15-oz. can 448
raviolios, beef, in meat sauce (*Franco-American*), 7½ oz. ..220
rotini in tomato sauce (*Franco-American*), 7½ oz. 200
rotini and meatballs in tomato sauce
  (*Franco-American*), 7¼ oz. 230
spaghetti:
  and beef (*Hormel* Short Order), 7½-oz. can 242
  w/franks, in tomato sauce (*Heinz*), 1 cup 280
  in meat sauce (*Franco-American*), 7¾ oz. 220
  in meat sauce (*Heinz*), 8 oz. 170
  w/meatballs (*Buitoni*), 15-oz. can 456
  w/meatballs (*Dia-Mel*), 8-oz. can 200
  w/meatballs (*Featherweight*), 8-oz. can 220
  w/meatballs (*Hormel* Short Order), 7½-oz. can 211
  w/meatballs (*Libby's*), 1 cup 206
  w/meatballs, in tomato sauce
    (*Franco-American*), 7¼ oz. 210
  w/tomato sauce and cheese (*Franco-American*), 7 oz. ..170
  w/tomato sauce and cheese (*Heinz*), 1 cup 160
  rings, w/little meatballs in tomato sauce
    (*Franco-American* SpaghettiOs), 7⅜ oz. 210
  rings, w/sliced franks in tomato sauce
    (*Franco-American* SpaghettiOs), 7⅜ oz. 210

spaghetti, continued

rings, in tomato and cheese sauce
  (*Franco-American* SpaghettiOs), 7⅜ oz. 160
twists, w/meatballs (*Buitoni*), 15-oz. can 456
twists, w/sauce (*Buitoni*), 15-oz. can 320

PASTA ENTREES, FROZEN,
one whole package*, except as noted
*See also "Pasta Entrees, Canned," "Dinner & Side Dish Mixes,"
"Macaroni Entrees, Frozen" and "Noodle Entrees, Canned &
Frozen"*

CALORIES

cannelloni Florentine (*Weight Watchers*), 13-oz. pkg. 450
fettuccine Alfredo (*Ronzoni*), 16-oz. pkg. 760
fettuccine Alfredo (*Ronzoni* Single Serving), 8-oz. pkg. ..430
lasagna:
  (*Stouffer's*), 10½-oz. pkg. 385
  (*Stouffer's*), 21-oz. pkg. 770
  (*Swanson Hungry-Man* Entree), 12¾-oz. pkg. 540
  beef (*Hormel*), 10-oz. pkg. 370
  w/cheese, veal and sauce
    (*Weight Watchers*), 13-oz. pkg. 350
  w/meat sauce (*Buitoni*), 14-oz. pkg. 596
  w/meat and sauce
    (*Green Giant* Baked Entree), 9-oz. pkg. 310
  w/ricotta cheese (*Ronzoni*), 23-oz. pkg. 800
linguine w/clam sauce (*Ronzoni*), 16-oz. pkg. 480
linguine w/clam sauce (*Stouffer's*), 10½-oz. pkg. 285
manicotti:
  jumbo (*Buitoni*), 18-oz. pkg. 887
  w/ricotta cheese (*Ronzoni*), 15-oz. pkg. 720
  in sauce (*Buitoni*), 13-oz. pkg. 570
mostaccioli and meat sauce
  (*Banquet Buffet Suppers*), 32-oz. pkg. 814

Pasta Entrees, Frozen, continued

ravioli:

    cheese (*Buitoni*), 15-oz. pkg. 1192

    cheese, Parmigiana (*Buitoni*), 12-oz. pkg. 452

    cheese, round (*Buitoni*), 11-oz. pkg. 912

    meat (*Buitoni*), 15-oz. pkg. 1280

    meat, Parmigiana (*Buitoni*), 12-oz. pkg. 581

rotelle alla Romana, w/sauce (*Ronzoni*), 15-oz. pkg. 480

shells:

    baked, in sauce (*Buitoni*), 8 oz. 269

    stuffed, w/ricotta cheese (*Ronzoni*), 15-oz. pkg. 750

    stuffed, w/sauce (*Buitoni*), 20-oz. pkg. 683

spaghetti:

    and meat casserole (*Morton*), 8-oz. pkg. 220

    w/meat sauce (*Stouffer's*), 14-oz. pkg. 445

    w/meat sauce, casserole (*Banquet*), 8-oz. pkg. 311

    and meatballs, w/tomato sauce

        (*Banquet Buffet Supper*), 32-oz. pkg. 1084

    and meatballs, w/tomato sauce

        (*Green Giant* Baked Entree), 9-oz. pkg. 280

    in tomato sauce, w/breaded veal

        (*Swanson TV Brand* Entree), 8¼-oz. pkg. 290

ziti:

    baked, in sauce (*Buitoni*), 10½-oz. pkg. 352

    baked, w/ricotta cheese and sauce

        (*Ronzoni*), 18-oz. pkg. 520

    baked, w/ricotta cheese and sauce

        (*Ronzoni* Single Serving), 8-oz. pkg. 250

    w/veal, cheese and sauce

        (*Weight Watchers*), 13-oz. pkg. 350

* *Pay attention to package sizes*

DINNER & SIDE DISH MIXES
See also "Rice, Flavored"

CALORIES

à la king* (*Lipton Lite-Lunch*), 7 fl. oz. 190
beef:
  noodle, dry (*Hamburger Helper*), ⅕ pkg. 140
  noodle, w/meat* (*Hamburger Helper*), ⅕ pkg. 320
  Romanoff, dry (*Hamburger Helper*), ⅕ pkg. 160
  Romanoff, w/meat* (*Hamburger Helper*), ⅕ pkg. 304
beef flavor* (*Lipton Lite-Lunch*), 7 fl. oz. 140
cheeseburger macaroni, dry (*Hamburger Helper*), ⅕ pkg. ...180
cheeseburger macaroni, w/meat*
  (*Hamburger Helper*), ⅕ pkg. 360
chicken flavor* (*Lipton Lite-Lunch*), 7 fl. oz. 140
chicken flavor noodles and šauce
  (*Mug•O•Lunch*), 1 pouch 150
chili tomato, dry (*Hamburger Helper*), ⅕ pkg. 140
chili tomato, w/meat* (*Hamburger Helper*), ⅕ pkg. 320
dumpling noodles, *see "noodles," below*
hamburger:
  hash, dry (*Hamburger Helper*), ⅕ pkg. 130
  hash, w/meat* (*Hamburger Helper*), ⅕ pkg. 300
  pizza dish, dry (*Hamburger Helper*), ⅕ pkg. 160
  pizza dish, w/meat* (*Hamburger Helper*), ⅕ pkg. 340
  stew, dry (*Hamburger Helper*), ⅕ pkg. 110
  stew, w/meat* (*Hamburger Helper*), ⅕ pkg. 290
lasagna, dry (*Hamburger Helper*), ⅕ pkg. 150
lasagna, w/meat* (*Hamburger Helper*), ⅕ pkg. 330
macaroni:
  and cheddar* (*Mac-A-Roni*), ¾ cup 141
  and cheese* (*Betty Crocker*), ¼ pkg. 310
  and cheese* (*Golden Grain* Stir & Serve), ½ cup 183
  and cheese* (*Kraft* Dinner), ¾ cup 300
  and cheese* (*Kraft* Deluxe Dinner), ¾ cup 250
  and cheese* (*Mug•O•Lunch*), 1 pouch 230

macaroni, continued

and cheese* (*Pennsylvania Dutch*), ½ cup 160
and cheese, freeze-dried (*Mountain House*), 1.05 oz. 200
w/cheese and meat, *see "cheeseburger macaroni," above*

noodles:

beef flavor (*Oodles of Noodles*), 3-oz. pkg. 390
and beef flavor sauce* (*Mug•O•Lunch*), 1 pouch 170
and beef flavor sauce* (*Pennsylvania Dutch*), ½ cup ..130
and butter sauce* (*Pennsylvania Dutch*), ½ cup 150
and cheese sauce* (*Pennsylvania Dutch*), ½ cup 150
w/cheese sauce and tuna, dry (*Tuna Helper*), ⅕ pkg. ...170
w/cheese sauce and tuna, with tuna*
   (*Tuna Helper*), ⅕ pkg. 230
and chicken, freeze-dried (*Mountain House*), 2-oz. 270
chicken flavor* (*Kraft* Dinner), ¾ cup 240
chicken flavor (*Oodles of Noodles*), 3-oz. pkg. 150
w/chicken flavor sauce* (*Pennsylvania Dutch*), ½ cup ..150
creamy, and tuna, dry (*Tuna Helper*), ⅕ pkg. 220
creamy, and tuna, w/tuna* (*Tuna Helper*), ⅕ pkg. 280
dumpling, and tuna, dry (*Tuna Helper*), ⅕ pkg. 170
dumpling, and tuna, w/tuna* (*Tuna Helper*), ⅕ pkg. ..230
onion flavor (*Oodles of Noodles*), 3-oz. pkg. 390
Oriental, and sauce* (*Mug•O•Lunch*), 1 pouch 190
Oriental flavor (*Oodles of Noodles*), 3-oz. pkg. 390
Oriental, beef flavor (*Ramen Pride*), 3-oz. pkg. 396
Oriental, chicken flavor (*Ramen Pride*), 3-oz. pkg. 401
Parmesano* (*Noodle-Roni*), ¾ cup 195
pork flavor (*Oodles of Noodles*), 3-oz. pkg. 390
Romanoff* (*Betty Crocker*), ¼ pkg. 230
Romanoff* (*Noodle-Roni*), ½ cup 181
Stroganoff* (*Betty Crocker*), ¼ pkg. 230
Stroganoff, w/meat* (*Noodle-Roni*), ½ cup 120

rice mixes, *see "Rice, Flavored," page 179*

spaghetti:

dry (*Hamburger Helper*), ⅕ pkg. 150
w/meat* (*Hamburger Helper*), ⅕ pkg. 330

spaghetti, continued

    w/mat sauce, freeze-dried (*Mountain House*), 1.7 oz. ..260
    and sauce* (*Mug•O•Lunch*), 1 pouch 160
vegetable, garden* (*Lipton Lite-Lunch*), 7 fl. oz. 160

* *Prepared according to package directions*

RICE, PLAIN, ½ cup cooked*
See also "Rice, Flavored"

	CALORIES
brown (*River Brand*)	110
brown (*Uncle Ben's*)	100
white:	
(*Carolina*)	90
(*Comet*)	102
(*River*)	100
(*Success*)	110
(*Uncle Ben's* Converted)	97
parboiled (*Comet*)	90
precooked (*Minute Rice*)	90
precooked (*Uncle Ben's* Quick)	89

* *Cooked according to package directions, without butter*

RICE, FLAVORED, ½ cup, except as noted
See also "Rice, Plain"

	CALORIES
beef flavor:	
mix* (*Comet*)	100
mix* (*Uncle Ben's* British Style)	141
w/vermicelli, mix* (*Carolina bake-it-easy*)	100
w/vermicelli, mix* (*Minute Rice* Rib Roast)	150
w/vermicelli, mix* (*Rice-A-Roni*)	160

Rice, Flavored, continued

w/broccoli in cheese sauce, frozen (*Green Giant*) 125
brown and wild rice, mix* (*Comet*) 100
brown and wild rice, mix* (*Uncle Ben's*) 150
w/cheese flavor sauce and vermicelli, mix*
  (*Rice-A-Roni*) 145
chicken flavor:
  mix* (*Comet*) 100
  mix* (*Uncle Ben's* French Style) 144
  w/vermicelli, mix* (*Carolina bake-it-easy*) 100
  w/vermicelli, mix* (*Minute Rice* Drumstick) 150
  w/vermicelli, mix* (*Rice-A-Roni*) 160
curry, mix* (*Uncle Ben's*) 106
French style, frozen (*Birds Eye*), 3.6 oz. 110
fried, Chinese:
  canned (*La Choy*) 207
  chicken, canned (*La Choy*) 209
  mix** (*Durkee* Seasoning Mix) 108
  mix* (*Minute Rice*) 160
  pork, frozen (*Chun King*), ½ pkg. 150
  pork, frozen (*La Choy*) 108
  w/vermicelli, mix* (*Rice-A-Roni*) 187
herb and butter flavor, w/vermicelli, mix*
  (*Carolina bake-it-easy*) 100
Italian style, frozen (*Birds Eye*), 3.6 oz. 110
long grain and wild rice:
  frozen (*Green Giant*) 110
  mix* (*Comet*) 100
  mix* (*Carolina*) 90
  mix* (*Uncle Ben's*) 113
  mix* (*Uncle Ben's* Fast) 127
Oriental style:
  fried, *see "fried, Chinese," above*
  frozen (*Birds Eye*), 3.6 oz. 100
  mix*** (*Hamburger Helper*—8-oz. pkg.), ⅕ pkg. 340
  mix*** (*Hamburger Helper*—6½-oz. pkg.), ⅕ pkg. 300
paella, mix* (*R. M. Quigg's*), 4½ oz. 153

Rice, Flavored, continued

w/peas and mushrooms, frozen (*Birds Eye*), 2.3 oz. 100

w/peas and mushrooms, frozen
    (*Green Giant* Rice Medley) 100

w/peppers and parsley, frozen
    (*Green Giant* Rice Verdi) 135

pilaf:

    frozen (*Green Giant* Rice Pilaf) 115

    mix* (*Uncle Ben's* Greek Style) 144

    w/vermicelli, mix* (*Carolina bake-it-easy*) 100

Spanish:

    canned (*Comstock*), 7½ oz. 130

    canned (*Featherweight*), 7½-oz. can 140

    canned (*Heinz*), 7½-oz. can 170

    canned (*Libby's*) 60

    canned (*Old El Paso*), 4 oz. 97

    canned (*Stokely-Van Camp*) 85

    frozen (*Birds Eye*), 3.6 oz. 100

    mix** (*Durkee* Seasoning Mix) 137

    mix* (*Minute Rice*) 150

    w/vermicelli, mix* (*Rice-A-Roni*) 118

turkey flavor, w/vermicelli, mix* (*Rice-A-Roni*) 182

wild rice, w/vermicelli, mix* (*Rice-A-Roni*) 134

   * *Prepared according to package directions*
  ** *Prepared according to package directions, with rice*
 *** *Prepared according to package directions, with hamburger*

CHAPTER 15

FATS, OILS
AND SALAD DRESSINGS

FATS & OILS,
one tablespoon, except as noted

CALORIES

butter:
 (*Land O Lakes*) 100
 (*Meadow Gold*) 100
 (*Sealtest*) 102
 whipped (*Breakstone*) 67
margarine:
 (*Allsweet*) 100
 (*Autumn*—stick or soft) 100
 (*Blue Bonnet*—stick or soft) 100
 (*Chiffon*—soft) 96
 (*Fleischmann's*—stick or soft) 100
 (*Holiday*) 100
 (*Imperial*—stick) 100
 (*Mazola*) 100
 (*Mazola*—unsalted) 100
 (*Mrs. Filberts*—stick or soft) 100
 (*Nucoa*) 100
 (*Nucoa*—soft) 90
 (*Parkay*) 100
 (*Promise*—stick or soft) 100
 (*Saffola*) 99

margarine, continued

    diet (*Blue Bonnet*) 50
    diet (*Fleischmann's*) 50
    diet (*Imperial*) 50
    diet (*Mazola*) 50
    diet (*Mrs. Filberts*) 50
    spread (*Blue Bonnet*) 80
    spread (*Fleischmann's*) 80
    spread (*Mrs. Filberts*) 80
    whipped (*Blue Bonnet*—stick or soft) 70
    whipped (*Fleischmann's*—soft) 70
    whipped (*Imperial*) 65

oil:

    all-blend (*Hain*) 120
    cod liver (*Hain*) 120
    cod liver, cherry or mint (*Hain*) 120
    corn (*Ann Page*) 120
    corn (*Hain*) 120
    corn (*Mazola*) 125
    olive (*Filippo Berio*) 125
    olive (*Hain*) 120
    peanut (*Hain*) 120
    peanut (*Planters*) 130
    safflower (*Hain*) 120
    salad (*Saffola*) 124
    sesame (*Hain*) 120
    soy (*Hain*) 120
    sunflower (*Hain*) 120
    sunflower (*Sunlite*) 120
    vegetable (*Crisco*) 120
    vegetable (*Hi Lite*) 120
    vegetable (*Pour 'N Fry*) 120
    vegetable (*Puritan*) 120
    vegetable (*Wesson*) 120
    vegetable-soy (*Jewel*) 120
oil, cooking spray (*Mazola No Stick*), 2-second spray 7

Fats & Oils, continued
shortening:
　(*Bake Rite*) 91
　(*Crisco*) 110
　(*Fluffo*) 110
　(*Hi Tone*) 120
　(*Light Spry*) 93
　(*Snowdrift*) 110

SALAD DRESSINGS, one tablespoon,
except as noted

　　　　　　　　　　　　　　　　　　　　　　CALORIES
avocado goddess, bottled (*Marie's Specialty Brands*) 96
bacon, creamy, bottled (*Seven Seas*) 60
blue cheese:
　bottled (*Marie's Specialty Brands*) 100
　chunky, bottled (*Seven Seas*) 70
　chunky, bottled (*Wish-Bone*) 80
　mix* (*Good Seasons*) 90
　mix *(*Good Seasons Thick 'n Creamy*) 80
　low-calorie, bottled (*Dia-Mel*) 15
　low-calorie, bottled (*Ann Page*) 18
　low-calorie, bottled (*Marie's Specialty Brands*) 27
　low-calorie, chunky, bottled (*Walden Farms*) 27
　low-calorie, chunky, bottled (*Wish-Bone*) 40
　low-calorie, mix* (*Weight Watchers*) 10
bottled (*Ann Page*) 70
bottled (*Bennett's*) 60
bottled (*Hellmann's Spin Blend*) 55
bottled (*Mrs. Filberts*) 70
bottled (*Saffola*) 56
bottled (*Seven Seas Capri*) 70
buttermilk farm style, mix* (*Good Seasons*) 60
buttermilk ranch style, bottled (*Marie's Specialty Brands*) ..105

Salad Dressings, continued

Caesar:

   bottled (*Hain*) 63

   bottled (*Lawry's*) 70

   bottled (*Pfeiffer*) 70

   bottled (*Seven Seas*) 60

   bottled (*Seven Seas Viva*) 60

   bottled (*Wish-Bone*) 80

   low-calorie, bottled (*Dia-Mel*) 50

   low-calorie, bottled (*Pfeiffer*) 10

Canadian, bottled (*Lawry's*) 72

cheese-garlic, mix* (*Good Seasons*) 90

cheese-Italian, mix* (*Good Seasons*) 90

chef-style, low-calorie, bottled (*Ann Page*) 20

farm-style, mix* (*Good Seasons*) 50

French:

   bottled (*Bennett's*) 60

   bottled (*Lawry's*) 60

   bottled (*Lawry's San Francisco*) 53

   bottled (*Pfeiffer*) 55

   bottled (*Saffola*) 54

   bottled (*Seven Seas* Family Style) 60

   bottled (*Wish-Bone* De Luxe) 50

   bottled (*Wish-Bone* Sweet 'n Spicy) 70

   creamy, bottled (*Hain*) 63

   creamy, bottled (*Seven Seas*) 60

   mix* (*Good Seasons*) 80

   mix* (*Good Seasons* Old Fashion) 80

   mix* (*Good Seasons* Riviera) 90

   mix* (*Good Seasons* Thick 'N Creamy) 75

   low-calorie, bottled (*Ann Page*) 25

   low-calorie, bottled (*Bennett's*) 25

   low-calorie, bottled (*Dia-Mel*) 30

   low-calorie, bottled (*Diet Delight*) 12

   low-calorie, bottled (*Pfeiffer*) 18

   low-calorie, bottled (*Walden Farms*) 33

French, continued

   low-calorie, bottled (*Wish-Bone*) 25
   low-calorie, bottled (*Wish-Bone* Sweet 'n Spicy) 30
   low-calorie, mix* (*Dia-Mel*) 18
   low-calorie, mix* (*Weight Watchers*) 4
garlic:
   creamy, bottled (*Wish-Bone*) 80
   mix* (*Good Seasons*) 80
   low-calorie, creamy, mix* (*Dia-Mel*) 22
garlic-French, bottled (*Wish-Bone*) 70
green goddess:
   bottled (*Lawry's*) 59
   bottled (*Seven Seas*) 60
   bottled (*Wish-Bone*) 70
Hawaiian, bottled (*Lawry's*) 77
herbs and spices, bottled (*Seven Seas*) 60
Italian:
   bottled (*Bennett's*) 60
   bottled (*Hain*) 64
   bottled (*Lawry's*) 80
   bottled (*Pfeiffer* Chef) 60
   bottled (*Saffola*) 50
   bottled (*Seven Seas* Family Style) 70
   bottled (*Seven Seas Viva*) 70
   bottled (*Wish-Bone*) 80
   w/cheese, bottled (*Marie's Specialty Brands*) 62
   w/cheese, bottled (*Wish-Bone*) 60
   creamy, bottled (*Seven Seas*) 70
   garlic, bottled (*Marie's Specialty Brands*) 100
   mix* (*Good Seasons*) 80
   mix* (*Good Seasons* Mild) 90
   mix* (*Good Seasons Thick 'n Creamy*) 85
   low-calorie, bottled (*Ann Page*) 14
   low-calorie, bottled (*Bennett's*) 6
   low-calorie, bottled (*Dia-Mel*) 2
   low-calorie, bottled (*Diet Delight*) 6
   low-calorie, bottled (*Pfeiffer*) 10

Italian, continued

   low-calorie, bottled (*Walden Farms Classico*) 9

   low-calorie, bottled (*Wish-Bone*) 30

   low-calorie, creamy, bottled (*Wish-Bone*) 35

   low-calorie, mix* (*Dia-Mel*) 2

   low-calorie, mix* (*Good Seasons*) 8

   low-calorie, mix* (*Weight Watchers*) 2

   low-calorie, creamy, mix* (*Weight Watchers*) 4

mayonnaise:

   bottled (*Ann Page*) 100

   bottled (*Bama*) 95

   bottled (*Bennett's*) 110

   bottled (*Best Foods*) 100

   bottled (*Cains*) 100

   bottled (*Hain*—safflower or unsalted) 100

   bottled (*Hellmann's*) 100

   bottled (*Kraft*) 100

   bottled (*Mrs. Filberts*) 100

   bottled (*Saffola*) 101

   imitation, bottled (*Bennett's*) 40

   imitation, bottled (*Dia-Mel*) 106

   imitation, bottled (*Mrs. Filberts*) 40

   imitation, bottled (*Saffola*) 59

   imitation, eggless, bottled (*Hain*) 85

   low-calorie, imitation, bottled (*Diet Delight Mayolite*) ...24

oil and vinegar, bottled (*Hain*) 90

onion, bottled (*Wish-Bone* California Onion) 80

onion, mix* (*Good Seasons*) 80

red wine, low-calorie, bottled (*Pfeiffer*) 10

red wine vinegar and oil, bottled (*Seven Seas Viva*) 60

Roquefort, bottled (*Marie's Specialty Brands*) 105

Russian:

   bottled (*Bennett's*) 70

   bottled (*Hain*) 66

   bottled (*Marie's Specialty Brands*) 88

   bottled (*Pfeiffer*) 65

   bottled (*Wish-Bone*) 60

Russian, continued

   creamy, bottled (*Seven Seas*) 80
   low-calorie, bottled (*Dia-Mel*) 9
   low-calorie, bottled (*Pfeiffer*) 15
   low-calorie, bottled (*Wish-Bone*) 25
   low-calorie, mix* (*Weight Watchers*) 4
sesame, creamy, bottled (*Sahadi*) 60
sesame, spice, bottled (*Sahadi*) 80
Thousand Island:
   bottled (*Hain*) 55
   bottled (*Lawry's*) 69
   bottled (*Marie's Specialty Brands*) 88
   bottled (*Pfeiffer*) 65
   bottled (*Seven Seas*) 50
   bottled (*Wish-Bone*) 70
   mix* (*Good Seasons Thick 'n Creamy*) 75
   low-calorie, bottled (*Ann Page*) 25
   low-calorie, bottled (*Dia-Mel*) 30
   low-calorie, bottled (*Diet Delight*) 18
   low-calorie, bottled (*Pfeiffer*) 15
   low-calorie, bottled (*Walden Farms*) 24
   low-calorie, bottled (*Wish-Bone*) 30
   low-calorie, mix* (*Dia-Mel*) 20
   low-calorie, mix* (*Weight Watchers*) 12

* *Prepared according to package directions*

CHAPTER 16

SAUCES, GRAVIES, CONDIMENTS AND SEASONINGS

SAUCES, ½ cup, except as noted
*See also "Gravies," "Condiments & Seasonings"
and "Seasoning & Roasting Mixes, Dry"*

	CALORIES
à la king, mix* (*Durkee*)	65
all-purpose, canned (*Ronzoni*), 4 oz.**	80
barbecue, in jars:	
(*Cris & Pitt's*)	120
(*French's*)	116
(*Heinz*)	110
(*Open Pit*), 4 oz.**	104
hickory smoke flavor (*Heinz*)	125
hickory smoke flavor (*Open Pit*), 4 oz.**	106
hot (*French's*)	116
hot (*Heinz*)	125
smoky flavor (*French's*)	116
w/mushrooms (*Heinz*)	125
w/onions (*Heinz*)	125
w/onions (*Open Pit*), 4 oz.**	109
browning sauce, microwave:	
beef (*Holland House*), ½ oz.	28
chicken (*Holland House*), ½ oz.	31
pork (*Holland House*), ½ oz.	33

spaghetti or pasta sauce, continued

marinara, canned (*Ann Page*), 4 oz.** 70
marinara, canned (*Buitoni*), 4 oz.** 88
marinara, canned (*Ronzoni*), 4 oz.** 80
meat, canned (*Ann Page*), 4 oz.** 80
meat, canned (*Ronzoni*), 4 oz.** 80
meat flavor, canned (*Buitoni*), 4 oz.** 120
meat flavor, canned (*Hunt's Prima Salsa*), 4 oz.** 120
meatless, canned (*Ann Page*), 4 oz.** 70
meatless, canned (*Buitoni*), 4 oz.** 92
meatless, w/mushrooms, canned (*Ann Page*), 4 oz.** ...70
mushroom, canned (*Buitoni*), 4 oz.** 88
w/mushrooms, canned (*Hunt's Prima Salsa*), 4 oz.** ..110
w/mushrooms, mix* (*Durkee*) 40
w/mushrooms, mix* (*French's*) 80
soy, *see "Condiments & Seasonings," page 197*
stroganoff, mix* (*French's*) 165
sweet dessert sauces, *see "Syrups & Toppings," page 241*
sweet and sour:
canned (*Contadina* Cookbook Sauces) 120
in jars (*La Choy*) 262
mix* (*Durkee*) 115
mix* (*French's*) 55
Swiss steak sauce, canned (*Contadina* Cookbook Sauces) ...40
taco sauce, *see "Condiments & Seasonings," page 197*
teriyaki, *see "Condiments & Seasonings," page 198*
tomato:
canned (*Contadina*), 4 oz.** 40
canned (*Del Monte*) 40
canned (*Hunt's*), 4 oz.** 35
canned (*Hunt's* Special), 4 oz.** 40
canned (*Libby's*) 45
canned (*Stokely-Van Camp*) 35
w/bits, canned (*Del Monte*) 40
w/bits, canned (*Heinz*), 4 oz.** 35
w/cheese, canned (*Hunt's*), 4 oz.** 70
w/mushrooms, canned (*Del Monte*) 50

tomato, continued

  w/mushrooms, canned *(Hunt's)*, 4 oz.** 40
  w/onions, canned *(Del Monte)* 50
  w/onions, canned *(Hunt's)*, 4 oz.** 45
  pizza sauce, *see "pizza," above*
  spaghetti sauce, *see "spaghetti or pasta," above*
  Spanish-style, canned *(Ann Page)*, 4 oz.** 40
tomato-herb, canned *(Hunt's)*, 4 oz.** 80
tomato paste or puree, *see "Tomato Paste & Puree," page 107*
white sauce, mix* *(Durkee)* 119
worcestershire, *see "Condiments & Seasonings," page 198*

  * *Prepared according to package directions*
** *Approximately ½ cup*

GRAVIES, ½ cup, except as noted
See also "Condiments & Seasonings," "Sauces"
and "Seasoning & Roasting Mixes, Dry"

                        CALORIES

au jus:
  mix* *(Ann Page)* 16
  mix* *(Durkee)* 16
  mix* *(French's* Gravy Makins) 16
  mix* *(French's* Pan Rich Gravy) 60
  mix* *(McCormick/Schilling)* 15
beef:
  canned *(Ann Page)*, 2.1 oz. 25
  canned *(Franco-American)*, 4 oz.** 60
  brown, canned *(Howard Johnson's)* 51
brown:
  in jars *(Heinz)* 60
  mix *(Ann Page)*, ¼ oz. dry 20
  mix* *(Ehler's)* 44
  mix* *(Durkee)* 30
  mix* *(French's* Gravy Makins) 40

brown, continued

mix* (*French's* Pan Rich Gravy) 120

mix* (*McCormick/Schilling*) 59

mix* (*McCormick/Schilling* Lite) 20

mix* (*Pillsbury*) 30

mix* (*Spatini*) 40

mix* (*Weight Watchers*) 16

w/mushroom broth, canned (*Dawn Fresh*), 4 oz.** 40

w/mushrooms, mix* (*Durkee*) 30

w/mushrooms, mix* (*Weight Watchers*) 24

w/onion, canned (*Franco-American*), 4 oz.** 50

w/onion, mix* (*Durkee*) 33

w/onion, mix* (*Weight Watchers*) 26

chicken:

canned (*Franco-American*), 4 oz.** 100

in jars (*Heinz*) 80

mix (*Ann Page*), ¼ oz. dry 30

mix* (*Durkee*) 44

mix* (*Ehler's*) 42

mix* (*French's* Gravy Makins) 50

mix* (*French's* Pan Rich Gravy) 120

mix* (*McCormick/Schilling*) 48

mix* (*McCormick/Schilling* Lite) 20

mix* (*Pillsbury*) 50

mix* (*Weight Watchers*) 20

creamy, mix* (*Durkee*) 78

chicken giblet, canned (*Franco-American*), 4 oz.** 70

herb, mix* (*McCormick/Schilling*) 41

home-style:

mix* (*Durkee*) 35

mix* (*French's* Gravy Makins) 50

mix* (*Pillsbury*) 30

mushroom:

canned (*Franco-American*), 4 oz.** 70

in jars (*Heinz*) 50

mix (*Ann Page*), ¼ oz. dry 20

mushroom, continued

   mix* (*Durkee*) 30

   mix* (*French's* Gravy Makins) 40

   mix* (*McCormick/Schilling*) 40

onion:

   in jars (*Heinz*) 60

   mix (*Ann Page*), ¼ oz. dry 30

   mix* (*Durkee*) 42

   mix* (*French's* Gravy Makins) 50

   mix* (*French's* Pan Rich Gravy) 100

   mix* (*McCormick/Schilling*) 51

pork, mix* (*Durkee*) 35

pork, mix* (*French's* Gravy Makins) 40

Swiss steak, mix* (*Durkee*) 23

turkey:

   mix* (*Ann Page*) 50

   mix* (*Durkee*) 47

   mix* (*French's* Gravy Makins) 50

   mix* (*McCormick/Schilling*) 41

turkey giblet, canned (*Howard Johnson's*) 55

* *Prepared according to package directions*
** *Approximately ½ cup*

CONDIMENTS & SEASONINGS

See also "Sauces," "Gravies," "Seasoning & Roasting Mixes, Dry," "Pure Herbs & Spices, Ground" and "Salad Dressings"

CALORIES

bacon bits:

   (*Oscar Mayer*), ½ oz. 45

   imitation (*Ann Page*), 1 tbsp. 25

   imitation (*Bac*Os*), 1 tbsp. 40

   imitation (*Durkee*), 1 tsp. 8

   imitation (*French's* Crumbles), 1 tsp. 6

   imitation (*McCormick/Schilling*), 1 tbsp. 30

barbecue sauce, *see "Sauces," page 189*

Condiments & Seasonings, continued

barbecue seasoning (*French's*), 1 tsp. 6
(*Bennett's* Special Sauce), 1 tbsp. 50
bitters (*Angostura*), ¼ tsp. 4
brown gravy sauce (*La Choy*), 1 tsp. 19
browning sauce, microwave, *see "Sauces," page 189*
burger sauce (*Hellmann's Big H*), 1 tbsp. 70
butter flavor, imitation (*Ehler's*), 1 tsp. 8
butter flavor, imitation (*Durkee*), 1 tsp. 3
capers (*Crosse & Blackwell*), 1 tbsp. 6
catsup:
   (*Del Monte*), 1 tbsp. 15
   (*Heinz*), 1 tbsp. 16
   (*Hunt's*), 1 tbsp. 18
   (*Smucker's*), 1 tbsp. 19
   hot (*Heinz*), 1 tbsp. 21
   imitation (*Hain* Natural), 1 tbsp. 16
   low-calorie (*Dia-Mel*), 1 tbsp. 7
   low-calorie (*Featherweight*), ½ oz. 6
celery salt, *see "salt, flavored," below*
chili powder (*Mexene*), 1 tbsp. 24
chili sauce:
   (*Heinz*), 1 tbsp. 17
   (*Hunt's*), 1 tbsp. 19
   low-calorie (*Featherweight*), ½ oz. 8
chili sauce relish (*Bennett's*), 1 tbsp. 15
chutney, Major Grey's (*Crosse & Blackwell*), 1 tbsp. 53
cocktail seafood sauce:
   (*Crosse & Blackwell*), 1 tbsp. 22
   (*Del Monte*), 1 tbsp. 18
   (*Pfeiffer*), ½ oz. 25
   (*Sau-Sea*), 1 tbsp. 16
coconut, cream of (*Holland House Coco Casa*), 1 tbsp. 59
curry powder (*Crosse & Blackwell*), 1 tbsp. 26
(*Durkee Famous Sauce*), 1 tbsp. 69
garlic flavoring, liquid (*Burton's*), ½ tsp. 21
garlic, salt, *see "salt, flavored," below*

Condiments & Seasonings, continued

garlic spread (*Lawry's*), 1 tbsp. 88
(*Gravymaster*), 1 tsp. 12
hot sauce:
  (*Frank's*), 1 tsp. 1
  (*Gebhardt*), 1 tsp. 1
  (*Tabasco*), 1 tsp. 1
hot sauce relish (*Bennett's*), 1 tbsp. 16
lemon-pepper seasoning (*French's*), 1 tsp. 6
marinade, meat, mix* (*Durkee*), ½ cup 47
marinade, meat, dry form, *see "Seasoning & Roasting Mixes,
Dry," page 199*
mayonnaise, *see "Salad Dressings," page 187*
meat-fish-poultry sauce:
  (*A.1.*), 1 tbsp. 12
  (*Crosse & Blackwell*), 1 tbsp. 21
  (*Escoffier Sauce Diable*), 1 tbsp. 20
  (*Escoffier Sauce Robert*), 1 tbsp. 19
  (*Heinz 57*), 1 tbsp. 14
  (*Heinz Savory Sauce*), 1 tbsp. 21
  (*H.P.*), 1 tbsp. 21
mint sauce (*Crosse & Blackwell*), 1 tbsp. 16
mustard, prepared:
  (*French's Cream Salad*), 1 tbsp. 10
  (*French's Medford*), 1 tbsp. 16
  (*Grey Poupon*), 1 tbsp. 15
  brown (*French's Brown 'N Spicy*), 1 tbsp. 15
  brown (*Heinz*), 1 tbsp. 11
  w/horseradish (*French's*), 1 tbsp. 15
  hot (*Mister Mustard*), 1 tsp. 11
  w/onion (*French's*), 1 tbsp. 25
  yellow (*Heinz*), 1 tbsp. 10
onion flavoring, liquid (*Burton's*), ½ tsp. 21
onion salt, *see "salt, flavored," below*
pepper, seasoned (*French's*), 1 tsp. 8
pepper, seasoned (*Lawry's*), 1 tsp. 8
pizza seasoning (*French's*), 1 tsp. 4

Condiments & Seasonings, continued

relish, *see specific kinds, and "Pickles & Relishes," page 108*

relish spread (*Mrs. Filberts*), 1 tbsp. 80

salad dressing:

    (*Durkee*), 1 tsp. 4

    (*French's Salad Lift*), 1 tsp. 6

    w/cheese (*Durkee*), 1 tsp. 10

salt, flavored:

    butter, imitation (*French's*), 1 tsp. 8

    butter, imitation (*McCormick/Schilling*), 1 tsp. 2

    celery (*French's*), 1 tsp. 2

    garlic (*French's*), 1 tsp. 4

    garlic, parslied (*French's*), 1 tsp. 6

    hickory smoke (*French's*), 1 tsp. 2

    onion (*French's*), 1 tsp. 6

    seasoned (*Lawry's*), 1 tsp. 1

    seasoning (*French's*), 1 tsp. 2

sandwich spread:

    (*Bennett's*), 1 tbsp. 45

    (*Best Foods*), 1 tbsp. 60

    (*Hellmann's*), 1 tbsp. 60

    (*Mrs. Filberts*), 1 tbsp) 50

seafood sauce, *see "cocktail seafood sauce," above and*
    "tartar sauce," below

seafood seasoning (*French's*), 1 tsp. 2

soy sauce:

    (*Chun King*), 1 tbsp. 6

    (*Kikkoman*), 1 tbsp. 12

    (*La Choy*), 1 tbsp. 8

stock base, beef flavor (*French's*), 1 tsp. 8

stock base, chicken flavor (*French's*), 1 tsp. 8

sweet and sour dressing (*Bennett's*), 1 tbsp. 70

sweet and sour sauce, *see "Sauces," page 191*

taco sauce:

    (*Gebhardt*), 1 tsp. 3

    (*Old El Paso*), 1 tsp. 3

    (*Ortega*), 1 tbsp. 21

Condiments & Seasonings, continued

tartar sauce:

   (*Bennett's*), 1 tbsp. 70

   (*Best Foods*), 1 tbsp. 70

   (*Kraft*), ½ oz. 72

   (*Hellmann's*), 1 tbsp. 70

   (*Mrs. Filberts*), 1 tbsp. 80

   mix (*Mrs. Paul's Create A Sauce*), ½ packet 22

   mix* (*Van de Kamp's*), ½ oz. 80

tenderizer, meat (*French's*), 1 tsp. 2

tenderizer, meat, seasoned (*French's*), 1 tsp. 2

teriyaki sauce:

   (*Chun King*), 1 tbsp. 12

   (*Kikkoman*), 1 tbsp. 17

   mix* (*French's*), 1 tbsp. 18

vinegar:

   cider (*Heinz*), 1 tbsp. 3

   red wine (*Regina*), 1 tbsp. 2

   red wine, w/garlic (*Regina*), 1 tbsp. 2

   white (*Heinz*), 1 tbsp.. 3

   white wine (*Regina*), 1 tbsp. 2

wine, cooking:

   Marsala (*Holland House*), 1 tbsp. 18

   red (*Holland House*), 1 tbsp. 13

   sauterne (*Regina*), 1 tbsp. 2

   sherry (*Holland House*), 1 tbsp. 20

   sherry (*Regina*), 1 tbsp. ....trace

   white (*Holland House*), 1 tbsp. 13

worcestershire sauce:

   (*Crosse & Blackwell*), 1 tbsp. 15

   (*French's*), 1 tbsp. 10

   (*Heinz*), 1 tbsp. 11

   (*Lea & Perrins*), 1 tbsp. 12

   smoky (*French's*), 1 tbsp. 10

* *Prepared according to package directions*

SEASONING & ROASTING
MIXES, DRY, 1 packet*
See also "Sauces," "Gravies" and "Seasoned Coating Mixes"

CALORIES

à la king (*Durkee*), 1⅛-oz. packet 133
au jus (*Durkee Roastin' Bag*), 1-oz. packet 64
beef:
   ground (*Durkee*), 1⅛-oz. packet 91
   ground, w/onion (*Ann Page*), 1⅛-oz. packet 100
   ground, w/onion (*Durkee*), 1⅛-oz. packet 102
   ground, w/onion (*French's*), 1⅛-oz. packet 100
   ground, w/onion (*McCormick/Schilling*), 1-oz. packet ..86
   hamburger, *see "hamburger," below*
   stew (*Durkee*), 1¾-oz. packet 99
   stew (*French's*), 1⅞-oz. packet 150
   stew (*McCormick/Schilling*), 1½-oz. packet 90
   stroganoff, *see "stroganoff," below*
chicken:
   creamy style (*Durkee Roastin' Bag*), 2-oz. packet 242
   gravy (*Durkee Roastin' Bag*), 1½-oz. packet 122
   Italian style (*Durkee Roastin' Bag*), 1½-oz. packet 144
chili:
   (*Ann Page*), 1¾-oz. packet 120
   (*Durkee*), 1¾-oz. packet 148
   (*French's Chili-O*), 1¾-oz. packet 150
chop suey (*Durkee*), 1½-oz. packet 128
hamburger (*Durkee*), 1-oz. packet 110
hamburger (*French's*), 1-oz. packet 100
hamburger and meat loaf
   (*McCormick/Schilling*), 1½-oz. packet 119
enchilada (*French's*), 1⅜-oz. packet 120
enchilada (*McCormick/Schilling*), 1½-oz. packet 113
   marinade, meat (*Durkee*), 1-oz. packet 47
   meatball (*French's*), 1½-oz. packet 140
   meatball, Italian (*Durkee*), 1-oz. packet 22

Seasoning & Roasting Mixes, Dry, continued

meat loaf:

    (*Contadina*), 3¾-oz. packet 363

    (*Durkee Roastin' Bag*), 1½-oz. packet 129

    (*French's*), 1½-oz. packet 160

pork gravy (*Durkee Roastin' Bag*), 1½-oz. packet 130

pot roast, onion (*Durkee Roastin' Bag*), 1½-oz. packet 124

pot roast and stew (*Durkee Roastin' Bag*), 1½-oz. packet ..125

sloppy hot dog (*French's*), 1½-oz. packet 160

sloppy Joe:

    (*Durkee*), 1½-oz. packet 118

    (*French's*), 1½-oz. packet 128

    (*McCormick/Schilling*), 1-5/16-oz. packet 102

    pizza flavor (*Durkee*), 1-oz. packet 99

sparerib sauce (*Durkee Roastin' Bag*), 1.9-oz. packet 162

stroganoff:

    (*Durkee*), 1¼-oz. packet 90

    (*French's*), 1 packet 55

    (*McCormick/Schilling*), 1½-oz. packet 113

Swiss steak (*Durkee Roastin' Bag*), 1½-oz. packet 115

Swiss steak (*McCormick/Schilling*), 1-oz. packet 44

taco:

    (*Durkee*), 1⅛-oz. packet 67

    (*French's*), 1¾-oz. packet 150

    (*McCormick/Schilling*), 1¼-oz. packet 61

tuna casserole (*McCormick/Schilling*), 1½-oz. packet 104

* *Note variation in packet sizes*

PURE HERBS & SPICES,
GROUND, one teaspoon
See also "Condiments & Seasonings"

Note: Since the composition of pure herbs and spices should not vary in caloric content by brand, it is assumed that the following values are the same for all brands—*Durkee, Ehler's, McCormick/Schilling,* etc.

	CALORIES
allspice (all brands)	6
basil leaves (all brands)	3
bay leaves (all brands)	5
caraway seed (all brands)	8
cardamon seed (all brands)	6
celery seed (all brands)	11
cinnamon (all brands)	6
cloves (all brands)	7
coriander seed (all brands)	6
cumin seed (all brands)	7
dill seed (all brands)	9
fennel seed (all brands)	8
garlic powder (all brands)	5
ginger (all brands)	6
mace (all brands)	10
marjoram (all brands)	4
mustard powder (all brands)	9
nutmeg (all brands)	11
onion powder (all brands)	8
oregano (all brands)	6
paprika, domestic (all brands)	7
parsley flakes (all brands)	4
pepper:	
black (all brands)	9
chili (all brands)	9
red (all brands)	9
white (all brands)	9

Pure Herbs & Spices, Ground, continued

poppy seed (all brands) 13
rosemary leaves (all brands) 5
sage (all brands) 4
savory (all brands) 5
sesame seed (all brands) 9
tarragon (all brands) 5
thyme (all brands) 5
turmeric (all brands) 7

CHAPTER 17

PUDDINGS, CUSTARDS AND GELATINS

CUSTARDS, PUDDINGS & PIE FILLINGS,
½ cup, except as noted
See also "Gelatin Desserts" and "Pie Fillings, Canned"

	CALORIES
banana:	
(*Del Monte Pudding Cup*), 5-oz. container	180
(*Hunt's Snack Pack*), 5-oz. container	180
mix* (*Royal*)	160
cream, mix* (*Ann Page*)	160
cream, mix* (*Jell-O*), ⅙ of 8" pie**	110
cream, mix* (*Jell-O* Instant)	180
butter pecan, mix* (*Jell-O* Instant)	170
butterscotch:	
(*Del Monte Pudding Cup*), 5-oz. container	180
(*Hunt's Snack Pack*), 5-oz. container	170
(*Rich's*), 3-oz. container	133
(*Swiss Miss*), 4¼-oz. container	160
mix* (*Ann Page*)	190
mix* (*Ann Page* Instant)	170
mix* (*Jell-O*)	170
mix* (*Jell-O* Instant)	170
mix* (*My-T-Fine*)	143
mix* (*Royal*)	160
mix* (*Royal* Instant)	180

butterscotch, continued

   low-calorie, mix* *(D-Zerta)* 70
   low-calorie, mix* *(Featherweight)*, 4 oz. 12
cherry, mix* *(Ann Page)* 170
chocolate:
   (Betty Crocker RTS) 180
   (Del Monte Pudding Cup), 5-oz. container 190
   (Hunt's Snack Pack), 5-oz. container 180
   (Rich's), 3-oz. container 140
   (Swiss Miss), 4¼-oz. container 180
   mix* *(Ann Page)* 180
   mix* *(Ann Page* Instant) 190
   mix* *(Jell-O)* 170
   mix* *(Jell-O* Instant) 190
   mix* *(My-T-Fine)* 133
   mix* *(Royal)* 180
   mix* *(Royal* Instant) 190
   low-calorie, mix* *(D-Zerta)* 70
   low-calorie, mix* *(Dia-Mel)*, 4 oz. 60
   low-calorie, mix* *(Featherweight)*, 4 oz. 14
chocolate, dark:
   (Rich's), 3-oz. container 140
   (Swiss Miss), 4¼-oz. container 180
   mix* *(Royal Dark 'N Sweet)* 180
   mix* *(Royal Dark 'N Sweet* Instant) 190
chocolate, German
   (Hunt's Snack Pack), 5-oz. container 170
chocolate, milk, mix* *(Jell-O)* 170
chocolate almond, mix* *(My-T-Fine)* 169
chocolate fudge:
   (Betty Crocker RTS) 180
   (Del Monte Pudding Cup), 5-oz. container 190
   (Hunt's Snack Pack), 5-oz. container 180
   mix* *(Jell-O)* 170
   mix* *(Jell-O* Instant) 190
   mix* *(My-T-Fine)* 151

Custards, Puddings & Pie Fillings, continued

chocolate marshmallow
    (*Hunt's Snack Pack*), 5-oz. container 170
chocolate sundae (*Swiss Miss*), 4¼-oz. container 190
coconut:
    mix* (*Royal* Instant) 170
    cream, mix* (*Ann Page*) 170
    cream, mix* (*Jell-O*), ⅙ of 8″ pie** 110
    cream, mix* (*Jell-O* Instant) 180
    toasted, mix* (*Ann Page* Instant) 170
    coffee, mix* (*Royal* Instant) 180
custard:
    (*Swiss Miss*), 4-oz. container 160
    mix* (*Royal*) 150
    egg (*Swiss Miss*), 4-oz. container 160
    egg, mix* (*Ann Page*) 150
    golden egg, mix* (*Jell-O Americana*) 160
flan, mix* (*Royal*) 150
lemon:
    (*Hunt's Snack Pack*), 5-oz. container 150
    mix* (*Ann Page*) 170
    mix* (*Ann Page* Instant) 180
    mix* (*Jell-O*), ⅙ of 9″ pie** 180
    mix* (*Jell-O* Instant) 180
    mix* (*My-T-Fine*) 164
    mix* (*Royal*) 160
    mix* (*Royal* Instant) 180
    low-calorie, mix* (*Dia-Mel*) 53
lime, key, mix* (*Royal*) 160
pineapple cream, mix* (*Jell-O* Instant) 180
pistachio:
    mix* (*Ann Page* Instant) 180
    mix* (*Jell-O* Instant) 180
    mix* (*Royal* Instant) 170
plum (*Crosse & Blackwell*), 4 oz. 340
plum (*Richardson & Robbins*) 300

Custards, Puddings & Pie Fillings, continued

rice pudding:
   (*Betty Crocker RTS*) 150
   (*Hunt's Snack Pack*), 5-oz. container 190
   mix* (*Jell-O Americana*) 170
tapioca:
   (*Betty Crocker RTS*) 150
   (*Hunt's Snack Pack*), 5-oz. container 140
   (*Swiss Miss*), 4¼-oz. container 170
   chocolate, mix* (*Ann Page*) 180
   chocolate, mix* (*Jell-O Americana*) 160
   chocolate, mix* (*Royal*) 180
   vanilla, mix* (*Ann Page*) 170
   vanilla, mix* (*Jell-O Americana*) 160
   vanilla, mix* (*My-T-Fine*) 130
   vanilla, mix* (*Royal*) 160
vanilla:
   (*Betty Crocker RTS*) 190
   (*Del Monte Pudding Cup*), 5-oz. container 190
   (*Hunt's Snack Pack*), 5-oz. container 180
   (*Rich's*), 3-oz. container 130
   (*Swiss Miss*), 4¼-oz. container 170
   mix* (*Ann Page*) 170
   mix* (*Ann Page* Instant) 170
   mix* (*Jell-O*) 160
   mix* (*Jell-O* Instant) 180
   mix* (*My-T-Fine*) 133
   mix* (*Royal*) 160
   mix* (*Royal* Instant) 180
   low-calorie, mix* (*D-Zerta*) 70
   low-calorie, mix* (*Dia-Mel*), 4 oz. 53
   low-calorie, mix* (*Featherweight*), 4 oz. 12
   French, mix* (*Jell-O*) 170
   French, mix* (*Jell-O* Instant) 180

  * *Prepared according to package directions*
 ** *Prepared according to package directions, without crust*

GELATIN DESSERTS, ½ cup,
except as noted
See also "Gelatin, Unflavored"

	CALORIES
all flavors, low-calorie (Dia-Mel), 4 oz.	1
all flavors, mix*:	
(Ann Page)	80
(Carmel Kosher Gelatin Dessert), 4 oz.	80
(Jell-O)	80
(Jells Best)	77
(Royal)	80
low-calorie (D-Zerta)	8
low-calorie (Dia-Mel), 4 oz.	10
low-calorie, fructose-sweetened (Featherweight), 4 oz.	35
low-calorie, artifically sweetened (Featherweight), 4 oz.	10
unsweetened (Royal Sweet As You Please)	6
vegetable gelatin, all flavors, mix* (Carmel Kosher), 4 oz.	90
vegetable gelatin, all flavors, low-calorie, mix* (Carmel Kosher), 4 oz.	8

* Prepared according to package directions

GELATIN, UNFLAVORED, one envelope*
See also "Gelatin Desserts"

	CALORIES
(Ann Page)	24
(Carmel Kosher)	30
(Knox)	28

* As packaged

CHAPTER 18

CAKES, COOKIES, PIES AND PASTRIES

DESSERT CAKES, FROZEN*
*See also "Dessert Cakes, Mixes," "Dessert Pies, Frozen"
and "Pastries, Cakes & Pies, Frozen & Refrigerated"*

CALORIES

apple walnut (*Sara Lee*), ⅛ of 12¼-oz. cake 166
banana:
   (*Pepperidge Farm* Cake Supreme), ¼ of 11½-oz. cake ..280
   (*Sara Lee*), ⅛ of 13¾-oz. cake 175
   nut layer (*Sara Lee*), ⅛ of 20-oz. cake 233
black forest (*Sara Lee*), ⅛ of 21-oz. cake 203
Boston cream
   (*Pepperidge Farm* Cake Supreme), ¼ of 11½-oz. cake ..270
Boston cream pie, see "Dessert Pies, Frozen," page 214
carrot (*Sara Lee*), ⅛ of 12¼-oz. cake 153
cheesecake:
   plain (*Sara Lee*), ⅙ of 17-oz. cake 240
   plain (*Sara Lee—small*), ⅓ of 10-oz. cake 287
   cherry (*Sara Lee*), ⅙ of 19-oz. cake 214
   French, plain (*Sara Lee*), ⅛ of 23½-oz. cake 274
   French, strawberry (*Sara Lee*), ⅛ of 26-oz. cake 258
   strawberry (*Sara Lee*), ⅙ of 19-oz. cake 214
chocolate:
   (*Pepperidge Farm* Cake Supreme), ¼ of 12-oz. cake ..310
   (*Sara Lee*), ⅛ of 13¼-oz. cake 185
   cream layer (*Sara Lee*), ⅛ of 18-oz. cake 209
   double chocolate layer (*Sara Lee*), ⅛ of 18-oz. cake ..214

chocolate, continued

    fudge (*Pepperidge Farm*), ⅛ of 17-oz. cake 225
    fudge (*Pepperidge Farm* Half Cake),
      ¼ of 8½-oz. cake 225
    German (*Pepperidge Farm*), ⅛ of 17-oz. cake 200
    German (*Sara Lee*), ⅛ of 12¼-oz. cake 172
    roll (*Rich's*), ⅛ of 14-oz. cake 150

coconut:
    (*Pepperidge Farm*), ⅛ of 17-oz. cake 225
    (*Pepperidge Farm* Half Cake), ¼ of 8½-oz. cake 225
    (*Sara Lee*), ⅛ of 10-oz. cake 144

coffee cake:
    almond (*Sara Lee* Coffee Ring), ⅛ of 11¾-oz. cake 169
    almond (*Sara Lee* Light Coffee Round),
      ⅛ of 8-oz. cake 120
    blueberry (*Sara Lee* Coffee Ring),
      ⅛ of 9¾-oz. cake 133
    blueberry (*Sara Lee* Light Coffee Round),
      ⅛ of 8-oz. cake 115
    butter streusel (*Sara Lee*), ⅛ of 11½-oz. cake 160
    cinnamon streusel (*Sara Lee*), ⅛ of 10⅞-oz. cake 154
    maple (*Sara Lee* Light Coffee Round), ⅛ of 8-oz. cake ..121
    maple crunch (*Sara Lee* Coffee Ring),
      ⅛ of 9¾-oz. cake 138
    pecan (*Sara Lee*), ⅛ of 11¼-oz. cake 165
    pecan (*Sara Lee*), ¼ of 6½-oz. cake 191
    raspberry (*Sara Lee* Coffee Ring), ⅛ of 9¾-oz. cake ..140
    raspberry (*Sara Lee* Light Coffee Round),
      ⅛ of 8-oz. cake 115

devil's food (*Pepperidge Farm*), ⅛ of 17-oz. cake 225
golden layer (*Pepperidge Farm*), ⅛ of 17-oz. cake 225
golden layer (*Pepperidge Farm* Half Cake),
    ¼ of 8½-oz. cake 225
lemon-coconut (*Pepperidge Farm* Cake Supreme),
    ¼ of 12-oz. cake 280
lemon cream roll (*Rich's*), ⅛ of 14-oz. cake 150
orange (*Sara Lee*), ⅛ of 13¾-oz. cake 175

Dessert Cakes, Frozen, continued

pound cake:

    plain (*Sara Lee*), 1/10 of 10¾-oz. cake 124

    plain (*Sara Lee* Homestyle), 1/10 of 9½-oz. cake 109

    plain (*Sara Lee* Family Size), 1/15 of 16½-oz. cake 127

    apple nut (*Pepperidge Farm*), 1/10 of 14-oz. cake 130

    banana nut (*Sara Lee*), 1/10 of 11-oz. cake 117

    butter (*Pepperidge Farm*), 1/10 of 10½-oz. cake 130

    carrot (*Pepperidge Farm*), 1/10 of 14-oz. cake 160

    chocolate (*Pepperidge Farm*), 1/10 of 10½-oz. cake 130

    chocolate (*Sara Lee*), 1/10 of 10¾-oz. cake 122

    chocolate swirl (*Sara Lee*), 1/10 of 11¾-oz. cake 130

    raisin (*Sara Lee*), 1/10 of 12.9-oz. cake 128

strawberry:

    cheese, *see "cheesecake," above*

    cream layer (*Sara Lee*), ⅛ of 20½-oz. cake 213

    shortcake (*Mrs. Smith's*), ⅛ of 20-oz. cake 235

    shortcake (*Sara Lee*), ⅛ of 21-oz. cake 193

    roll (*Rich's*), ⅛ of 14-oz. cake 130

vanilla (*Pepperidge Farm*), ⅛ of 17-oz. cake 237

walnut layer (*Sara Lee*), ⅛ of 18-oz. cake 211

* *Note variation in cake sizes*

DESSERT CAKES, MIXES*,
1/12 of whole cake
See also "Dessert Cakes, Frozen," "Snack & Coffee Cakes,
Mixes," "Cake Frosting, Ready to Spread"
and "Cake Frostings, Mixes"

                                      CALORIES

angel food:

    (*Betty Crocker* One-Step) 140

    (*Betty Crocker* Traditional) 130

    (*Duncan Hines*) 140

Dessert Cakes, Mixes, continued

devil's food:

    (*Betty Crocker Supermoist*) 270

    (*Duncan Hines* Layer) 200

    (*Duncan Hines* Pudding Recipe) 250

    (*Pillsbury Plus*) 250

    (*Pillsbury Streusel Swirl*) 330

    (*Swans Down*) 187

fudge:

    marble (*Duncan Hines* Layer) 200

    marble (*Pillsbury Plus*) 270

    marble (*Pillsbury Streusel Swirl*) 350

    nut crown (*Pillsbury Bundt*) 290

    triple (*Pillsbury Bundt*) 300

golden vanilla (*Duncan Hines* Pudding Recipe) 250

lemon:

    (*Betty Crocker Supermoist*) 270

    (*Duncan Hines* Pudding Recipe) 250

    (*Pillsbury Plus*) 250

    (*Pillsbury Streusel Swirl*) 350

    chiffon (*Betty Crocker*) 190

    supreme (*Duncan Hines* Layer) 200

lemon-blueberry (*Pillsbury Bundt*) 280

marble (*Betty Crocker Supermoist*) 290

marble, fudge, *see "fudge," above*

marble supreme (*Pillsbury Bundt*) 330

orange (*Betty Crocker Supermoist*) 270

orange supreme (*Duncan Hines* Layer) 200

pineapple supreme (*Duncan Hines* Layer) 200

pound (*Pillsbury Bundt*) 310

pound, golden (*Betty Crocker*) 190

sour cream:

    chocolate (*Betty Crocker Supermoist*) 270

    chocolate (*Duncan Hines* Layer) 200

    white (*Betty Crocker Supermoist*) 200

spice (*Betty Crocker Supermoist*) 270

spice (*Duncan Hines* Layer) 200

Dessert Cakes, Mixes, continued

strawberry:
    (*Betty Crocker Supermoist*) 270
    (*Pillsbury Plus*) 250
    supreme (*Duncan Hines* Layer) 200

white:
    (*Betty Crocker Supermoist*) 190
    (*Duncan Hines* Layer) 190
    (*Duncan Hines* Pudding Recipe) 240
    (*Pillsbury Plus*) 240
    (*Swans Down*) 178

yellow:
    (*Betty Crocker Supermoist*) 270
    (*Duncan Hines* Layer) 200
    (*Duncan Hines* Pudding Recipe) 250
    (*Pillsbury Plus*) 250
    (*Swans Down*) 188

* *Prepared according to package directions, without added frosting*

DESSERT PIES, FROZEN,
⅙ of whole pie*
See also "Pies, Mixes" and "Pastries, Cakes &
Pies, Frozen & Refrigerated"

                                            CALORIES

apples:
    (*Banquet*), ⅙ of 20-oz. pie 240
    (*Morton*), ⅙ of 24-oz. pie 290
    (*Mrs. Smith's*), ⅙ of 26-oz. pie 295
    (*Sara Lee*), ⅙ of 31-oz. pie 421
    Dutch apple (*Mrs. Smith's*), ⅙ of 26-oz. pie 312
    Dutch apple (*Sara Lee*), ⅙ of 30-oz. pie 391
    lattice crust (*Christopher Edwards* Bak'd For You),
      ⅙ of 38-oz. pie 528
    natural juice (*Mrs. Smith's*), ⅙ of 37-oz. pie 477
apple tart (*Mrs. Smith's*), ⅙ of 26-oz. pie 250

lemon, continued

cream (*Morton*), ⅙ of 16-oz. pie 180

krunch (*Mrs. Smith's*), ⅙ of 26-oz. pie 380

meringue (*Mrs. Smith's*), ⅙ of 20-oz. pie 260

meringue, cond.

   (*Christopher Edwards*), ⅙ of 34-oz. pie 504

yogurt (*Mrs. Smith's*), ⅙ of 16-oz. pie 200

mince, (*Morton*), ⅙ of 24-oz. pie 310

mince (*Mrs. Smith's*), ⅙ of 26-oz. pie 333

peach:

   (*Banquet*), ⅙ of 20-oz. pie 219

   (*Morton*), ⅙ of 24-oz. pie 280

   (*Mrs. Smith's*), ⅙ of 26-oz. pie 298

   (*Sara Lee*), ⅙ of 31-oz. pie 432

   natural juice (*Mrs. Smith's*), ⅙ of 37-oz. pie 462

Neopolitan cream (*Morton*), ⅙ of 16-oz. pie 190

pecan (*Mrs. Smith's*), ⅙ of 24-oz. pie 430

pecan, southern

   (*Christopher Edwards* Bak'd For You), ⅙ of 32-oz. pie. .597

pineapple (*Mrs. Smith's*), ⅙ of 26-oz. pie 300

pumpkin:

   (*Banquet*), ⅙ of 20-oz. pie 208

   (*Morton*), ⅙ of 24-oz. pie 230

   (*Mrs. Smith's*), ⅙ of 25-oz pie 240

   (*Sara Lee*), ⅙ of 45-oz. pie 473

strawberry:

   cream (*Banquet*), ⅙ of 14-oz. pie 169

   cream (*Morton*), ⅙ of 16-oz. pie 180

   yogurt (*Mrs. Smith's*), ⅙ of 16-oz. pie 200

strawberry-rhubarb (*Mrs. Smith's*), ⅙ of 26-oz. pie 315

strawberry-rhubarb, natural juice

   (*Mrs. Smith's*), ⅙ of 37-oz. pie 448

* *Note variation in pie sizes*

PIES, MIXES*

See also "Dessert Pies, Frozen," and "Snack Cakes & Pies, Packaged" and "Pastries, Cakes & Pies, Frozen & Refrigerated"

CALORIES

banana cream (*Jell-O*), ⅙ of 8" pie** 110
Boston cream (*Betty Crocker*), ⅛ pie or pkg. 260
cheesecake:
   (*Jell-O*), ⅛ of 8" pie 250
   (*Royal*), ⅛ of pie or pkg. 230
   creamy (*Pillsbury* No Bake), ⅙ of pie or pkg. 410
chocolate cream (*Pillsbury* No Bake), ⅙ of pie or pkg. ...410
coconut cream (*Jell-O*), ⅙ of 8" pie** 110
lemon (*Jell-O*), ⅙ of 9" pie** 180
lemon chiffon (*Pillsbury* No Bake), ⅙ of pie or pkg. 330
vanilla marble (*Pillsbury* No Bake), ⅙ of pie or pkg. 390

   * *Prepared according to package directions*
  ** *Prepared according to package directions with whole milk—does not include crust*

SNACK CAKES & PIES, PACKAGED,

one piece*, except as noted
See also "Pastries, Cakes & Pies, Frozen & Refrigerated," "Snack and Coffee Cakes, Mixes" and "Cookies"

CALORIES

apricot cake (*El Molino*), 2-oz. piece 250
banana (*Hostess Suzy Q's*), 2¼-oz. piece 240
brownie:
   (*Hostess*), 1¼-oz. piece 150
   (*Hostess*), 2-oz. piece 240
   carob (*El Molino*), 2-oz. piece 220
butterscotch (*Tastykake Krimpets*), 1¾-oz. pkg. 192

Snack Cakes & Pies, Packaged, continued

chocolate or devil's food:
    (*Drake's Devil Dogs*), 1½-oz. piece 180
    (*Drake's Funny Bones*), 1¼-oz. piece 160
    (*Drake's Ring Ding Jr.*), 1¼-oz. piece 165
    (*Drake's Swiss Roll*), 3-oz. piece 350
    (*Drake's Yodels*), .9-oz. piece 120
    (*Hostess Big Wheels*), 1⅓-oz. piece 170
    (*Hostess Choco-Dile*), 2.2-oz. piece 250
    (*Hostess Ding Dongs*), 1⅓-oz. piece 170
    (*Hostess Ho Ho's*), 1-oz. piece 120
    (*Tastykake Chocolate Cream Tempty*), 2-oz. pkg. 197
    (*Tastykake Chocolate Creamies*), 2⅓-oz. pkg. 257
    (*Tastykake Chocolate Juniors*), 2¾-oz. pkg. 307
    (*Tastykake Chocolate Tasty Klairs*), 4-oz. pkg. 435
    (*Tastykake Kandy Kake*), 1⅓-oz. pkg. 181
cinnamon crumb cake (*El Molino*), 2-oz. piece 250
coffee cake:
    (*Drake Junior*), 1.1-oz. piece 125
    (*Hostess Crumb Cakes*), 1¼-oz. piece 130
    (*Tastykake Koffee Kake*), 2-oz. pkg. 247
    (*Tastykake Koffee Kake Juniors*), 2½-oz. pkg. 313
coconut (*Tastykake Coconut Juniors*), 2¾-oz. pkg. 330
coconut patties (*Frito-Lay's Choc-o-Roon*), 2-oz. pkg. 290
cup cakes:
    chocolate (*Drake's*), 1½-oz. piece 170
    chocolate (*Drake's Yankee Doodles*), 1-oz. piece 105
    chocolate (*Hostess*), 1¾-oz. piece 160
    chocolate (*Tastykake*), 2-oz. pkg. 200
    orange (*Hostess*), 1½-oz. piece 150
date cake (*El Molino*), 2-oz. piece 240
doughnuts:
    cinnamon (*Hostess*), 1-oz. piece 110
    enrobed (*Hostess*), 1-oz. piece 130
    krunch (*Hostess*), 1-oz. piece 100
    old fashioned (*Hostess*), 1½-oz. piece 170

doughnuts, continued

plain (*Hostess*), 1-oz. piece 110
powdered sugar (*Hostess*), 1-oz. piece 110
fruit and spice cake (*El Molino*), 2-oz. piece 230
granola cake (*El Molino*), 2-oz. piece 220
honey and bran cake (*El Molino*), 1½-oz. piece 160
honeybun (*Hostess*), 4¾-oz. piece 580
(*Hostess Twinkies*), 1½-oz. piece 140
(*Hostess Sno Ball*), 1½-oz. piece 140
(*Hostess Tiger Tail*), 2.2-oz. piece 215
jelly (*Tastykake* Jelly Krimpets), 1¾-oz. pkg. 168
lemon (*Tastykake* Lemon Juniors), 2¾-oz. pkg. 297
oatmeal, creme filled (*Frito-Lay's*), 2-oz. pkg. 260
oatmeal raisin bar (*Tastykake*), 1¾-oz. pkg. 267
pie:

apple (*Drake's*), 2-oz. piece 200
apple (*Hostess*), 4½-oz. piece 400
apple (*Tastykake*), 4-oz. pkg. 348
apple, French (*Tastykake*), 4¼-oz. pkg. 405
berry (*Hostess*), 4½-oz. piece 400
blueberry (*Hostess*), 4½-oz. piece 390
blueberry (*Tastykake*), 4-oz. pkg. 366
cherry (*Drake's*), 2-oz. piece 200
cherry (*Hostess*), 4½-oz. piece 420
cherry (*Tastykake*), 4-oz. pkg. 381
lemon (*Drake's*), 2-oz. piece 200
lemon (*Hostess*), 4½-oz. piece 420
lemon (*Tastykake*), 4-oz. pkg. 370
peach (*Hostess*), 4½-oz. piece 400
peach (*Tastykake*), 4-oz. pkg. 349
pecan (*Frito-Lay's*), 3-oz. pkg. 350
pound cake, butter (*Drake's*), 1-oz. piece 100
pound cake, butter, marble (*Drake's*), 1-oz. piece 100
raspberry crumb cake (*El Molino*), 2-oz. piece 260
spice cake (*Tastykake* Spice Creamie), 2¾-oz. pkg. 272
strawberry-filled cake (*El Molino*), 2-oz. piece 240

* *Note variations in sizes*

PASTRIES, CAKES & PIES,
FROZEN & REFRIGERATED, one piece*
See also "Dessert Cakes, Frozen" and "Dessert Pies, Frozen"

CALORIES

brownie, chocolate, frozen (*Sara Lee*), 1.62-oz. piece 200
buns:
    caramel sticky, frozen (*Sara Lee*), 1.1-oz. piece 118
    honey, frozen (*Morton*), 2.3-oz. piece 230
    honey, mini, frozen (*Morton*), 1.3-oz. piece 130
cheesecake:
    cherry, frozen (*Morton*), 6½-oz. piece 470
    cream, frozen (*Morton*), 6½-oz. piece 480
    pineapple, frozen (*Morton*), 6½-oz. piece 470
    strawberry, frozen (*Morton*), 6½-oz. piece 480
crumb cake, blueberry, frozen (*Sara Lee*), 1¾-oz. piece ..155
crumb cake, French, frozen (*Sara Lee*), 1.7-oz. piece 172
cupcakes:
    chocolate, frozen (*Sara Lee*), 1¾-oz. piece 190
    double chocolate, frozen (*Sara Lee*), 1¾-oz. piece 191
    yellow, frozen (*Sara Lee*), 1¾-oz. piece 174
danish:
    apple, frozen (*Sara Lee*), 1.3-oz. piece 121
    caramel, w/nuts, refrigerator (*Pillsbury*), 1 piece** 160
    cheese, frozen (*Sara Lee*), 1.3-oz. piece 131
    cinnamon raisin, frozen (*Sara Lee*), 1.3-oz. piece 146
    cinnamon raisin, refrigerator (*Pillsbury*), 1 piece 150
    orange, refrigerator (*Pillsbury*), 1 piece** 130
devil's food cake, frozen
    (*Morton Donut Holes*), 1½-oz. piece 160
doughnuts:
    Bavarian creme, frozen (*Morton*), 2-oz. piece 180
    Boston creme, frozen (*Morton*), 2⅓-oz. piece 210
    chocolate iced, frozen (*Morton*), 1½-oz. piece 150
    glazed, frozen (*Morton*), 1½-oz. piece 150
    jelly, frozen (*Morton*), 1.8-oz. piece 180
    mini, frozen (*Morton*), 1.1-oz. piece 120

Pastries, Cakes & Pies, Frozen, continued

dumpling, apple, frozen (*Pepperidge Farm*), 1 piece** 280
eclair, chocolate, frozen (*Rich's*), 2.62-oz. piece 291
honey wheat cake, frozen
  (*Morton Donut Holes*), 1½-oz. piece 160
muffins, sweet:
  blueberry, frozen
    (*Howard Johnson Toastees*), 1 piece** 121
  blueberry, frozen (*Morton*), 1½-oz. piece 110
  blueberry, rounds, frozen (*Morton*), 1.58-oz. piece 120
  corn, frozen (*Howard Johnson Toastees*), 1 piece** 112
  corn, frozen (*Morton*), 1½-oz. piece 130
  corn, rounds, frozen (*Morton*), 1⅔-oz. piece 130
  orange, frozen (*Howard Johnson Toastees*), 1 piece** ..127
pie tarts:
  apple, frozen (*Pepperidge Farm*), 1 piece** 280
  blueberry, frozen (*Pepperidge Farm*), 1 piece** 280
  cherry, frozen (*Pepperidge Farm*), 1 piece** 280
  lemon, frozen (*Pepperidge Farm*), 1 piece** 320
  raspberry, frozen (*Pepperidge Farm*), 1 piece** 320
pies:
  apple, frozen (*Morton*), 8-oz. piece 590
  apple, Dutch, frozen (*Morton*), 7.8-oz. piece 600
  banana cream, frozen (*Morton*), 3½-oz. piece 230
  blueberry, frozen (*Morton*), 8-oz. piece 580
  cherry, frozen (*Morton*), 8-oz. piece 590
  chocolate cream, frozen (*Morton*), 3½-oz. piece 260
  coconut cream, frozen (*Morton*), 3½-oz. piece 260
  coconut custard, frozen (*Morton*), 6½-oz. piece 370
  lemon cream, frozen (*Morton*), 3½-oz. piece 240
puffs, vanilla, frozen (*Rich's*), 2.17-oz. piece 167
rolls, sweet:
  apple crunch, frozen (*Sara Lee*), 1-oz. piece 102
  caramel pecan, frozen (*Sara Lee*), 1.3-oz. piece 154
  cinnamon, frozen (*Sara Lee*), .9-oz. piece 100

rolls, sweet, continued

   cinnamon, iced, refrigerator (*Ballard*), 1 piece** 100
   cinnamon, iced, refrigerator
      (*Hungry Jack Butter Tastin'*), 1 piece** 145
   cinnamon, iced, refrigerator (*Pillsbury*), 1 piece** 115
   honey, frozen (*Sara Lee*), 1-oz. piece 112
strudel, apple, frozen (*Pepperidge Farm*), 3-oz. piece 250
turnovers:
   apple, frozen (*Pepperidge Farm*), 1 piece** 310
   apple, refrigerator (*Pillsbury*), 1 piece** 180
   blueberry, frozen (*Pepperidge Farm*), 1 piece** 320
   blueberry, refrigerator (*Pillsbury*), 1 piece** 180
   cherry, frozen (*Pepperidge Farm*), 1 piece** 340
   cherry, refrigerator (*Pillsbury*), 1 piece** 190
   peach, frozen (*Pepperidge Farm*), 1 piece** 320
   raspberry, frozen (*Pepperidge Farm*), 1 piece** 340
vanilla cake, frozen (*Morton Donut Holes*), 1½-oz. piece..160

* *Note variation in size*
** *As packaged*

SNACK & COFFEE CAKES, MIXES*
See also "Snack Cakes & Pies, Packaged,"
"Pies, Mixes" and "Dessert Cakes, Mixes"

                                                    CALORIES

apple raisin, spicy
   (*Duncan Hines* Moist & Easy), 1/9 cake 180
applesauce raisin
   (*Betty Crocker Snackin' Cake*), 1/9 pkg. 200
banana nut (*Duncan Hines* Moist & Easy), 1/9 cake 200
banana walnut (*Betty Crocker Snackin' Cake*), 1/9 pkg. ...200
brownies, *see "Cookies, Mixes," page 229*
cheesecake, *see "Pies, Mixes," page 216*

Snack & Coffee Cakes, Mixes, continued

chocolate:

    (*Betty Crocker* Pudding Cake), ⅙ pkg. ....:.230

    chip, double (*Duncan Hines* Moist & Easy), 1/9 cake ...180

    chip, fudge (*Betty Crocker Snackin' Cake*), 1/9 pkg. ...220

    chip, golden (*Betty Crocker Snackin' Cake*), 1/9 pkg. ..220

    devil's food, chocolate frosting

        (*Betty Crocker Stir 'n Frost*), ⅙ pkg. 280

    fudge, vanilla frosting

        (*Betty Crocker Stir 'n Frost*), ⅙ pkg. 290

chocolate almond (*Betty Crocker Snackin' Cake*), 1/9 pkg..210

coconut pecan (*Betty Crocker Snackin' Cake*), 1/9 pkg ..220

coffee cake:

    (*Aunt Jemima* Easy Mix), ⅛ cake 170

    apple cinnamon (*Pillsbury*), ⅛ cake 235

    butter pecan (*Pillsbury*), ⅛ cake 310

    cinnamon streusel (*Pillsbury*), ⅛ cake 250

    sour cream (*Pillsbury*), ⅛ cake 270

cup cake (*Flako*), 1 cake 150

date nut (*Betty Crocker Snackin' Cake*), 1/9 pkg. ....210.

devil's food, *see "chocolate," above*

lemon (*Betty Crocker* Pudding Cake), ⅙ cake 230

lemon, w/lemon frosting

    (*Betty Crocker Stir 'n Frost*), ⅙ pkg. 230

pineapple upside-down, w/topping

    (*Betty Crocker*), 1/9 cake 270

spice, w/vanilla frosting

    (*Betty Crocker Stir 'n Frost*), ⅙ pkg. 270

spice raisin (*Betty Crocker Snackin' Cake*), 1/9 pkg. 200

white, w/milk chocolate frosting

    (*Betty Crocker Stir 'n Frost*), ⅙ pkg. 230

yellow, w/chocolate frosting

    (*Betty Crocker Stir 'n Frost*), ⅙ pkg. 230

* *Prepared according to package directions, without frosting unless indicated*

COOKIES, one piece*
See also "Cookies, Frozen, Mixes & Refrigerator"

CALORIES

almond flavor:
    (*Stella D'Oro* Almond Toast—Mandel) 55
    (*Stella D'Oro* Breakfast Treats) 105
    (*Stella D'Oro* Chinese Dessert) 165
animal crackers:
    (*Barnum's*) 12
    (*Keebler*) 12
    (*Sunshine*) 11
    honey (*El Molino*) 14
    iced (*Keebler 100's*) 24
anise flavor:
    (*Stella D'Oro* Anisette Sponge) 49
    (*Stella D'Oro* Anisette Toast) 43
    (*Stella D'Oro* Anisette Toast—large) 129
    (*Stella D'Oro* Roman Egg Biscuits) 128
apple (*Stella D'Oro* Apple Pastry) 92
arrowroot (*Nabisco*) 60
assorted (*Stella D'Oro* Hostess) 43
assorted (*Stella D'Oro* Lady Stella) 40
bran (*El Molino* Breakfast Biscuit) 20
brown edge (*FFV*) 40
brown edge (*Nabisco*) 28
brown sugar, *see "sugar," below*
butter flavor:
    (*Jacob's Petit Beurre*) 110
    (*Keebler 100's*) 65
    (*Nabisco*) 23
    (*Pepperidge Farm Bordeaux*) 37
    (*Pepperidge Farm Chessman*) 43
    (*Sunshine*) 28
carob chip (*El Molino*) 80
carob, wheat-free (*El Molino*) 80

shortbread, continued

   pecan (*Nabisco*) 80
   pecan (*Pecan Sandies*) 86
(*Social Tea Biscuits*) 20
spice (*Keebler Spiced Windmills*) 60
spice (*Nabisco* Wafers) 33
(*Stella D'Oro Angel Puffs*) 18
(*Stella D'Oro Angelica Goodies*) 101
(*Stella D'Oro Como Delights*) 143
(*Stella D'Oro Love Cookies*) 110
(*Stella D'Oro Royal Nuggets*) 1
(*Stella D'Oro Sorrento*) 58
(*Stella D'Oro Taste of Vienna*) 85
sugar:
   (*Nabisco* Sugar Rings) 70
   (*Pepperidge Farm*).................................53
   brown (*Pepperidge Farm*) 50
sugar wafers:
   (*Bisco*) 19
   (*Bisco* Waffle Cremes) 43
   (*Sunshine*) 42
   chocolate covered (*Nabisco* Creme Wafer Sticks) 50
   iced (*Sunshine Yum Yums*) 83
sunflower-raisin (*Pepperidge Farm*) 53
toy cookies (*Sunshine*) 13
vanilla:
   (*FFV* Wafers) 18
   (*Keebler* Wafers) 19
   (*Nilla* Wafers) 19
   (*Stella D'Oro Margherite*) 74
   (*Stella D'Oro* Roman Egg Biscuit) 128
   (*Sunshine Dixie Vanilla*) 58
   (*Sunshine* Wafers) 14
   chocolate center (*Stella D'Oro* Swiss Fudge) 67
   creme wafer, low-calorie (*Sug'r Like*) 49
   low-calorie (*Sug'r Like*) 40
   rolls (*Pepperidge Farm Pirouette*) 40

vanilla, continued

    rolls, chocolate laced (*Pepperidge Farm Pirouette*) 40
    sandwich, chocolate filled (*Pepperidge Farm Brussels*) ...57
    sandwich, chocolate filled (*Pepperidge Farm Lido*) 95
    sandwich, chocolate filled (*Pepperidge Farm Milano*) 63
    wafer, chocolate covered (*Pepperidge Farm Orleans*) 33
wheat-free (*El Molino*) 80

---

* As packaged. Bear in mind that cookies are available in dozens of sizes and shapes; therefore, it is hard—indeed, just about impossible —to accurately compare the caloric content of different brands and types. (See "What You Should Know About Using This Book," pages 11–16)

COOKIES, FROZEN, MIXES & REFRIGERATOR,
one piece, except as noted
See also "Cookies"

                                                CALORIES

brownie:
    mix* (*Betty Crocker* Fudge), 1/16 of pkg. 150
    mix* (*Betty Crocker* Fudge Family Size), 1/24 of pkg...130
    mix* (*Betty Crocker* German Chocolate), 1/16 of pkg...150
    mix* (*Betty Crocker* Supreme Fudge), 1/24 of pkg. 120
    mix* (*Duncan Hines* Double Fudge—Cake or Chewy) ..140
    mix* (*Pillsbury*), 1½" square 65
    mix* (*Pillsbury* Family Size), 1½" square 75
    chocolate chip butterscotch, mix*
      (*Betty Crocker*), 1/16 of pkg. 130
    w/walnuts, mix* (*Betty Crocker*), 1/16 of pkg. 160
    w/walnuts, mix*
      (*Betty Crocker* Family Size), 1/24 of pkg. 130
    w/walnuts, mix* (*Pillsbury*), 1½" square 65
    w/walnuts, mix* (*Pillsbury* Family Size), 1½" square ..80
    refrigerator (*Pillsbury* Slice 'N Bake Fudge) 130

Cookies, Frozen, Mixes & Refrigerator, continued

chocolate, mix*
  (*Betty Crocker Big Batch* Double Chocolate) 70
chocolate chip:
  frozen (*Mrs. Goodcookie*) 57
  mix* (*Betty Crocker Big Batch*) 75
  mix* (*Quaker*) 75
  low-calorie, mix* (*Dia-Mel*), 2″ cookie 50
  refrigerator (*Pillsbury Oven Lovin*) 57
  refrigerator (*Pillsbury* Slice 'N Bake) 53
  refrigerator (*Pillsbury* Slice 'N Bake Cookie Lover) 53
chocolate fudge, frozen (*Mrs. Goodcookie*) 57
coconut macaroon, mix*
  (*Betty Crocker* Dessert Mix), 1/24 of pkg. 80
date bar, mix* (*Betty Crocker*), 1/32 of pkg. 60
gingerbread, mix*
  (*Betty Crocker* Dessert Mix), 1/9 of pkg. 210
gingerbread, mix* (*Pillsbury*), 3″ square 190
oatmeal:
  mix* (*Betty Crocker Big Batch*) 70
  mix* (*Quaker*) 65
  low-calorie, mix* (*Dia-Mel*) 50
  refrigerator (*Pillsbury Oven Lovin*) 57
  refrigerator (*Pillsbury* Slice 'N Bake) 57
  w/raisins, frozen (*Mrs. Goodcookie*) 53
  w/raisins, refrigerator (*Pillsbury* Slice 'N Bake) 53
peanut butter:
  frozen (*Mrs. Goodcookie*) 60
  mix* (*Betty Crocker Big Batch*) 70
  mix* (*Quaker*) 75
  refrigerator (*Pillsbury Oven Lovin*) 60
  refrigerator (*Pillsbury* Slice 'N Bake) 53
  w/chips, mix* (*Betty Crocker Big Batch*) 70
sugar:
  frozen (*Mrs. Goodcookie*) 53
  mix* (*Betty Crocker Big Batch*) 65

sugar, continued
   refrigerator (*Pillsbury Oven Lovin*) 57
   refrigerator (*Pillsbury* Slice 'N Bake) 63
Vienna bar, mix*
   (*Betty Crocker* Vienna Dream Bar), 1/24 of pkg. 90

* *Prepared according to package directions*

TOASTER PASTRIES, one piece*

                                  CALORIES
all varieties (*Nabisco Toastettes*), 1.7-oz. pastry 190
apple, Dutch, frosted
   (*Kellogg's Danish Rings*), 1.5-oz. pastry 180
apple, Dutch, frosted
   (*Kellogg's Frosted Pop-Tarts*), 1.8-oz. pastry 210
blueberry:
   (*Kellogg's Pop-Tarts*), 1.8-oz. pastry 210
   frosted (*Kellogg's Danish Rings*), 1.5-oz. pastry 180
   frosted (*Kellogg's Frosted Pop-Tarts*), 1.8-oz. pastry ...210
brown sugar-cinnamon
   (*Kellogg's Pop-Tarts*), 1.8-oz. pastry 210
brown sugar-cinnamon, frosted
   (*Kellogg's Frosted Pop-Tarts*), 1.8-oz. pastry 210
cherry:
   (*Kellogg's Pop-Tarts*), 1.8-oz. pastry 210
   chip (*Kellogg's Pop-Tarts*), 1.8-oz. pastry 200
   frosted (*Kellogg's Danish Rings*), 1.5-oz. pastry 180
   frosted (*Kellogg's Frosted Pop-Tarts*), 1.8-oz. pastry ...210
chocolate chip (*Kellogg's Pop-Tarts*), 1.8-oz. pastry 200
chocolate fudge, frosted
   (*Kellogg's Frosted Pop-Tarts*), 1.8-oz. pastry 220
chocolate-vanilla creme, frosted
   (*Kellogg's Frosted Pop-Tarts*), 1.8-oz. pastry 210
grape, Concord (*Kellogg's Pop-Tarts*), 1.8-oz. pastry 210

Toaster Pastries, continued

grape, Concord, frosted
 (*Kellogg's Frosted Pop-Tarts*), 1.8-oz. pastry 210
raspberry (*Kellogg's Pop-Tarts*), 1.8-oz. pastry 210
raspberry, frosted
 (*Kellogg's Frosted Pop-Tarts*), 1.8-oz. pastry 210
strawberry:
 (*Kellogg's Pop-Tarts*), 1.8-oz. pastry 210
 frosted (*Kellogg's Danish Rings*), 1.5-oz. pastry 180
 frosted (*Kellogg's Frosted Pop-Tarts*), 1.8-oz. pastry ...210

* *As packaged; note variations in size*

FOOD STICKS & BARS, one piece*

CALORIES

caramel (*Pillsbury*), 1 stick 45
caramel nut (*Figurines*), 1 bar 138
chocolate:
 (*Figurines*), 1 bar 138
 (*Pillsbury*), 1 stick 45
 (*Slender*), 1 bar 138
 double (*Figurines*), 1 bar 138
chocolate caramel (*Figurines*), 1 bar 138
chocolate malt (*Pillsbury*), 1 stick 45
chocolate mint (*Figurines*), 1 bar 138
chocolate mint (*Pillsbury*), 1 stick 45
chocolate peanut butter (*Slender*), 1 bar 138
cinnamon (*Slender*), 1 bar 138
orange (*Pillsbury*), 1 stick 45
peanut butter (*Figurines*), 1 bar 138
raspberry (*Figurines*), 1 bar 138
vanilla (*Figurines*), 1 bar 138
vanilla (*Slender*), 1 bar 138

* *As packaged*

CAKE FROSTINGS, READY TO SPREAD,
1/12 of container, except as noted
See also "Cake Frostings, Mixes"

	CALORIES
butter pecan (*Betty Crocker Creamy Deluxe*)	170
cherry (*Betty Crocker Creamy Deluxe*)	170
chocolate and fudge:	
(*Betty Crocker Creamy Deluxe*)	170
double Dutch (*Pillsbury Frosting Supreme*)	160
dark Dutch fudge (*Betty Crocker Creamy Deluxe*)	170
fudge (*Pillsbury Frosting Supreme*)	160
milk chocolate (*Betty Crocker Creamy Deluxe*)	170
milk chocolate (*Pillsbury Frosting Supreme*)	160
nut (*Betty Crocker Creamy Deluxe*)	170
decorator, all colors (*Pillsbury*), 1 tbsp.	70
lemon (*Betty Crocker Sunkist Creamy Deluxe*)	170
lemon (*Pillsbury Frosting Supreme*)	160
orange (*Betty Crocker Creamy Deluxe*)	170
sour cream:	
chocolate (*Betty Crocker Creamy Deluxe*)	170
vanilla (*Pillsbury Frosting Supreme*)	160
white (*Betty Crocker Creamy Deluxe*)	160
strawberry (*Pillsbury Frosting Supreme*)	160
vanilla (*Betty Crocker Creamy Deluxe*)	170
vanilla (*Pillsbury Frosting Supreme*)	160

CAKE FROSTINGS, MIXES*,
1/12 of package
See also "Cake Frostings, Ready to Spread"

	CALORIES
banana (*Betty Crocker Chiquita* Fluffy)	170
butter (*Betty Crocker Butter Brickle* Fluffy)	170
butter pecan (*Betty Crocker* Fluffy)	170
caramel (*Pillsbury Rich 'n Easy*)	170
cherry, creamy (*Betty Crocker* Fluffy)	170

Cake Frostings, Mixes, continued

chocolate and fudge:
  dark fudge (*Betty Crocker*) 170
  double Dutch (*Pillsbury Rich 'n Easy*) 170
  double Dutch (*Pillsbury* Smooth and Creamy) 180
  fudge (*Betty Crocker*) 180
  fudge (*Pillsbury Rich 'n Easy*) 170
  .fudge (*Pillsbury* Smooth and Creamy) 180
  milk chocolate (*Betty Crocker*) 170
  milk chocolate (*Pillsbury Rich 'n Easy*) 170
  milk chocolate (*Pillsbury* Smooth and Creamy) 190
coconut almond (*Pillsbury*) 170
coconut pecan (*Betty Crocker* Fluffy) 140
coconut pecan (*Pillsbury*) 150
lemon:
  (*Betty Crocker Sunkist*) 170
  (*Pillsbury Rich 'n Easy*) 170
  (*Pillsbury* Smooth and Creamy) 180
sour cream, chocolate (*Betty Crocker*) 170
sour cream, white (*Betty Crocker*) 180
strawberry (*Pillsbury Rich 'n Easy*) 170
strawberry (*Pillsbury* Smooth and Creamy) 180
vanilla (*Pillsbury Rich 'n Easy*) 170
vanilla (*Pillsbury* Smooth and Creamy) 180
white:
  (*Betty Crocker* Fluffy) 60
  (*Pillsbury* Fluffy) 70
  creamy (*Betty Crocker* Fluffy) 190

* *Prepared according to package directions*

PIE FILLINGS, CANNED,
⅓ cup*, except as noted
See also "Custards, Puddings & Pie Fillings"

	CALORIES
apple (*Comstock*), 3½ oz.	110
apricot (*Comstock*)	100
banana cream (*Comstock*)	110
blueberry (*Comstock*)	100
butterscotch (*Comstock*)	110
cherry (*Comstock*)	100
chocolate (*Comstock*)	130
coconut cream (*Comstock*)	120
lemon (*Comstock*), 3½ oz.	150
mincemeat:	
(*Comstock*)	150
(*Borden None Such*)	220
with brandy and rum (*Borden None Such*)	220
peach (*Comstock*)	100
pineapple (*Comstock*)	100
pumpkin (*Comstock*), 4½ oz.	150
pumpkin (*Stokely-Van Camp*)	117
raisin (*Comstock*)	140
strawberry (*Comstock*)	100

* *Approximately 3½ ounces*

PASTRY SHELLS & PIE CRUSTS

	CALORIES
pastry sheet, frozen (*Pepperidge Farm*), 1 sheet*	570
pastry shell (*Stella D'Oro*), 1 shell*	149
patty shell, frozen (*Pepperidge Farm*), 1 shell*	240
pie crusts:	
frozen (*Mrs. Smith's*), ⅙ of 8″ crust	129
frozen (*Mrs. Smith's*), ⅙ of 9″ crust	233

pie crusts, continued

 * *As packaged*
** *Prepared according to package directions*

CHAPTER 19

NUT BUTTERS, JAMS AND JELLIES

NUT BUTTERS, one tablespoon,
except as noted

	CALORIES
almond butter (*Hain*)	95
cashew butter (*Hain*)	95
peanut butter:	
creamy or smooth (*Ann Page*)	105
creamy or smooth (*Jif*)	95
creamy or smooth (*Peter Pan*)	95
creamy or smooth (*Planters*)	95
creamy or smooth (*Smucker's*)	90
creamy or smooth (*Skippy/Skippy* Old Fashioned)	95
creamy or smooth (*Teddie*)	100
creamy or smooth (*Velvet*)	97
crunchy or chunk (*Ann Page*)	105
crunchy or chunk (*Jif*)	95
crunchy or chunk (*Peter Pan*)	95
crunchy or chunk (*Planters*)	95
crunchy or chunk (*Skippy/Skippy* Old Fashioned)	95
crunchy or chunk (*Smucker's*)	90
low-sodium (*Cellu*), ½ oz.	90
low-sodium (*Peter Pan*)	95
low-sodium (*S & W Nutradiet*)	93

peanut butter, continued
  natural (*Elam's*) 102
  natural (*Smucker's*) 103
peanut butter w/grape jelly
  (*Smucker's Goober Grape*), ½ oz. 63
sesame butter (*Hain*) 90

JAMS, JELLIES & PRESERVES,
one tablespoon

CALORIES

butter, apple:
  (*Bama*) 31
  (*Ma Brown*) 32
  (*Musselman's*) 33
  cider and spiced (*Smucker's*) 37
butter, peach (*Smucker's*) 45
jams:
  all flavors (*Ann Page*) 43
  all flavors (*Smucker's*) 53
  all flavors, except apricot, peach, pear and plum (*Bama*) ..54
  all flavors, low-calorie (*S & W Nutradiet*) 12
  apricot, peach, pear and plum (*Bama*) 51
  grape (*Welch's*) 53
  strawberry (*Musselman's*) 54
  strawberry (*Welch's*) 53
jellies:
  all flavors (*Ann Page*) 43
  all flavors (*Bama*) 51
  all flavors (*Crosse & Blackwell*) 51
  all flavors (*Kraft*) 46
  all flavors (*Ma Brown*) 49
  all flavors (*Musselman's*) 53
  all flavors (*Smucker's*) 53
  all flavors, low-calorie (*Dia-Mel*) 6

CHAPTER 20

SYRUPS, TOPPINGS AND SWEET BAKING INGREDIENTS

SUGAR, one tablespoon
See also "Honey, Molasses & Syrups"

	CALORIES
brown, firm-packed (all brands)	52
granulated (all brands)	46
powdered, stirred (all brands)	31

HONEY, MOLASSES & SYRUPS,
one tablespoon
*See also "Sugar," "Dessert Toppings & Syrups"
and "Sweet Flavorings & Extracts"*

	CALORIES
honey, strained or extracted (all brands)	64
molasses, dark (*Brer Rabbit*)	53
molasses, light (*Brer Rabbit*)	60
syrups:	
corn, dark (*Karo*)	60
corn, light (*Karo*)	60
maple, pure (*Cary's*)	50
maple, blended (*Log Cabin*)	52
maple, imitation (*Karo*)	55
maple, imitation, low-calorie (*S & W Nutradiet*)	15
maple, low-calorie (*Cary's*)	0

Honey, Molasses & Syrups, continued

pancake syrup, maple-flavored:

    (*Aunt Jemima*) 53

    (*Golden Griddle*) 50

    (*Happy Jack*) 50

    (*Karo*) 60

    (*Log Cabin* Country Kitchen) 50

    (*Smucker's*) 43

    buttered (*Log Cabin*) 54

    buttered (*Mrs. Butterworth's*) 53

    w/honey (*Log Cabin* Maple Honey) 50

    low-calorie (*Dia-Mel*) 16

    low-calorie (*Diet Delight*) 6

    low-calorie (*Featherweight*) 16

DESSERT TOPPINGS & SYRUPS,
one tablespoon, except as noted
See also "Honey, Molasses & Syrups"

	CALORIES
black cherry concentrate (*Hain*)	46
blueberry, low-calorie (*Featherweight*)	14
butterscotch (*Smucker's*)	70
caramel (*Smucker's*)	70

chocolate:

    (*Bosco* Milk Amplifier) 50

    (*Hershey* Syrup) 40

    (*Milk Mate*) 50

    (*Smucker's*) 65

    low-calorie (*Dia-Mel*) 15

    low-calorie (*Diet Delight*) 8

chocolate fudge:

    (*Hershey* Topping) 50

    (*Kraft*) 46

    (*Smucker's*) 65

    (*Smucker's* Swiss Milk) 70

Dessert Toppings & Syrups, continued

chocolate mint fudge *(Smucker's)* 70
cranberry concentrate *(Hain)* 19
cream, *see "Whipped," below*
fruit *(Smucker's)* 50
hard sauce *(Crosse & Blackwell)* 64
marshmallow creme *(Kraft)* 21
peanut butter caramel *(Smucker's)* 75
pecans, in syrup *(Smucker's)* 65
pineapple *(Smucker's)* 65
strawberry *(Smucker's)* 60
walnuts, in syrup *(Smucker's)* 65
whipped:
    cream, aerosol *(Reddi-Wip)* 8
    non-dairy *(Birds Eye Cool Whip)* 14
    non-dairy *(Pet)* 14
    non-dairy *(Richwhip)* 10
    non-dairy *(Rich's Spoon 'N Serve)*, ¼ .oz.............24
    non-dairy, aerosol *(Lucky Whip)* 12
    non-dairy, aerosol *(Rich's)*, ¼ oz. 20
    non-dairy, mix* *(Dream Whip)* 8
    non-dairy, mix* *(D-Zerta)* 8

* *Prepared according to package directions*

SWEET FLAVORINGS & EXTRACTS*,
one teaspoon
See also "Honey, Molasses & Syrups"
and "Dessert Toppings & Syrups"

                                              CALORIES

almond:
    extract *(Virginia Dare)* 7
    extract, pure *(Durkee)* 13
    extract, pure *(Ehlers)* 12
anise extract, pure *(Ehlers)* 26
anise extract, imitation *(Durkee)* 16

Sweet Flavorings & Extracts, continued

banana extract, imitation (*Durkee*) 15
banana extract, imitation (*Ehlers*) 20
black walnut flavor, imitation (*Durkee*) 4
brandy extract, imitation (*Durkee*) 15
brandy flavor, pure (*Ehlers*) 16
cherry extract, pure (*Burton's*) 9
cherry extract, imitation (*Ehlers*) 16
chocolate extract, imitation (*Durkee*) 7
chocolate flavor, imitation (*Ehlers*) 10
coconut flavor, imitation (*Durkee*) 8
coconut flavor, imitation (*Ehlers*) 17
coffee flavor, pure (*Burton's*) 9
grenadine (*Garnier*) 17
grenadine (*Holland House*) 15
lemon:
    extract (*Virginia Dare*) 14
    extract, pure (*Ehlers*) 30
    extract, imitation (*Durkee*) 17
maple extract, imitation (*Durkee*) 6
maple flavor, imitation (*Ehlers*) 9
orange:
    extract (*Virginia Dare*) 15
    extract, pure (*Ehlers*) 30
    extract, imitation (*Durkee*) 14
orgeat syrup (*Garnier*) 17
peppermint extract, pure (*Burton's*) 12
peppermint extract, pure (*Ehlers*) 24
pineapple:
    extract, imitation (*Ehlers*) 14
    flavor, pure (*Burton's*) 12
    flavor, imitation (*Durkee*) 9
raspberry:
    extract, pure (*Burton's*) 8
    extract, imitation (*Burton's*) 10
    extract, imitation (*Ehlers*) 14
rose extract, pure (*Burton's*) 9

Sweet Flavorings & Extracts, continued

rum:

  extract, imitation (*Burton's*) 11

  extract, imitation (*Durkee*) 14

  flavor, pure (*Ehlers*) 19

strawberry:

  extract, pure (*Burton's*) 10

  extract, imitation (*Durkee*) 12

  extract, imitation (*Ehlers*) 16

vanilla:

  extract (*Virginia Dare*) 7

  extract, pure (*Durkee*) 8

  extract, pure (*Ehlers*) 13

  extract, imitation (*Durkee*) 3

  extract, imitation (*Gold Medal*) ....trace

* *Note: If a flavoring which contains alcohol is added to a recipe
  before cooking, the alcohol (which frequently contributes a major
  portion of the calories) will be evaporated and the calories reduced.*

MISCELLANEOUS SWEET BAKING
INGREDIENTS, one ounce, except as noted

	CALORIES
butterscotch (*Nestlé* Morsels)	150
chocolate:	
baking (*Hershey*)	190
milk (*Hershey* Chips)	147
milk (*Nestlé* Morsels)	150
pre-melted (*Nestlé Choco-Bake*)	170
semisweet (*Baker's*)	130
semisweet (*Baker's* Chips)	130
semisweet (*Ghirardelli* Chips)	150
semisweet (*Hershey* Chips/Mini Chips)	147
semisweet (*Nestlé* Morsels)	150
sweet (*Baker's* German)	130
unsweetened (*Baker's*)	140

CHAPTER 21

CANDY AND CHEWING GUM

CANDY

CALORIES

almonds, w/milk chocolate, *see "chocolate w/fruit
  and/or nuts," below*
(*Baby Ruth*), 1.8-oz. bar 260
bridge mix (*Nabisco*), 1 oz. 125
bridge mix (*Nabisco*), 1 piece* 9
(*Black Cow* Sucker), 1 oz. 103
(*Butterfinger*), 1.6-oz. bar 220
(*Butternut*), 1.75-oz. bar 230
(*Butternut*), 1.5-oz. bar 194
butterscotch:
  (*Nestlé* Morsels), 1 oz. 150
  (*Rothchild's*), 1 piece* 19
  drops (*Nabisco* Skimmers), 1 oz. 116
  drops (*Nabisco* Skimmers), 1 piece* 25
candy corn (*Heide*), 1 piece* 4
(*CaraCoa Nuggets*), 1 oz. 140
caramel:
  (*CaraCoa*), 1 oz. 110
  (*Pearson* Caramel Nip), 1 oz. 125
  (*Whirligigs*), .22-oz. piece 26
  chocolate (*Sugar Daddy* Junior), .45-oz. piece 51
  chocolate center (*Tootsie* Pops/Pop Drops), 1 oz. ...113

caramel, continued

vanilla (*Sugar Babies*), 1 oz. 117
vanilla (*Sugar Babies*), .05-oz. piece 6
vanilla (*Sugar Daddy*), 1.07-oz. piece 121
vanilla (*Sugar Daddy* Giant), 1-lb. piece 1806
vanilla (*Sugar Daddy* Junior), .45-oz. piece 50
vanilla (*Sugar Daddy* Nuggets), .43-oz. piece 48
vanilla (*Sugar Mama*), .84-oz. piece 101

caramel, chocolate-covered:

(*Milk Duds*), 1 oz. 111
(*Pom Poms*), 1 oz. 126
(*Pom Poms*), 1 piece* 14
(*Rolo*), 1 oz. or 5 pieces 140

carob-coated bars:

(*CaraCoa* Milk Free), 1-oz. bar 145
(*CaraCoa* Natural), 1-oz. bar 160
(*Tiger's Milk*), 2-oz. bar 250
crunchy (*CaraCoa*), ⅞-oz. bar 140
fruit and nut (*CaraCoa*), 1-oz. bar 155
mint (*CaraCoa*), 1-oz. bar 160
peanut (*CaraCoa*), 1-oz. bar 160
peanut butter (*Tiger's Milk*), 1.7-oz. bar 210
peanut butter and honey (*Tiger's Milk*), 1.7-oz. bar 210
peanut butter and jelly (*Tiger's Milk*), 1.7-oz. bar 210
orange (*CaraCoa*), 1-oz. bar 160

cherries:

dark chocolate covered (*Nabisco/Welch's*), 1 oz. 113
dark chocolate covered (*Nabisco/Welch's*), 1 piece* 67
milk chocolate covered (*Nabisco/Welch's*), 1 oz. 112
milk chocolate covered (*Nabisco/Welch's*), 1 piece* 66

chocolate, solid:

milk (*Cadbury*), 1 oz. 151
milk (*Ghirardelli* Bars), 1 oz. 150
milk (*Ghirardelli* Block), 1 oz. 149
milk (*Hershey*), 1.2-oz. bar 180
milk (*Hershey* Chips), 1.5 oz. or ¼ cup 220

chocolate, solid, continued

milk (*Hershey* Kisses), 1 oz. or 6 pieces 150
milk (*Nabisco* Stars), 1 oz. or 10 pieces 152
milk (*Nestlé*), 1 oz. 150
mint (*Ghirardelli*), 1 oz. 150
semisweet (*Eagle*), 1 oz. 149
semisweet (*Ghirardelli* Chips), 1 oz. 150
semisweet (*Hershey* Chips), 1.5 oz. or ¼ cup 220
semisweet (*Hershey* Mini Chips), 1.5 oz. or ¼ cup 220
semisweet (*Hershey Special Dark*), 1.2-oz. bar 180
semisweet (*Lindt Excellence*), 1 oz. 162
semisweet (*Nestlé* Morsels), 1 oz. 150
semisweet, w/vanilla (*Lindt*), 1 oz. 163
chocolate, w/caramel (*Cadbury Caramello*), 1 oz. 144
chocolate, candy coated:
    (*M & M's*), 1.5-oz. pkg. 215
    (*M & M's*), 1-oz. pkg. 138
    (*M & M's* Fun Size), .63-oz. pkg. 88
chocolate-coated candy, *see specific kinds (fudge, coconut,
    peanuts, etc.)*
chocolate, w/crisps:
    (*Ghirardelli*), 1 oz. 150
    (*Krackel*), 1.2-oz. bar 180
    (*Nestlé Crunch*), 1 oz. 150
chocolate, w/fruit and/or nuts:
    w/almonds (*Cadbury*), 1 oz. 155
    w/almonds (*Ghirardelli*), 1 oz. 152
    w/almonds (*Hershey*), 1.15-oz. bar 180
    w/almonds (*Nestlé*), 1 oz. 150
    w/almonds, toasted (*Hershey Golden Almond*), 1 oz. ..160
    w/Brazil nuts (*Cadbury*), 1 oz. 156
    w/fruit and nuts (*Cadbury*), 1 oz. 152
    w/fruit and nuts (*Chunky*), 1 oz. 135
    w/hazel nuts (*Cadbury*), 1 oz. 155
    w/peanuts (*Mr. Goodbar*), 1.5-oz. bar 230
    w/raisins (*Ghirardelli*), 1 oz. 142

Candy, continued

coconut, chocolate covered:
 (*Mounds*), 1 oz. 147
 (*Nabisco* Cocoanut Squares), .54-oz. piece 64
 (*Welch's*), 1.07-oz. bar 132
 w/almonds (*Almond Joy*), 1 oz. 151
coffee (*Pearson* Coffee Nip), 1 oz. 125
cough drops (*Halls*—Square and Oval), 1 piece* 15
crisps, chocolate covered, w/caramel (*Caravelle*), 1 oz. ..137
crisps, chocolate covered, w/caramel (*$100,000*), 1 oz. ...140
dates, carob coated (*CaraCoa*), 1 oz. 125
(*Forever Yours*), 1.37-oz. bar 175
fruit chews (*Starburst*), 1.68-oz. pkg. 186
fruit chews (*Starburst*), 1-oz. pkg. 113
fruit roll, *see "Fruit, Dried," page 75*
fudge:
 (*Nabisco Home Style*), .7-oz. bar 90
 chocolate covered (*Welch's*), 1.07-oz. bar 144
 w/nuts (*Nabisco*), .54-oz. bar 70
 w/nuts (*Nabisco* Squares), 1 oz. 132
 w/nuts (*Nabisco* Squares), 1 piece* 70
(*Good & Fruity*), 1.5-oz. pkg. 136
gum candy, *see "jellied and gum candy," below*
hard candy (*see also specific flavors*):
 all flavors (*Bonomo*), 1 oz. 110
 all flavors (*Jolly Rancher Stix* Bars), 1 oz. 102
 all flavors (*Jolly Rancher Stix* Kisses), 1 oz. 110
 all flavors (*Reed's*), 1 oz. 110
 all flavors, low-calorie (*Sug'r Like*), 1 piece* 12
(*Heide* Chocolate Babies), 1 piece* 9
(*Heide* Red Hot Dollars), 1 piece* 15
(*Heide* Witchcraft), 1 piece* 5
(*Heide* Wet'm 'n Wear'm), 1 piece* 15
honey nougat (*Bit-O-Honey*), 1 oz. 116
jellied and gum candy:
 (*Chuckles* Variety Pack), 2-oz. pkg. 205
 (*Chuckles Ju-Jubes*), 1 oz. 103

jellied and gum candy, continued

    (*Heide Jujubes*), 1 piece* 3
    (*Just Born*), 1.25 oz. 117
    (*Mason Dots*), 1 oz. 95
    (*Mason Crows*), 1 oz. 95
    beans (*Heide*), 1 piece* 9
    eggs (*Chuckles*), 1 oz. 109
    eggs (*Chuckles*), 1 piece* 10
    fruit flavor (*Jujyfruits*), 1 piece* 9
    gum drops, low-calorie (*Sug'r Like*), 1 piece* 3
    licorice, *see "licorice," below*
    nougat center (*Chuckles*), 1 oz. 109
    nougat center (*Chuckles*), 1 piece* 17
    orange flavor slices (*Chuckles*), 1 oz. 97
    orange flavor slices (*Chuckles*), 1 piece* 29
    rings (*Chuckles*), 1 oz. 95
    rings (*Chuckles*), 1 piece* 37
    spearmint flavor leaves (*Chuckles*), 1 oz. 96
    spearmint flavor leaves (*Chuckles*), 1 piece* 27
    spice flavor (*Chuckles*), 1 oz. 98
    spice flavor sticks or drops (*Chuckles*), 1 piece* 14
    spice flavor strings (*Chuckles*), 1 piece* 18
(*KitKat*), 1.25-oz. bar 180
licorice:
    (*Pearson* Licorice Nip), 1 oz. 125
    (*Switzer*), 1 oz. 101
    candy coated (*Good & Plenty*), 1.5-oz. pkg. 136
    drops (*Diamond*), 1 piece* 14
    jellies (*Chuckles*), 1 oz. 95
    jellies (*Chuckles*), 1 piece* 36
    red (*Switzer*), 1 oz. 101
(*Marathon*), 1.37-oz. bar 179
(*Marathon* Fun Size), .44-oz. bar 58
(*Mars*), 1.25-oz. bar 170
marshmallow:
    (*Campfire*), 1 oz. 100
    (*Just Born*), 1.1-oz. pkg. 94

marshmallow, continued

eggs (*Chuckles*), 1 oz. 111
eggs (*Chuckles*), 1 piece* 38
(*Mary Jane*), 1 oz. 74
(*Mary Jane* Bite Size), ¼-oz. piece 18
(*Milky Way*), 2.25-oz. bar 286
(*Milky Way*), 1.81-oz. bar 232
(*Milky Way* Fun Size), .84-oz. bar 106
mints:
  (*Certs* Clear), 1 piece* 8
  (*Certs* Pressed), 1 piece* 6
  (*Clorets*), 1 piece* 6
  (*Delson Merri-Mints*), 1 piece* 25
  (*Delson* Thin Mints), 1 piece* 52
  (*Jamaica Mints*), 1 oz. 113
  (*Jamaica Mints*), 1 piece* 24
  (*Nabisco* Liberty Mints), 1 oz. 113
  (*Nabisco* Liberty Mints), 1 piece* 24
  (*Pearson* Mint Parfait), 1 oz. 136
  (*Rolaids*), 1 piece* 4
  (*Tic Tac*), 1 piece* 2
  (*Trident*), 1 piece* 8
  butter (*Richardson*), 1 oz. 109
  chocolate covered (*Junior*), 1 oz. 118
  chocolate covered (*Junior*), 1 piece* 10
  chocolate covered (*Nabisco* Mint Wafers), 1 oz. 166
  chocolate covered (*Nabisco* Mint Wafers), 1 piece* 10
  chocolate covered (*Nabisco* Peppermint Patties), 1 oz. ...122
  chocolate covered
     (*Nabisco* Peppermint Patties), 1 piece* 63
  chocolate covered (*Nabisco Thin Mints*), 1 oz. 119
  chocolate covered (*Nabisco Thin Mints*), 1 piece* 42
  chocolate covered (*York* Peppermint Patties), 1 oz. 124
  jelly center (*Richardson*), 1 oz. 104
  midget (*Richardson*), 1 oz. 109
  striped (*Richardson*), 1 oz. 109

Candy, continued

(*Nabisco* Coco-Mello), .7-oz. bar 91
(*Nabisco* Crispy Clusters), 1 oz. 114
(*Nabisco* Crispy Clusters), 1 piece* 65
(*Nabisco* Malted Milk Crunch), 1 oz. 152
(*Nabisco* Malted Milk Crunch), 1 piece* 8
(*Nabisco* Nutty Crunch), .54-oz. bar 71
(*Nestlé Choco Lite*), 1 oz. 150
party mix, carob coated (*CaraCoa*), 1 oz. 145
(*Payday*), 1.75-oz. bar 239
(*Payday*), 1.5-oz. bar 200
peanut bar (*Munch*), 1.5-oz. bar 229
peanut brittle (*Planter's* Peanut Block), 1 oz. 140
peanut brittle (*Stuckey's*), 1 oz. 122
peanut butter, chocolate covered:
  (*Peter Paul*), 1 oz. 157
  (*Reese's Peanut Butter Cups*), 1.4 oz. or 2 pieces 210
  (*Reese's Peanut Butter Flavor Chips*), 1 oz. 150
peanut cluster, chocolate covered (*Royal Cluster*), 1 oz. ..137
peanut cluster, chocolate covered (*Royal Cluster*), 1 piece* ..78
peanuts, carob coated (*CaraCoa*), 1 oz. 160
peanuts, chocolate covered:
  (*Goober's*), 1 oz. 153
  (*Nabisco*), 1 oz. 168
  (*Nabisco*), 1 piece* 24
peanuts, chocolate covered, candy coated:
  (*M & M's*), 1.5-oz. pkg. 215
  (*M & M's*), 1-oz. pkg. 143
  (*M & M's* Fun Size), .82-oz. pkg. 117
(*Pearson* Chocolate Parfait), 1 oz. 136
(*Pearson Coffioca*), 1 oz. 136
pecan roll (*Stuckey's* Log), 1 oz. 135
peppermint, *see* "mint," *above*
popcorn, *see* "Popcorn," *page 263*
popcorn, caramel coated (*Bachman*), 1 oz. 130
popcorn, caramel coated, w/nuts (*Cracker Jack*), 1 oz. ..120

* *Average-size piece, as packaged*

CHEWING GUM, one piece*

	CALORIES
(*Adams* Sour Gum)	9
(*Beechnut*)	10
(*Big Red*)	10
(*Bubble Yum*)	20
(*Bubblicious*)	24
(*Chicklets*)	6
(*Clorets*)	6
(*Dentyne*)	5
(*Doublemint*)	10
(*Freedent*)	10
(*Freshen-Up*)	10
(*Juicy Fruit*)	10
(*Orbit*)	8
(*Trident*—all flavors except bubble gum)	5
(*Trident* Bubble Gum)	7
(*Wrigley's Spearmint*)	10

* *As packaged*

CHAPTER 22

ICE CREAM AND FROZEN CONFECTIONS

ICE CREAM & FROZEN CONFECTIONS,
½ cup, except as noted
See also "Frozen Yogurt"

	CALORIES

ice cream:

butter almond (*Breyer's*)	170
butter almond and chocolate (*Breyer's*)	160
butter pecan (*Good Humor*)	200
cherry vanilla (*Breyer's*)	140
chocolate (*Breyer's*)	160
chocolate (*Foremost*)	130
chocolate (*Good Humor*)	180
chocolate (*Meadow Gold*)	129
chocolate (*Sealtest*)	140
chocolate (*Swift's* Sweet Cream)	130
chocolate chip (*Good Humor*)	210
chocolate chip (*Sealtest*)	150
chocolate chip mint (*Breyer's*)	170
chocolate eclair (*Sealtest*)	160
chocolate peanut sundae (*Sealtest*)	170
coffee (*Breyer's*)	140
coffee (*Sealtest*)	140
heavenly hash (*Sealtest*)	150

Ice cream, continued

mint (*Foremost* San Francisco Mint) 140

peach (*Breyer's*) 140

peach (*Sealtest*) 130

strawberry (*Breyer's*) 130

strawberry (*Foremost*) 110

strawberry (*Meadow Gold*) 126

strawberry (*Good Humor*) 200

strawberry (*Swift's* Sweet Cream) 120

vanilla (*Breyer's*) 150

vanilla (*Foremost*) 130

vanilla (*Good Humor*) 130

vanilla (*Hood*) 130

vanilla (*Hood Coronet*) 150

vanilla (*Meadow Gold*) 126

vanilla (*Swift's* Sweet Cream) 130

vanilla, w/fudge (*Breyer's* Fudge Royale) 150

vanilla, w/fudge (*Breyer's* Vanilla Fudge Twirl) 160

vanilla, w/fudge (*Good Humor* Royal Fudge) 170

ice cream, non-dairy, all flavors (*Meadow Gold*) 126

ice cream bars:

(*Good Humor* Milky Pop), 1.5 fl. oz. 60

assorted (*Good Humor Whammy*), 1.6 fl. oz. 100

chocolate chip, crunch coated

(*Good Humor Whammy* Chip Crunch), 1.6 fl. oz. 110

strawberry ripple, cake-coated

(*Good Humor* Strawberry Shortcake), 3 fl. oz. 200

vanilla, chocolate coated (*Eskimo Pie*), 3 fl. oz. 180

vanilla, chocolate coated (*Good Humor*), 3 fl. oz. 170

vanilla, toasted almond-coated

(*Good Humor* Toasted Almond), 3 fl. oz. 220

vanilla with chocolate fudge, cake coated

(*Good Humor* Chocolate Eclair), 3 fl. oz. 220

ice cream sandwich (*Good Humor*), 3 fl. oz. 220

ice cream sandwich, mint

(*Foremost* San Francisco Mint), 1 sandwich* 140

Ice Cream & Frozen Confections, continued

ice milk:

    chocolate (*Foremost Big Dip*) 100

    chocolate (*Light 'N Easy*) 110

    strawberry (*Foremost Big Dip*) 110

    strawberry (*Light 'N Easy*) 100

    vanilla (*Foremost Big Dip*) 110

    vanilla (*Hood Nuform*) 110

    vanilla (*Light 'N Easy*) 110

    vanilla (*Meadow Gold*) 95

ice milk, non-dairy, all flavors (*Meadow Gold*) 106

sherbet:

    fruit flavors (*Meadow Gold*) 120

    lime (*Foremost*) 110

    orange (*Foremost*) 110

    orange (*Hood*) 110

    pineapple (*Foremost*) 100

    raspberry (*Foremost*) 110

    strawberry (*Foremost*) 100

sherbet bar, fudge (*Fudgsicle*), 2½ fl. oz. 110

* *As packaged*

ICE CREAM CONES & CUPS,
one piece, as packaged

                                           CALORIES

cones, all flavors (*Comet*) 18

cones, rolled sugar (*Comet*) 45

cups, all flavors (*Comet*) 18

CHAPTER 23

NUTS, CHIPS, PRETZELS AND RELATED SNACKS

NUTS & SEEDS, SHELLED,
one ounce, except as noted
See also "Nut Butters"

	CALORIES
almonds, whole, slivered or sliced (*Ann Page*)	190
almonds, dry roasted (*Planters*)	170
Brazil nuts, raw unblanched (*Ann Page*)	200
cashews:	
(*Frito-Lay's*), ⅝-oz. pkg.	110
(*Planters*)	170
dry roasted (*Ann Page*)	180
dry roasted (*Planters*)	160
salted or fancy (*Ann Page*)	180
unsalted (*Planters*)	160
mixed nuts:	
dry roasted (*Ann Page*)	180
dry roasted (*Planters*)	160
with peanuts (*Planters*)	180
without peanuts (*Planters*)	180
salted (*Ann Page*)	190
salted, fancy, without peanuts (*Ann Page*)	190
unsalted (*Planters*)	170
nut and snack mix (*Flavor Tree*)	162

Nuts & Seeds, Shelled, continued

peanuts:

    cocktail (*Planters*) 170

    dry roasted (*Ann Page*) 180

    dry roasted (*Planters*) 160

    dry roasted, unsalted (*Ann Page*) 180

    in shell, raw (*Ann Page*) 170

    in shell, roasted (*Ann Page*) 170

    in shell, salted (*Frito-Lay's*) 160

    old fashioned (*Planters*) 170

    redskin, Virginia (*Planters*) 170

    salted (*Ann Page*) 180

    salted (*Frito-Lay's*) 170

    salted, party (*Ann Page*) 180

    Spanish (*Ann Page*) 180

    Spanish (*Frito-Lay's*) 170

    Spanish (*Planters*) 170

    Spanish, dry roasted (*Planters*) 160

    unsalted (*Planters*) 170

pecans, whole, chopped or pieces (*Ann Page*) 200

pecans, dry roasted (*Planters*) 190

pistachios:

    (*Ann Page*) 180

    (*Frito-Lay's*) 180

    dry roasted (*Planters*) 170

sesame buds (*Flavor Tree*) 160

sesame buds w/garlic (*Flavor Tree*) 160

sesame nut mix (*Planters*) 160

soy nuts:

    (*Flavor Tree* Peanuts) 150

    (*Planters*) 130

    roasted, all varieties (*Malt-O-Meal*) 140

sunflower kernels:

    (*Frito-Lay's*) 180

    dry roasted (*Planters*) 160

    unsalted (*Planters*) 170

Nuts & Seeds, Shelled, continued

sunflower kernels and sesames (*Flavor Tree*) 158
tavern nuts (*Planters*) 170
walnuts:
   (*Ann Page*) 200
   (*Diamond*) 192
   black, pieces (*Ann Page*) 190
   chopped (*Ann Page*) 190
wheat "nuts" (*Pillsbury Wheat Nuts*) 200

CHIPS, PUFFS & SIMILAR
SNACKS, one ounce
*See also "Popcorn," "Pretzels," "Crackers" and
"Nuts & Seeds, Shelled"*

                                                CALORIES

corn chips:
   (*Bachmans* Indian) 160
   (*Frito's*) 160
   (*Planters*) 170
   (*Wise*) 160
   (*Wonder*) 162
   barbecue flavor (*Frito's* Bar-B-Q) 150
corn crisps and puffs:
   (*Bachman's* Cheese Twists) 150
   (*Chee • tos*) 160
   (*Cheez Bursts*) 160
   (*Cheez Doodles*) 160
   (*Diggers*) 160
   (*Doo Dads*) 140
   (*Flings*) 160
   (*Jax*) 150
   (*Korkers*) 150
   (*Planters* Cheez Balls) 160
   (*Planters* Cheez Curls) 160
corn nuggets, toasted (*Frito-Lay's*) 180

Chips, Puffs & Similar Snacks, continued

(Fiddle Faddle) 125
grain chips (*Hain* 7-Grain Chips) 131
pork rinds, fried (*Baken • Ets*) 140
potato chips:
   (*Bachman*) 150
   (*Cains*) 160
   (*Chipsters*) 130
   (*Kas*) 160
   (*Kitty Clover*) 160
   (*Lay's*) 160
   (*Planters*) 150
   (*Pringle's*) 150
   (*Pringle's* Country Style) 160
   (*Pringle's* Rippled Style) 160
   (*Ruffles*) 160
   (*Snack Time*) 160
   (*Snack Time* Rippled) 160
   (*Wise*) 150
   (*Wise Light*) 170
   barbecue flavor (*Lay's* Bar-B-Q) 160
   barbecue flavor (*Wise*) 150
   sour cream and onion flavor (*Lay's*) 160
   sour cream and onion flavor (*Wise*) 170
potato crisps (*Munchos*) 150
onion flavor rings (*Funyuns*) 140
onion flavor rings (*Wise*) 130
(*Screaming Yellow Zonkers*) 121
snack cracker chips (*Skittle Chips*) 140
sticks (*Lil' Loaf*) 140
sticks (*Twigs*) 140
tortilla chips:
   (*Doritos*) 140
   (*Pinata*) 140
   (*Tor-Tico*) 160
   (*Tostitos*) 150
   nacho cheese flavor (*Bachman*) 150

tortilla chips, continued

nacho cheese flavor (*Bravos*) 150
nacho cheese flavor (*Doritos*) 140
nacho cheese flavor (*Pinata*) 140
nacho cheese flavor (*Planters*) 130
nacho cheese flavor (*Wise*) 150
taco flavor (*Bachman*) 150
taco flavor (*Doritos*) 140
taco flavor (*Pinata*) 140
taco flavor (*Planters*) 130
taco flavor (*Wise*) 150
yogurt chips (*Hain*) 144

POPCORN, one ounce,
except as noted

	CALORIES
(*Bachman*)	160
(*Belvins*), 1 cup	55
(*Golden Pop*)	160
(*Mary Poppin'*), 1 cup	60
(*Super Pop*), ⅛ cup unpopped	100
(*TV Time*), 1 cup	70
caramel coated, *see "Candy," page 253*	
cheese flavor (*Bachman*)	180
cheese flavor (*Golden Pop*)	150
salted (*Frito-Lay's*)	150

PRETZELS

	CALORIES
all varieties (*Quinlan*), 1 oz.	109
bite-size (*Bachman B's*), 1 piece*	8
bite-size (*Bachman Nutzels*), 1 piece*	7
logs (*Bachman*), 1 piece*	18
(*Mister Salty Veri-Thin*), .9 oz. or 5 pieces	100

Pretzels, continued

rings:

    (*Bachman Beers*), 1 piece* 56

    (*Bachman* Medium), 1 piece* 20

    (*Bachman* Teeny), 1 piece* 11

    (*Bachman Thin*), 1 piece* 18

    (*Mr. Salty* Pretzelettes), 1 oz. or 17 pieces 110

    (*Rold Gold*), 1 oz. 110

rods (*Bachman*), 1 piece* 50

rods (*Rold Gold*), 1 oz. 110

sticks:

    (*Bachman*), 1 piece* 3

    (*Mister Salty Veri-Thin*), 1 oz. or 94 sticks 100

    (*Rold Gold*), 1 oz. 110

twists (*Rold Gold*), 1 oz. 110

* *As packaged*

CHAPTER 24

COCOA, COFFEE, TEA AND SOFT DRINKS

COCOA & FLAVORED MIXES, DRY,
once ounce, except as noted
See also "Dessert Toppings & Syrups" and
"Flavored Milk Beverages"

	CALORIES
egg nog flavor (*Ovaltine*)	113
carob (*CaraCoa*), 4 heaping tsp.	45
chocolate flavor:	
(*Flick* Instant)	111
(*Hershey* Instant), 3 tbsp.	80
(*Nestlé Quik*), ¾ oz.	70
(*Ovaltine*), ¾ oz.	80
cocoa:	
(*Hershey*)	120
(*Hershey* Hot Cocoa Mix)	120
(*Nestlé* Hot Cocoa Mix)	110
(*Ovaltine* Hot Cocoa Mix)	120
chocolate, w/mini marshmallows	
(*Carnation* Instant Hot Cocoa Mix)	109
milk chocolate (*Carnation* Instant Hot Cocoa Mix)	112
rich chocolate (*Carnation* Instant Hot Cocoa Mix)	112

Cocoa & Flavored Mixes, Dry, continued
malted flavor:
   (*Ovaltine*), ¾ oz. 80
   chocolate (*Carnation* Instant), ¾ oz. 85
   natural (*Carnation* Instant), ¾ oz. 90
strawberry flavor (*Nestlé Quick*), ¾ oz. 80
strawberry flavor (*Ovaltine*), .54 oz. 60

COFFEE, six fluid ounces

CALORIES

plain:
   ground roasted, prepared* (*Chase & Sanborn*) 2
   ground roasted, prepared* (*Maxwell House*) 2
   ground roasted, prepared* (*Sanka*) 2
   ground roasted, prepared* (*Yuban*) 2
   instant* (*Decaf*) 4
   instant* (*Kava*) 3
   instant* (*Maxwell House*) 3
   instant* (*Nescafé*) 4
   instant (*Nescafé* Decaffeinated) 4
   instant*, freeze-dried (*Maxim*) 3
   instant*, freeze-dried (*Taster's Choice*) 4
   instant*, freeze-dried (*Taster's Choice* Decaffeinated) 4
flavored, prepared*:
   café Francais (*General Foods* International Coffees) 60
   café Vienna (*General Foods* International Coffees) 60
   Irish Mocha Mint
      (*General Foods* International Coffees) 50
   orange cappucino (*General Foods* International Coffees)..60
   Suisse mocha (*General Foods* International Coffees) 60
   imitation (*Celestial Seasoning Roastaroma*) 10

---

* *Prepared according to package directions, without added cream or sugar*

TEA, six fluid ounces,
except as noted

CALORIES

regular, loose or bags*:
   (*Bigelow Constant Comment*) 1
   (*Lipton*) 2
   (*Tender Leaf*) 1
   (*Tetley*) 3
   black (*Lipton Black Rum*) 2
   cinnamon (*Bigelow Cinnamon Stick*) 1
   cinnamon (*Lipton*) 2
   lemon (*Bigelow Lemon Lift*) 1
   lemon and spice (*Lipton*) 2
   mint (*Bigelow Peppermint Stick*) 1
   mint (*Bigelow Plantation Mint*) 1
   mint (*Lipton*) 2
   orange and spice (*Lipton*) 2
herbal, loose or bags*:
   (*Bigelow Feeling Free*) 1
   (*Bigelow Mint Medley*) 1
   (*Bigelow Sweet Dreams*) 1
   (*Bigelow Take-A-Break*) 3
   (*Celestial Seasoning Brazilian Breakfast*) 1
   (*Celestial Seasoning Pelican Punch*) 1
canned or dairy pack:
   lemon flavor, presweetened (*Hood*) 55
   lemon flavor, presweetened (*Lipton*), 12-fl.-oz. can 130
   lemon flavor, sugar-free (*Lipton*), 12-fl.-oz. can 2
instant and mixes*:
   plain (*Lipton*) 2
   plain (*Nestea*) 0
   lemon flavored (*Lipton*), 8 fl. oz. 4
   lemon flavored (*Nestea*) 2

Tea, continued

lemon flavored, presweetened
  (*Lipton* Iced Tea Mix), 8 fl. oz. 60
lemon flavored, presweetened (*Nestea*) 70
orange flavored, presweetened
  (*Lipton* Iced Tea Mix), 8 fl. oz. 60

* *Prepared according to package directions*

SOFT DRINKS & MIXERS,
eight fluid ounces, except as noted
*See also "Fruit & Fruit-Flavored Drinks," "Flavored
Milk Beverages" and "Cocktail Mixes, Nonalcoholic"*

                                            CALORIES
birch beer (*Canada Dry*) 110
bitter lemon (*Canada Dry*) 100
bitter lemon (*Schweppes*) 88
blended flavors:
  (*Canada Dry* Purple Passion) 120
  (*Canada Dry* Tahitian Treat) 130
  (*Shasta* Fruit Punch) 112
(*Bubble-Up*) 97
(*Canada Dry* Cactus Cooler) 120
(*Canada Dry* Hi Spot) 100
(*Canada Dry* Rooti) 110
(*Canada Dry* Vostok) 90
cherry:
  (*Fanta*) 117
  black (*Shasta*) 105
  wild (*Canada Dry*) 130
chocolate (*Yoo-Hoo*), 9 fl. oz. 170
club soda (all brands) 0
coconut shake (*Yoo-Hoo*), 9½ fl. oz. 150

Soft Drinks & Mixers, continued

cola:

(*Canada Dry* Jamaican Cola) 110

(*Coca-Cola*) 96

(*Pepsi Cola*) 104

(*Royal Crown*) 109

(*Shasta*) 95

cherry flavored (*Shasta*) 90

Collins mixer (*Canada Dry*) 80

cream (*Canada Dry* Vanilla) 130

cream (*Shasta*) 100

(*Dr Pepper*) 94

fruit punch, *see "blended flavors," above*

ginger ale:

(*Canada Dry*) 90

(*Canada Dry* Golden) 100

(*Schweppes*) 88

(*Shasta*) 78

grape:

(*Canada Dry* Concord) 130

(*Crush*) 119

(*Shasta*) 115

grapefruit (*Shasta*) 105

grapefruit (*Wink*) 120

half and half mixer (*Canada Dry*) 110

lemon, bitter, *see "bitter lemon," above*

lemonade (*Shasta*) 95

lemon-lime (*Shasta*) 93

lime (*Canada Dry*) 130

orange:

(*Canada Dry* Sunripe) 130

(*Crush*) 114

(*Shasta*) 115

(*Mello Yello*) 116

pineapple (*Canada Dry*) 110

Soft Drinks & Mixers, continued

root beer:

    (*Canada Dry* Barrelhead) 110

    (*Dads*) 105

    (*Hires*) 100

    (*Shasta*) 100

(*7-Up*) 97

(*Schweppes* Rondo) 102

(*Squirt*) 105

strawberry:

    (*Canada Dry* California) 120

    (*Shasta*) 95

    shake (*Yoo-Hoo*), 9½ fl. oz. 150

tonic water (*Canada Dry*) 90

tonic water (*Schweppes*) 88

vanilla shake (*Yoo-Hoo*), 9½ fl. oz. 150

whiskey sour mix (*Canada Dry*) 90

CHAPTER 25

BONUS SECTION: "FAST-FOOD" CHAINS AND RESTAURANTS

Note: The listings in this section—which are broken down by restaurant, rather than by food category—are based on an "average" or a "standard" serving. The caloric content of a serving may vary slightly according to restaurant location. And, of course, individual orders that result in a change of ingredients or quantity of ingredients will alter the caloric value. Wherever possible, the weight of a serving has been included as a guide.

ARBY'S*

	CALORIES
Beef and Cheese, 6-oz. sandwich	450
Club, 9-oz. sandwich	560
Ham and Cheese, 5½-oz. sandwich	380
Roast Beef, 5-oz. sandwich	350
Roast Beef, Junior, 3-oz. sandwich	220
Roast Beef, Super, 9¾-oz. sandwich	620
Turkey Deluxe, 8.51-oz. sandwich	510

* *See Note above*

ARTHUR TREACHER'S*

	CALORIES
Chicken, 2 pieces	369
Chicken Sandwich, 5½-oz. sandwich	413
Fish, 2 pieces	355
Fish Sandwich, 5½-oz. sandwich	440
Shrimp, 7 pieces	381
Soup and Side Dishes:	
Chowder, 6-oz. serving	112
Chips, 4-oz. serving	276
Cole Slaw, 3-oz. serving	123
Krunch Pup, 2-oz. serving	203
Lemon Luvs, 3-oz. serving	276

* See Note on page 271

BASKIN-ROBBINS*

	CALORIES
Ice Cream:	
Chocolate, 1 scoop	165
Chocolate Fudge, 1 scoop	178
French Vanilla, 1 scoop	181
Pralines 'N Cream, 1 scoop	177
Strawberry, 1 scoop	141
Vanilla, 1 scoop	147
Ice, Daiquiri, 1 scoop	84
Sherbet, Orange, 1 scoop	99

* See Note on page 271

BURGER KING*

CALORIES

Cheeseburger, 1 sandwich 350
Double Cheeseburger, 1 sandwich 530
Hamburger, 1 sandwich 290
Whopper, 1 sandwich 630
Whopper w/Cheese, 1 sandwich 740
Whopper, Double Beef, 1 sandwich 850
Whopper, Double Beef w/Cheese, 1 sandwich 950
Whopper Jr., 1 sandwich 370
Whopper Jr. w/Cheese, 1 sandwich 420

Side Dishes and Dessert:
Apple Pie, 1 piece 240
French Fries, 1 regular serving 210
Onion Rings, 1 regular serving 270

Beverages:
Chocolate Shake, 1 serving 340
Vanilla Shake, 1 serving 340
Coca-Cola, 1 medium serving 121
Diet Pepsi, 1 medium serving 7

* See Note on page 271

CARVEL*

CALORIES

Ice Cream, Chocolate, 3 fl. oz. 147
Ice Cream, Vanilla, 3 fl. oz. 148
Lo-Yo, Plain, 3 fl. oz. 110
Sherbet, 3 fl. oz. 105
Thinny-Thin, Coffee, Mint, Strawberry or Vanilla, 3 fl. oz. ..56
Thinny-Thin, Chocolate or Chocolate Mint, 3 fl. oz. 56

* See Note on page 271

CHURCH'S FRIED CHICKEN*

CALORIES

Chicken, boned, dark meat, 3½-oz. piece 305
Chicken, boned, white meat, 3½-oz. piece 327

* See Note on page 271

DAIRY QUEEN/BRAZIER*

CALORIES

Dairy Queen:

Banana Split, 13½-oz. serving 540
Cone, 2½-oz. small cone 110
Cone, 5-oz. regular cone 230
Cone, 7½-oz. large cone 340
Cone, Dipped**, 2¾-oz. small cone 150
Cone, Dipped**, 5½-oz. regular cone 300
Cone, Dipped**, 8¼-oz. large cone 450
Dilly Bar, 3-oz. bar 240
DQ Sandwich, 2.12-oz. sandwich 140
Fiesta Sundae, 9½-oz. serving 570
Float, 14-oz. serving 330
Freeze, 14-oz. serving 520
Malt**, 8½-oz. small serving 340
Malt**, 20¾-oz. large serving 840
Mr. Misty Float, 14¼-oz. serving 440
Mr. Misty Freeze, 14½-oz. serving 500
Mr. Misty Kiss, 3.125-oz. serving 70
Parfait, 10-oz. serving 460
Sundae**, 3¾-oz. small serving 170
Sundae**, 6¼-oz. regular serving 290
Sundae**, 8¾-oz. large serving 400

Dairy Queen, continued

Brazier:

Fish Sandwich, 6-oz. sandwich 400
Fish Sandwich w/Cheese, 6¼-oz. sandwich 440
Hamburger, "Single," ⅙ lb. precooked,
    5.4-oz. sandwich 370
Hamburger, "Single" w/Cheese, 6.4-oz. sandwich 470
Hamburger, "Double," ⅓ lb. precooked,
    7.55-oz. sandwich 540
Hamburger, "Double" w/Cheese, 8.55-oz. sandwich 650
Hamburger, "Triple," ½ lb. precooked,
    10½-oz. sandwich 740
Hamburger, "Triple" w/Cheese, 11½-oz. sandwich 840
Hot Dog, 3½-oz. sandwich 270
Hot Dog w/Cheese, 4-oz. sandwich 330
Hot Dog w/Chili, 4½-oz. sandwich 330
French Fries, 2½-oz. regular serving 200
French Fries, 4-oz. large serving 320
Onion Rings, 3-oz. serving 300

* *See Note on page 271*
** *Chocolate*

GINO'S*

CALORIES

Sandwiches and Entrees:

Cheese Hero, 1 sandwich 738
Cheese Sirloiner, 1 sandwich 532
Cheeseburger, 1 sandwich 300
Fish Sandwich, 1 sandwich 450
Fish Platter, 1 platter 650
Giant, 1 sandwich 569
Hamburger, 1 sandwich 254
Hero, 1 sandwich 647
Sirloiner, 1 sandwich 441

Gino's, continued

Salad Bar Items:

Bac-O Bits, ¼ oz. 29

Bean Sprouts, 1 oz. 8

Beets, 1 oz. 10

Carrots, ¼ oz. 3

Celery, ½ oz. 2

Chick Peas, 1 oz. 102

Cucumbers, ½ oz. 2

Grated Cheese, ¼ oz. 28

Green Beans, 1 oz. 7

Kidney Beans, 1 oz. 26

Lettuce, 2 oz. 7

Pepperoncini, ½ oz. 5

Peppers, ¾ oz. 5

Onions, 1 oz. 11

Radishes, ¾ oz. 4

Tomato, 2 oz. 13

Blue Cheese Dressing, 1 tbsp. 80

French Dressing, 1 tbsp. 60

Italian Dressing, 1 tbsp. 60

Russian Dressing 60

Side Dishes:

French Fries, 1 serving 156

Beverages:

Coke—medium, 1 serving 117

Hot Chocolate, 1 serving 90

Milk, 1 serving 160

Milkshake, Chocolate, 1 serving 324

Milkshake, Vanilla, 1 serving 310

Orange—medium, 1 serving 140

Root Beer—medium, 1 serving 122

Dessert:

Apple Pie, 1 serving 238

* *See Note on page 271*

HARDEE'S*

CALORIES

Egg and Biscuit Dishes:

Biscuit, 2.9-oz. biscuit 275
Biscuit w/Jelly, 3½-oz. serving 324
Biscuit w/Egg, 5.6-oz. serving 383
Fried Egg, 1¾-oz. medium egg 108
Ham Biscuit, 3.8-oz. serving 349
Ham Biscuit w/Egg, 6½-oz. serving 458
Sausage Biscuit, 4-oz. serving 413
Sausage Biscuit w/Egg, 5.7-oz. serving 521
Steak Biscuit, 4¾-oz. serving 419
Steak Biscuit w/Egg, 5.7-oz. serving 527

Sandwiches:

Big Roast Beef, 6.6-oz. sandwich 485
Big Twin, 5.8-oz. sandwich 447
Cheeseburger, 4.1-oz. sandwich 335
Deluxe, 8.9-oz. sandwich 675
Double Cheeseburger, 6-oz. sandwich 495
Ham and Cheese, 5.22-oz. sandwich 376
Fish Sandwich, 5.1-oz. sandwich 468
Hamburger, 3.9-oz. sandwich 305
Hot Dog, 4.2-oz. sandwich 346
Roast Beef Sandwich, 5.1-oz. sandwich 390

Side Dishes:

French Fries, 2½-oz. small serving 239
French Fries, 4-oz. large serving 381

Beverage and Dessert:

Apple Turnover, 3.07-oz. turnover 282
Milkshake, 11½-oz. serving 391

* See Note on page 271

JACK IN THE BOX*

CALORIES

Breakfast Dishes:

Breakfast Jack Sandwich, 1 sandwich 301
Double Cheese Omelette, 1 serving 423
French Toast Breakfast, 1 serving 537
Ham & Cheese Omelette, 1 serving 425
Pancakes Breakfast, 1 serving 626
Ranchero Style Omelette, 1 serving 414
Scrambled Eggs Breakfast, 1 serving 719

Sandwich Entrees:

Bonus Jack Hamburger, 1 sandwich 461
Cheeseburger, 1 sandwich 310
Cheeseburger Deluxe, 1 sandwich 314
Hamburger, 1 sandwich 263
Hamburger Deluxe, 1 sandwich 260
Jack Burrito, 1 piece 448
Jack Steak Sandwich, 1 sandwich 428
Jumbo Jack Hamburger, 1 sandwich 551
Jumbo Jack Hamburger w/Cheese, 1 sandwich 628
Moby Jack Sandwich, 1 sandwich 455
Regular Taco, 1 taco 189
Super Taco, 1 taco 285

Side Dishes:

French Fries, 1 serving 270
Onion Rings, 1 serving 351

Beverages:

Chocolate Shake**, 1 serving 365
Chocolate Shake***, 1 serving 325
Strawberry Shake**, 1 serving 380
Strawberry Shake***, 1 serving 323
Vanilla Shake**, 1 serving 342
Vanilla Shake***, 1 serving 317

Jack in the Box, continued

Desserts:

Apple Turnover, 1 piece 411

Lemon Turnover, 1 piece 446

* *See Note on page 271*

** *Formulation for shakes sold in all states, except Arizona, California, Texas and Washington*

*** *Special formulation for shakes sold in Arizona, California, Texas and Washington*

KENTUCKY FRIED CHICKEN*

CALORIES

Chicken Pieces, Original Recipe:

Drumstick, 1.66-oz. piece** 117

Keel, 3.35-oz. piece** 236

Rib, 2.45-oz. piece** 199

Thigh, 3.1-oz. piece**...............................257

Wing, 1.5-oz. piece** 136

Chicken Pieces, Extra Crispy:

Drumstick, 2.05-oz. piece** 155

Keel, 3.7-oz. piece** 297

Rib, 3-oz. piece** 286

Thigh, 3.8-oz. piece** 343

Wing, 1.9-oz. piece** 201

Extras:

Potatoes, 3-oz. serving 63

Gravy, ½-oz. serving 23

Potatoes and gravy, 3.5-oz. serving 86

Roll, ¾-oz. roll 61

Corn (2"–3"), 2 6-oz. pieces 92

Corn (4"–5"), 4 3.4-oz. pieces 169

Cole Slaw, 3.2-oz. serving 122

Kentucky Fried Chicken, continued

Dinners***, Original Recipe:

#1—Wing and Rib, extras, 11.4-oz. dinner 604
#2—Wing and Thigh, extras, 12-oz. dinner 662
#3—Drumstick and Thigh, extras, 12.2-oz. dinner 643

Dinner***, Extra Crispy:

#1—Wing and Rib, extras, 12.3-oz. dinner 755
#2—Wing and Thigh, extras, 13.1-oz. dinner 812
#3—Drum and Thigh, extras, 13.2-oz. dinner 765

* *See Note on page 271*
** *Average Edible Serving Weight*
*** *Dinner consists of 2 pieces of chicken, with potatoes and gravy,
   cole slaw and a roll*

LONG JOHN SILVER'S*

CALORIES

Breaded Clams, 1 serving 465
Breaded Oysters, 1 serving 460
Chicken Planks, 4-piece serving 458
Fish w/Batter, 2-piece serving 409
Fish w/Batter, 3-piece serving 613
Ocean Scallops, 6-piece serving 257
Peg Legs w/Batter, 5-piece serving 514
Shrimp w/Batter, 6-piece serving 269
S.O.S. Super Ocean Sandwich, 1 sandwich 554
Treasure Chest, 1 piece Fish and 3 Peg Legs 467

Side Orders:

Cole Slaw, 4-oz. serving 138
Corn on the Cob, 1 piece 174
Fryes, 3-oz. serving 275
Hush Puppies, 3-piece serving 153

* *See Note on page 271*

McDONALD'S*

CALORIES

Breakfast Dishes:

Egg McMuffin, 4.67-oz. sandwich 352

English Muffin, Buttered, 2.2-oz. muffin 186

Hot Cakes w/Butter and Syrup, 7.26-oz. serving 472

Pork Sausage, 1.7-oz. sausage patty 184

Scrambled Eggs, 2¾-oz. serving 162

Sandwiches:

Big Mac, 6.58-oz. sandwich 541

Cheeseburger, 4-oz. sandwich 306

Filet-O-Fish, 4.63-oz. sandwich 402

Hamburger, 3½-oz. sandwich 257

Quarter Pounder, 5¾-oz. sandwich 418

Quarter Pounder w/Cheese, 6.8-oz. sandwich 518

Side Dishes:

French Fries, 2.45-oz. serving 211

Hashbrown Potatoes, 2.05-oz. serving 130

Beverages:

Chocolate Shake, 10.2-oz. serving 364

Strawberry Shake, 10.2-oz. serving 345

Vanilla Shake, 10.3-oz. serving 323

Desserts:

Apple Pie, 3.22-oz. pie 300

Cherry Pie, 3¼-oz. pie 298

McDonaldland Cookies, 2¼-oz. serving 294

Sundaes:

Caramel, 5.1-oz. serving 282

Hot Fudge, 5.33-oz. serving 290

Pineapple, 5.1-oz. serving 230

Strawberry, 5.1-oz. serving 229

* See Note on page 271

PIZZA HUT* **

CALORIES

Thick'N Chewy Pizza:

Cheese, Standard, 2 slices of 13" medium pizza 390

Cheese, SuperStyle, 2 slices of 13" medium pizza 450

Pepperoni, Standard, 2 slices of 13" medium pizza 450

Pepperoni, SuperStyle, 2 slices of 13" medium pizza 490

Pork/Mushroom, Standard,
    2 slices of 13" medium pizza 430

Pork/Mushroom, SuperStyle,
    2 slices of 13" medium pizza 500

Supreme, Standard, 2 slices of 13" medium pizza 480

Supreme, Superstyle, 2 slices of 13" medium pizza 590

Thin'N Crispy Pizza:

Cheese, Standard, 2 slices of medium 13" pizza 340

Cheese, SuperStyle, 2 slices of 13" medium pizza 410

Pepperoni, Standard, 2 slices of 13" medium pizza 370

Pepperoni, SuperStyle, 2 slices of 13" medium pizza 430

Pork/Mushroom, Standard,
    2 slices of 13" medium pizza 380

Pork/Mushroom, SuperStyle,
    2 slices of 13" medium pizza 450

Supreme, Standard, 2 slices of 13" medium pizza 400

Supreme, SuperStyle, 2 slices of 13" medium pizza 520

* Pizza Hut, Thick 'N Chewy *and* Thin 'N Crispy *are all trademarks of Pizza Hut, Inc.*
** *See Note on page 271*

PONDEROSA*

CALORIES

entree**:

Chopped Beef, 5.3-oz. serving 324
Prime Rib, 4.2-oz. serving 286
Prime Rib, Extra-Cut, 5.99-oz. serving 409
Rib-Eye, 3.8-oz. serving 259
Rib-Eye, Extra-Cut, 5.2-oz. serving 358
Strip Sirloin, 4.7-oz. serving 277
Super Sirloin, 6.5-oz. serving 383
T-Bone, 6.7-oz. serving 374
Shrimp, 2.2 oz. or 4 pieces 139
Shrimp Dinner, 3.5 oz. or 7 pieces 220
Filet of Sole Dinner, 6 oz. or 2 pieces 251

sandwiches**:

Double Deluxe, 5.9 oz. 362
Junior Patty, 1.6 oz. 98
Steakhouse Deluxe, 2.96 oz. 181
Filet of Sole, 1 piece fish 125

rolls and buns:

Junior Bun, 1.4-oz. bun 118
Kaiser Roll, 2.2-oz. roll 184
Steakhouse Deluxe Bun, 2.4-oz. bun 190

side dishes and condiments:

Baked Potato, 7.2-oz. potato 145
Catsup, 1 tbsp. 18
Cocktail Sauce, 1½ oz. 57
Dill Pickle, 3 slices 2
French Fries, 3-oz. serving 230
Lemon Wedge, 1 piece 5
Lettuce, 3 oz. 12
Lettuce, .5 oz. 2
Mustard, 1 tsp. 4
Onion, chopped, 1 tbsp. 4

Ponderosa, continued
Salad Dressings:
Blue Cheese, 7/16 oz. 56
Creamy Italian, 7/16 oz. 60
French, 7/16 oz. 56
Thousand Islands, 7/16 oz. 51
Oil and Vinegar, 7/16 oz. 54
Steak Sauce, 7/16 oz. 10
Tartar Sauce, 1 tbsp. 95
Tomato, 3.5-oz. tomato 22
Tomato Slices, 2 slices 6

* *See Note on page 271*
** *Meat or Fish portion only—does not include bun, condiments and/or side dishes*

RUSTLER*

CALORIES
Individual Items:
Filet Mignon, 1 serving 308
Patty, 4-oz. serving 263
Patty, 8-oz. serving 526
Rib-Eye, 1 serving 224
Steak and Crab, 1 serving 479
Strip Steak, 1 serving 337
T-Bone, 1 serving 374
Platters**:
Filet Mignon, 1 platter 886
Patty, 4 oz., 1 platter 841
Patty, 8 oz., 1 platter 1104
Rib-Eye, 1 platter 802
Steak and Crab, 1 platter 1057
Strip Steak, 1 platter 915
T-Bone, 1 platter 952

Rustler, continued

Sandwiches***:

Trailboss, 1 sandwich	553
Westerner, 1 standwich	512

Sandwich Accessories:

Cheese, 2 slices	92
Ketchup, ½-oz. serving	15
Pickles, 2 slices	2
Potato Chips, ½-oz. serving	82

* *See Note on page 271*
** *Salad is not included*
*** *Roll and meat only*

TACO BELL*

	CALORIES
Beefy Tostado, 1 piece	232
Bellbeefer, 1 piece	243
Bean Burrito, 1 piece	345
Burrito Supreme, 1 piece	387
Enchirito, 1 piece	391
Pintos & Cheese, 1 piece	231
Taco, 1 piece	146
Tostada, 1 piece	206

* *See Note on page 271*

WENDY'S*

	CALORIES
Chili, 8.8-oz. serving	229
French Fries, 4.2-oz. serving	327
Frosty, 8.8-oz. serving	391

Wendy's, continued

Hot 'n Juicy Hamburgers:

Single, 7-oz. sandwich	472
Double, 10-oz. sandwich	669
Triple, 12.7-oz. sandwich	853
Single Cheese, 8.5-oz. sandwich	577
Double Cheese, 11.5-oz. sandwich	797
Triple Cheese, 14.1-oz. sandwich	1036

* *This study was conducted by Medallion Laboratories, an independent laboratory. Because "Hot 'n Juicy" hamburgers are prepared according to each customer's order, much as they would be prepared at home, significant variations in the test results will occur. The values derived from this study provide only a general guideline. We feel the number of sample items tested, though not scientifically selected, are adequate for the purposes of this book. (See Note on page 271)*

WHITE CASTLE*

	CALORIES
Cheeseburger, 2.33-oz. sandwich	185
Hamburger, 1.96-oz. sandwich	160
Fish, 2.27-oz. sandwich	192
French fries, 2.62-oz. serving	225
Bun alone**, .79-oz. bun	65

* *See Note on page 271*
** *All sandwich information includes the bun; the "bun-alone" information is suppied for the convenience of those who convert two sandwiches into a double, using only one bun, or who eat products such as fish, alone, without eating the bun.*

CHAPTER 26

SPIRITS, WINES, LIQUEURS, BEER AND RELATED DRINKS

DISTILLED SPIRITS*, one fluid ounce

Unlike other products in this book, distilled spirits are not listed by brand name. The caloric content in *any* distilled spirit is determined entirely by the amount of alcohol it contains. The higher the proof (alcoholic content), the more calories in the spirit. Different brands of liquor may not taste the same, but if they are the same proof there is no difference in their caloric content. This only applies to distilled spirits. The calories in other kinds of alcoholic beverages—wines, liqueurs, etc.—are likely to vary by brand, depending on proof and sugar content.

	CALORIES
80 proof	67
84 proof	70
86 proof	72
86.8 proof	72
90 proof	75
90.4 proof	75
94 proof	78
94.6 proof	79
97 proof	81
100 proof	83
104 proof	87

* *Applejack, bourbon, brandy, gin, rum, tequila and vodka; blended Canadian, Irish and rye whiskey; Scotch whisky*

COCKTAILS, BOTTLED, ALCOHOLIC,
one fluid ounce
See also "Cocktail Mixes, Nonalcoholic" and "Distilled Spirits"

CALORIES

daiquiri (*Calvert*), 60 proof 63
mai tai (*Lemon Hart*), 48 proof 60
Manhattan (*Calvert*), 60 proof 54
Margarita (*Calvert*), 55 proof 59
martini, gin (*Calvert* Martini), 70 proof 59
martini, vodka (*Calvert* Vodka Martini), 75 proof 63
screwdriver, vodka (*Old Mr. Boston*), 25 proof 39
sour, gin (*Calvert*), 60 proof 65
sour, tequila (*Calvert*), 55 proof 61
sour, whiskey (*Calvert*), 60 proof 65
Tom Collins (*Calvert*), 60 proof 65

COCKTAIL MIXES, NONALCOHOLIC*
See also "Cocktails, Bottled, Alcoholic" and
"Soft Drinks & Mixers"

CALORIES

liquid, bottled:
  Amaretto (*Holland House*), 1 fl. oz. 79
  apricot sour (*Holland House*), 1 fl. oz. 48
  black Russian (*Holland House*), 1 fl. oz. 92
  blackberry sour (*Holland House*), 1 fl. oz. 50
bloody Mary:
  regular (*Holland House*), 1 fl. oz. 10
  extra tangy (*Holland House*), 1 fl. oz. 10
  smooth 'n spicy (*Holland House*), 1 fl. oz. 6
cocktail host (*Holland House*), 1 fl. oz. 47
daiquiri (*Holland House*), 1 fl. oz. 51
dry martini (*Holland House*), 1 fl. oz. 10

Cocktail Mixes, Nonalcoholic, continued

gimlet (*Holland House*), 1 fl. oz. 40

mai-tai (*Holland House*), 1 fl. oz. 33

Manhattan (*Holland House*), 1 fl. oz. 29

Margarita (*Holland House*), 1 fl. oz. 39

old fashioned (*Holland House*), 1 fl. oz. 36

piña colada (*Holland House*), 1 fl. oz. 60

sip 'n slim (*Holland·House*), 1 fl. oz. 9

strawberry sting (*Holland House*), 1 fl. oz. 35

Tom Collins (*Holland House*), 1 fl. oz. 67

whiskey sour (*Holland House*), 1 fl. oz. 55

instant mixes, dry:

   Alexander (*Holland House*), 1 packet 69

   banana daiquiri (*Holland House*), 1 packet 66

   bloody Mary (*Holland House*), 1 packet 56

   daiquiri (*Holland House*), 1 packet 69

   gimlet (*Holland House*), 1 packet 69

   grasshopper (*Holland House*), 1 packet 69

   mai-tai (*Holland House*), 1 packet 69

   Margarita (*Holland House*), 1 packet 69

   mint julep (*Holland House*), 1 packet 67

   piña colada (*Holland House*), 1 packet 66

   pink squirrel (*Holland House*), 1 packet 69

   screwdriver (*Holland House*), 1 packet 69

   strawberry Margarita (*Holland House*), 1 packet 62

   strawberry sting (*Holland House*), 1 packet 74

   tequila sunrise (*Holland House*), 1 packet 63

   Tom Collins (*Holland House*), 1 packet 69

   vodka sour (*Holland House*), 1 packet 65

   wallbanger (*Holland House*), 1 packet 65

   whiskey sour (*Holland House*), 1 packet 69

* When using a drink mix, be sure to include the caloric content of the alcoholic beverage (see page 287) for the total calories per drink.

TABLE WINES, four fluid ounces
See also "Apertif & Dessert Wines"

CALORIES

Beaujolais, *see "Burgundy, red," below*
Bordeaux, red (*see also "claret," below*):
    (Château La Garde) 108
    (Château Olivier) 108
    (Château Pontet-Canet, *Cruse & Fils Frères*) 96
    Bordeaux Rouge (*Chanson Père & Fils*) 108
    Bordeaux Rouge (*Cruse & Fils Frères*) 84
    Margaux (*B & G*) 84
    Medoc (*Cruse & Fils Frères*) 96
    St. Emilion (*B & G*) 84
    St. Emilion (*Crus & Fils Frères*) 92
    St. Julien (*Crus & Fils Frères*) 92
Bordeaux, white, Graves (Château Olivier) 108
Bordeaux, white, Graves (*Crus & Fils Frères*) 92
Burgundy, red:
    domestic (*Gold Seal*) 109
    domestic (*Italian Swiss Colony*) 86
    domestic (*Taylor*) 96
    imported, Beaujolais (*Crus & Fils Frères*) 96
    imported, Beaune (*Chanson Père & Fils* St. Vincent) 108
    imported, Gevrey-Chambertin (*Crus & Fils Frères*) 96
    imported, Nuits St. George (*B & G*) 92
    imported, Pommard (*Chanson Père & Fils* St. Vincent) ..108
    imported, Pommard (*Crus & Fils Frères*) 96
Burgundy, sparkling, domestic (*Gold Seal*) 116
Burgundy, sparkling, domestic (*Taylor*) 104
Burgundy, white:
    domestic, Chablis (*Gold Seal*) 108
    domestic, Chablis (*Italian Swiss Colony*) 86
    imported, Chablis (*Chanson Père & Fils* St. Vincent) ..108
    imported, Chablis (*Crus & Fils Frères*) 88
    imported, Pouilly-Fuissé (*Crus & Fils Frères*) 96

Table Wines, continued

Catawba (*Gold Seal*) 167

Chablis, *see "Burgundy, white," above*

Champagne:

    domestic (*Charles Fournier* New York State Brut) 110

    domestic (*Gold Seal* New York State Brut) 113

    domestic (*Korbel* California Brut) 104

    domestic (*Lejon*) 94

    domestic (*Taylor* Dry Royal Quality New York State) ..104

    domestic (*Taylor* New York State Brut) 100

    imported (*Bollinger* Extra Dry) 114

    imported (*Mumm's* Cordon Rouge Brut) 88

    imported (*Mumm's* Extra Dry) 108

    imported (*Veuve Clicquot* Brut) 104

    pink, domestic (*Gold Seal* New York State Extra Dry) ..116

    pink, domestic (*Taylor* New York State) 108

Châteauneuf du Pape (*B & G*) 92

Châteauneuf du Pape (*Crus & Fils Frères*) 96

Chianti:

    domestic (*Italian Swiss Colony Tipo*) 86

    imported (*Brolio* Classico) 88

    imported (*Gancia* Classico) 100

claret:

    (*Gold Seal*) 109

    (*Italian Swiss Colony*) 86

    (*Taylor*) 96

    (*Taylor* Lake Country Red) 108

concord (*Gold Seal*) 167

Delaware (*Gold Seal*) 116

(*Fournier Nature*) 109

kosher:

    all dry varieties (*Manischewitz*) 91

    all medium varieties (*Manischewitz*) 112

    all sweet varieties (*Manischewitz*) 170

    concord (*Mogen David*) 200

Liebfraumilch (*Anheuser & Fehrs*) 84

Table Wines, continued

Liebfraumilch (*Dienhard & Co.*) 96
Moselle Bernkasteler (*Dienhard & Co.*) 92
(*Pink Carousel*) 167
Pouilly Fumé (*B & G*) 80
(*Red Carousel*) 139
Rhine:
   domestic (*Gold Seal*) 108
   domestic (*Italian Swiss Colony*) 86
   domestic (*Taylor*) 92
rosé
   domestic (*Italian Swiss Colony*) 86
   domestic (*Taylor*) 92
   imported (*Cruse & Fils Frères* Vin Rosé) 96
Sancerre (*B & G*) 80
sauterne:
   (*Gold Seal*) 116
   dry (*Gold Seal*) 108
   dry (*Taylor*) 108
Sauternes, *see "Apertif & Dessert Wines," page 293*
(*White Carousel*) 167
zinfandel (*Italian Swiss Colony* Gold Medal) 86

APERITIF & DESSERT WINES,
two fluid ounces
See also "Table Wines"

	CALORIES
Asti Spumante (*Gancia*)	84
(*Dubonnet* Blonde)	76
(*Dubonnet* Rouge)	95
Madeira:	
(*Hiram Walker*)	84
(*Leacock*)	80
(*Sandeman & Co.*)	84
muscatel (*Gold Seal*)	105

Aperitif & Dessert Wines, continued

port:

   (*Hiram Walker Porto Branco*) 92

   (*Partners* Port) 94

   all varieties, domestic (*Gold Seal*) 105

   ruby (*Hiram Walker*) 92

   ruby, domestic (*Italian Swiss Colony* Gold Medal) 86

   ruby, domestic (*Taylor*) 100

   ruby, imported (*Robertson Bros. & Co.* Black Label) 92

   ruby, imported (*Sandeman & Co.*) 92

   tawny (*Hiram Walker*) 92

   tawny, domestic (*Taylor*) 96

   tawny, imported (*Sandeman & Co.*) 92

Sauternes:

   (*B & G*) 64

   (*Château Voigny*) 64

sherry:

   (*Hiram Walker* Armada Cream) 82

   domestic (*Gold Seal* Private Reserve New York State) ..93

   domestic (*Taylor* New York State) 88

   domestic (*Taylor* New York State Cream) 100

   imported (*Williams & Humbert* Dry Sack) 80

sherry, dry:

   (*Hiram Walker* Cocktail) 70

   domestic (*Gold Seal* Private Reserve

     New York State Cocktail) 81

   domestic (*Taylor* New York State Pale Dry Cocktail) 76

   imported (*Sandeman* Cocktail) 72

vermouth, dry:

   domestic (*Lejon* Extra Dry) 68

   domestic (*Taylor* Extra Dry) 68

   imported (*C & P* Extra Dry) 74

   imported (*Gancia* Dry) 84

   imported (*Noilly Prat* Extra Dry) 68

vermouth, sweet:

   domestic (*Lejon*) 88

   domestic (*Taylor*) 88

vermouth, continued

imported (*C & P*) 94
imported (*Gancia* Bianco) 88
imported (*Gancia* Rosso) 102
imported (*Noilly Prat*) 86
white tokay (*Taylor*) 96

LIQUEURS & OTHER FLAVORED SPIRITS,
one fluid ounce

                                                    CALORIES
Amaretto (*Hiram Walker*) 76
Amaretto and cognac (*Hiram Walker*) 62
anise-licorice liqueur:
    (*DuBouchett Absant*) 84
    (*Pernod*) 79
anisette liqueur:
    red or white (*Bols*) 111
    red or white (*DuBouchett*) 85
    red or white (*Hiram Walker*) 92
    white (*Dolfi*) 102
    white (*Garnier*) 82
    white (*Old Mr. Boston*—60 proof) 90
    white (*Old Mr. Boston* Connoisseur—42 proof) 64
apricot brandy, *see "brandy, flavored," below*
apricot liqueur:
    (*Bols*) 96
    (*Dolfi*) 100
    (*DuBouchett*) 63
    (*Hiram Walker*) 79
(*B & B*) 94
Benai (*DuBouchett*) 110
Benai and brandy (*DuBouchett*) 89
(*Benedictine*) 112
blackberry, *see "brandy, flavored," below*

triple sec, continued

  (*Leroux*) 105

  (*Old Mr. Boston*—60 proof) 105

  (*Old Mr. Boston* Connoisseur—42 proof) 97

vodka, flavored:

  cherry, wild (*Old Mr. Boston*) 100

  grape (*Old Mr. Boston*) 100

  lemon (*Old Mr. Boston*) 100

  lime (*Old Mr. Boston*) 100

  orange (*Old Mr. Boston*) 100

  peppermint (*Old Mr. Boston*) 90

yellow plum (*Dolfi* Mirabelle) 78

yellow plum (*Dolfi* Cordon d'Or Mirabelle) 83

BEER, ALE & MALT LIQUOR,
12 fluid ounces

	CALORIES
ale (*Red Cap*)	159

beer:

  (*Blatz*) 150

  (*Brauhaus*) 150

  (*Budweiser*) 157

  (*Busch Bavarian*) 157

  (*Carling Black Label*) 162

  (*Carlsberg Light de Luxe*) 153

  (*Falstaff*) 150

  (*Grand Union*) 150

  (*Heidelberg*) 147

  (*Heidelberg Light Pilsner*) 130

  (*Heileman Grain Belt*) 150

  (*Heileman National Bohemian*) 150

  (*Heileman National Premium*) 170

beer, continued

(Heileman Old Style) 150
(Heileman Special Export) 170
(Michelob) 160
(Old Dutch) 150
(Old Ranger) 150
(Pabst) 150
(Pearl) 147
(Pilsner's Original) 150
(Rainier) 150
(Rupert-Knickerbocker) 158
(Schaefer) 160
(Schlitz) 153
(Schmidt) ....,...................................150
(Schmidt Extra Special) ..:........................190
(Stag) 150
(Sterling) 150
(Tudor) 150
(Wiedemann) 150
light (Blatz) 96
light (Heileman) 96
light (Rainier) 96
malt liquor:
(Champale) 156
(Colt 45) 160
(Country Club) 163
(Malt Duck Apple) 250
(Malt Duck Grape) 210
(Mickeys) 160
near beer:
(Kingsbury) 60
(Maltcrest) 70
(Metbrew) 70
(Schmidt Select) 60
(Zing) 60

WHAT YOU SHOULD WEIGH

height (with shoes—2-in. heels)	small frame	medium frame	large frame
WOMEN			
4 ft. 10 in.	92-98	96-107	104-119
4 ft. 11 in.	94-101	98-110	106-122
5 ft. 0 in.	96-104	101-113	109-125
5 ft. 1 in.	99-107	104-116	112-128
5 ft. 2 in.	102-110	107-119	115-131
5 ft. 3 in.	105-113	110-122	118-134
5 ft. 4 in.	108-116	113-126	121-138
5 ft. 5 in.	111-119	116-130	125-142
5 ft. 6 in.	114-123	120-135	129-146
5 ft. 7 in.	118-127	124-139	133-150
5 ft. 8 in.	122-131	128-143	137-154
5 ft. 9 in.	126-135	132-147	141-158
5 ft. 10 in.	130-140	136-151	145-163
5 ft. 11 in.	134-144	140-155	149-168
6 ft. 0 in.	138-148	144-159	153-173

For girls 18-25, subtract 1 pound for each year under 25.

WHAT YOU SHOULD WEIGH

height (with shoes—1-in. heels)	MEN small frame	medium frame	large frame
5 ft. 2 in.	112-120	118-129	126-141
5 ft. 3 in.	115-123	121-133	129-144
5 ft. 4 in.	118-126	124-136	132-148
5 ft. 5 in.	121-129	127-139	135-152
5 ft. 6 in.	124-133	130-143	138-156
5 ft. 7 in.	128-137	134-147	142-161
5 ft. 8 in.	132-141	138-152	147-166
5 ft. 9 in.	136-145	142-156	151-170
5 ft. 10 in.	140-150	146-160	155-174
5 ft. 11 in.	144-154	150-165	159-179
6 ft. 0 in.	148-158	154-170	164-184
6 ft. 1 in.	152-162	158-175	168-189
6 ft. 2 in.	156-167	162-180	173-194
6 ft. 3 in.	160-171	167-185	178-199
6 ft. 4 in.	164-175	172-190	182-204

Prepared by the Metropolitan Life Insurance Co. from data of the Build and Blood Pressure Study, Society of Actuaries.

HOW MANY CALORIES TO MAINTAIN YOUR DESIRABLE WEIGHT?

Desirable weight	18-35 years	35-55 years	55-75 years
WOMEN DAILY MAINTENANCE CALORIES*			
99	1,700	1,500	1,300
110	1,850	1,650	1,400
121	2,000	1,750	1,550
128	2,100	1,900	1,600
132	2,150	1,950	1,650
143	2,300	2,050	1,800
154	2,400	2,150	1,850
165	2,550	2,300	1,950
MEN DAILY MAINTENANCE CALORIES*			
110	2,200	1,950	1,650
121	2,400	2,150	1,850
132	2,550	2,300	1,950
143	2,700	2,400	2,050
154	2,900	2,600	2,200
165	3,100	2,800	2,400
176	3,250	2,950	2,500
187	3,300	3,100	2,600

* Based on moderate activity. If your life is very active, add calories; if you lead a sedentary life, subtract calories. Prepared by the Food and Nutrition Board of the National Academy of Sciences, National Research Council.

INDEX

Roquefort cheese, 66
  salad dressing, 187
Rose extract, 244
Rosé wine, 292
Rosemary leaves, 202
Rotini, 174
Rum, 299
  and brandy flavor cookies,
    227
  extract, 245
  flavoring, 245
Russian salad dressing, 187–
  188
Rustler, 284–285
Rutabagas, 103
Rye
  bread, 32
  crackers, 47
  flour, 44

Sable, smoked, 163
Sage, 202
Salad
  chicken, 153
  herring, 157
  tuna, 153, 155
  turkey, 153
Salad dressing, 184–188, 197
  blue cheese, 184
  Caesar, 185
  French, 185–186
  Italian, 186
  Russian, 187–188
  Thousand Island, 188
  see also specific dressing

Salami, 150
  cheese food, 68
  cocktail, Danish, 127
  vegetarian, 114
Salisbury steak, 139, 143
  dinner, 133–134
Salmon, 157
  smoked, 163
Salt, flavored, 197
Saltines, 47–48
Sancerre wine, 292
Sandwich cookies, 224–225,
  226
Sandwich spread, 153, 197
  vegetarian, 113
Sap Sago cheese, 66
Sardines, 157
Sardo Romano cheese, 66
Sauces, 189–192
  à la king, 189
  barbecue, 189
  burger, 195
  chili, 190
  clam, 190
  cocktail seafood, 195
  hollandaise, 190
  spaghetti, 190–191
  sweet and sour, 191
  tomato, 191–192
  white, 192
  see also specific sauces
Sauerkraut, 92
Sausage(s), 151
  beef, 150, 151
  New England, 149
  and peppers, 143
  pizza, 170–171

THE DARK HORSEMAN

Marianne Harvey
author of *The Proud Hunter*

Beautiful Donna Penroze had sworn to her
dying father that she would save her sole leg-
acy, the crumbling tin mines and the ancient,
desolate estate *Trencobban*. But the mines
were failing, and Donna had no one to turn to.
No one except the mysterious Nicholas Tre-
varvas—rich, arrogant, commanding. Donna
would do anything but surrender her pride, anything but admit her irresistible longing for *The
Dark Horseman*.

A Dell Book $3.25